Praise for *The Wrong Men*

"For many, injustice is easier to define than justice. Stanley Cohen helps us articulate what justice should be by clearly reviewing how our system often fails, through his profiles of these wrongly condemned prisoners. *The Wrong Men* is a book that will keep you reading as you fervently hope for a better day, when justice will prevail instead of fail."—Joseph B. Ingle, minister to condemned prisoners and author of *Last Rights: Thirteen Fatal Encounters with the State's Justice*

"Some day, the number of mistakes in death penalty cases will become intolerable. Thankfully, *The Wrong Men* brings that day closer. By providing more than 100 stories, arranged so that the patterns of error become clear, while never losing sight of the individual tragedies in each case, Stanley Cohen shows why the death penalty is the wrong punishment. Over 100 mistakes in less than thirty years reveals that far too high a risk is being taken with innocent lives. If the people in these stories had been executed before the truth came out, nothing could be done to right the wrong."—Richard Dieter, Director, Death Penalty Information Center

"A spellbinding book, in the same mesmerizing sense of watching an unscrolling catastrophe. Cohen has carefully catalogued the tales of one hundred men (and two women) wrongfully sentenced to die in America's death chambers, then exonerated. *The Wrong Men* is an essential book for anyone concerned with the inequities of today's criminal justice system."—Joe Jackson, coauthor of *Dead Run: The Shocking Story of Dennis Stockton and Life on Death Row in America* and author of *Leavenworth Train: A Fugitive's Search for Justice in the Vanishing West*

"Stanley Cohen's powerful, shocking book is a landmark in the fight against the death penalty. Extensively researched and brilliantly written, the book tells the heart-wrenching stories of 102 wrongfully convicted Americans. This seminal book should be read by every American, both by those who agree with the author and those who disagree with him. *The Wrong Men* is a gem. It is an important book and will help lead the courts, the legislature and the people to abolish capital punishment."—Martin Garbus, criminal defense attorney and author of *Courting Disaster: The Supreme Court and the Unmaking of American Law*

Also by
STANLEY COHEN

The Game They Played (1977)

The Man in the Crowd (1981)

A Magic Summer: The '69 Mets (1988)

Dodgers! The First 100 Years (1990)

Willie's Game (with Willie Mosconi, 1993)

Tough Talk (with Martin Garbus, 1998)

The Wrong Men

AMERICA'S EPIDEMIC OF WRONGFUL DEATH ROW CONVICTIONS

STANLEY COHEN

CARROLL & GRAF PUBLISHERS
NEW YORK

THE WRONG MEN

Carroll & Graf Publishers
An Imprint of Avalon Publishing Group Inc.
161 William St., 16th Floor
New York, NY 10038

First Carroll & Graf edition 2003

Library of Congress Cataloging-in-Publication Data is available.

ISBN: 0-7867-1258-9

Interior design by Paul Paddock

Printed in the United States of America
Distributed by Publishers Group West

CONTENTS

To Betty,
whose resourceful, industrious research made possible the timely
completion of this project.

Together, we dedicate this book
to all those who suffered the deprivations of the criminal
justice system, to the memory of those who paid with their lives,
and to the undaunted men and women who toil tirelessly on
behalf of the innocent.

Perhaps the bleakest fact of all is that the death penalty is imposed not only in a freakish and discriminatory manner, but also in some cases upon defendants who are actually innocent.

—Supreme Court Justice William J. Brennan Jr.

There isn't, I submit, a single admissible argument in favor of capital punishment. Nature loves life. We believe that life should be protected and preserved. The thing which keeps one from killing is the emotion they have against it; and the greater the sanctity that the State pays to life, the greater the feeling of sanctity the individual has for life.

—Clarence Darrow

Preface

Justice is an idea that is best understood in its absence. Throughout the ages, its essence has eluded the close study of scholars and the musings of poets, prophets, and philosophers. They were perhaps the wrong people looking in the wrong places. Experience tells us that we can most easily identify justice in places where it never existed; we discern its nature in circumstances where it was applied too loosely or not at all. The ultimate irony is that justice is comprehended most clearly by those who have been denied its benedictions.

Even at its best, fine-tuned through a network of statutory and constitutional laws, viewed through a prism that refracts the light of evolving moods and shifting attitudes, justice is at best an inexact process. It depends on too many variables for it to function with precision: the quality of the defense attorneys, the intensity of the prosecution, the disposition of the judge, the reliability of witnesses, the makeup of a jury whose members rarely resemble the defendant's peers. Guilt or innocence is determined in an atmosphere of competition, a contest in which each side is committed to a particular outcome rather than to a concept as abstract as justice. It is little wonder, then, that the judicial process is as quixotic and unpredictable as any other contest. What troubles one's sleep is that here the stakes are so much higher.

It is no secret of course that the guilty are sometimes acquitted while innocent people are often convicted and sent to prison. The possibility of error is built into the system. But the random nature of the process becomes acute when the crime is a capital one and the innocent person is sentenced to death. It is not an uncommon occurrence. The Death Penalty Information Center, which gathers statistics on capital cases at its Washington, D.C., headquarters, lists 102 cases between 1973 and 2002 in which innocent people were freed from death row. Many had spent more than a decade in isolated death-watch chambers before they were exonerated of the crimes with which they were charged. Sentenced to death in 1968, Peter Limone spent thirty-three years in a Massachusetts prison before being released in 2001.

The problem of wrongful conviction is not a new one in America. The first documented case in the United States dates to 1820 when the presumed victim of a murder for which two men had been sentenced to death turned up alive and well in New Jersey. Since then, hundreds of additional cases, many of them involving a death sentence, have come to light. Not until recently, however, did the gravity of the issue attract sustained national attention. It had been ignored perhaps not because of public indifference but because the depth of the problem—the sheer volume of numbers—was unknown. The turning point came in the fall of 1998 when the National Conference on Wrongful Convictions and the Death Penalty was held at the Northwestern University School of Law in Illinois. The meeting featured the appearance of twenty-eight innocent former prisoners from all over the country who had been sentenced to death for crimes they did not commit.

A few months later, Illinois death-row prisoner Anthony Porter was exonerated just two days before his scheduled execution. The reprieve prompted Northwestern professor David Protess and several of his students at the Medill School of Journalism to probe deeper into the circumstances surrounding Porter's conviction, and they uncovered conclusive evidence of his innocence. The two events stirred further interest and the Center on Wrongful Convictions was launched with private funding at the start of the 1999–2000 academic year. Its mission was to identify and rectify wrongful convictions and other serious miscarriages of justice. The effects of its efforts were felt almost immediately. In January 2000, Governor George H. Ryan declared a moratorium on executions in Illinois, where thirteen innocent men have been released from the state's death row over the past few years. Soon, a nationwide examination of the death penalty was under way.

The most compelling argument against capital punishment is that innocent people will inevitably be put to death. While few can doubt that such executions have occurred, it is difficult to document the cases. The courts do not entertain claims of innocence when the defendant is dead. Attorneys move on to new cases. They do not seek fresh evidence that would exonerate those whose fates have already been sealed. All the same, there are a significant number of cases in which subsequent findings strongly suggest that an innocent man has been executed. Often, such cases involve a defendant with a criminal background that makes him a likely suspect and might inure the jury, and even the judge, to the possibility of error. He is, in the end, convicted not by the evidence but by his past.

Dennis Stockton

Dennis Stockton insisted on his innocence from the very beginning. There was, after all, no physical evidence to tie him to the murder with which he was charged. In fact, he was convicted solely on the testimony of an ex-con who in many respects was a more likely suspect in the killing and who later championed a campaign to save Stockton when he was awaiting execution. But despite mounting evidence that he was innocent, Stockton was executed by lethal injection on September 27, 1995, more than ten years after his conviction.

The victim of the crime was a friend of Stockton's, a young man named Kenny Arnder. Arnder's body was found in a gully near a dirt road in North Carolina not far from the Virginia border, on a July day in 1978. His arms were splayed wide in the form of a cross and his hands were chopped off at the wrist. He had been shot between the eyes. The body was covered with branches and had begun to decompose, making identification difficult.

Stockton had been with Arnder shortly before he was murdered. Arnder had called him at his home and asked Stockton to drive him to Kibler Valley, a remote wooded area in south-western Virginia. He said he was worried because a man he feared had seen him stealing tires off a car. Stockton drove him to Kibler Valley and dropped him off at about six P.M. Arnder's body was discovered five days later. It was assumed that he had been killed in Virginia and his body moved across the border.

The police questioned Stockton, since he was one of the last people to see Arnder alive. He was the type of suspect who was easy pickings for the authorities. At age thirty-eight, he had spent most of his adult life in criminal custody. As a juvenile he was held in jail over a weekend for passing bad checks. At seventeen he served three to five years on similar charges. When he was released, he was already prison-tough. He became involved with drugs, both as a user and dealer, and did time on a variety of charges including arson by contract, safecracking, and carrying a gun. He was at the top of the police's "usual suspects" list. During one investigation, police said they found a human body part preserved in a jar in Stockton's home. He told them he had gotten it from a biker gang and kept it to show to his friends. When police questioned him about the Arnder murder, he readily showed them the selection of guns he kept at home. None of them matched the murder weapon. The police left, apparently satisfied that Stockton was not their man.

His involvement in the case might have ended right there had he not responded to jailhouse rumors two years after Arnder's death by going to the police. In prison on other charges, Stockton heard it bruited around the prison that the police suspected him of committing the murder. He believed he knew the source of the rumors and decided to act on his own. He went to the police and told them he had new information on the crime. The police accompanied him to his house, where he showed them letters he had received from a prominent citizen offering to pay him to commit a murder. He said he had received $3,000 but never killed anyone and suspected that the man who paid him might be circulating the rumors as a means of taking revenge. The letters, in police custody, never surfaced again; they apparently had been lost. But Stockton, who had tried to deflect suspicion, was again a prime suspect.

Two years later, he was charged by the Commonwealth of Virginia with the murder-for-hire killing of Kenny Arnder. The basis for the charge was the offer of testimony by a convict named Randy Bowman who was serving a prison sentence for larceny and possession of firearms. Bowman claimed to have been at a meeting during which Stockton was hired by a man named Tommy McBride to kill Arnder for a fee of $1,500. McBride allegedly was angry with Arnder for crossing him on a drug deal and wanted him killed as a message to other dealers.

Stockton was tried in the rural town of Stuart, Virginia, in 1983. Bowman testified that he was at McBride's house trying to sell some stolen goods when he overheard the deal being made. He also said he had not been promised anything in return for his testimony. His was the only evidence linking Stockton to the crime. Nonetheless, Stockton was convicted of murder for hire, a capital charge. At a separate sentencing hearing, he was sentenced to death.

In 1987, a federal judge set aside the death sentence when he learned that the jury deliberations had been tainted. The judge offered Stockton the choice of life imprisonment or a new sentencing hearing. Insisting on his innocence, Stockton opted for the new hearing. It was a mistake. Federal law generally does not allow evidence concerning guilt or innocence to be heard at a resentencing procedure, and Stockton again was sentenced to death.

During his twelve years on death row, Stockton kept a detailed diary on life in what he called "the monster factory." He also helped plan the only mass escape from a death row in American history, although he did not take part in the plan's execution. He remained in his cell during the breakout and documented the event carefully, still hoping that he would someday be granted a new trial. It appeared that his hopes were not unfounded. Questions continued to emerge regarding the credibility of Bowman's testimony. There was speculation that he had been offered incentives to testify against Stockton, but the prosecution denied it. Anthony Giorno, the prosecuting attorney, sent a letter to Stockton's defense attorneys in 1990, in which he said: "I am not aware of any promises made to Bowman other than that I told him I would endeavor to see that he would be transferred [to a different penitentiary]." Giorno also enclosed a letter written by Bowman to the prosecution two weeks before the trial in which he said: "I am writing to let you know that I'm not going to court [to testify] unless you can get this 6 or 7 months I've got left cut off where I don't have to come back to prison." So it was clear that Bowman expected to be rewarded for his testimony, but the prosecution denied making any deal.

In 1994, Stockton's attorneys obtained affidavits from law-enforcement officials stating that Bowman had become angry after Stockton's trial "because promises allegedly made to him were not kept." According to the affidavits, Bowman said he had been promised a reduction in sentence or a transfer to another prison in return for his testimony.

Seventeen days after Stockton was sentenced to death, prosecutors dropped charges against Bowman for obtaining stolen property. Fourteen months after the trial Bowman was released on parole.

On September 25, 1995, a district court judge ordered a sixty-day stay of execution when defense attorneys presented separate affidavits from Bowman's former wife, his son, and a friend stating that Bowman had admitted committing the murder. It was also rumored that Bowman had confessed his guilt to a journalist. The Fourth District court of appeals apparently found the new evidence to be unconvincing. The district court's stay was lifted a day after it had been ordered. The following day Dennis Stockton was executed.

Though it probably will never be known to a certainty, the likelihood is that an innocent man was put to death that day. The awareness that the judicial machinery is imperfect and that the consequences of the death penalty can never be remedied has led to a reexamination of capital punishment at both the federal and state levels. States other than Illinois have begun to consider the wisdom of instituting a moratorium until the issue has been studied more closely.

The Center on Wrongful Convictions (CWC) has proposed a series of reforms that would reduce the possibility of innocent people being executed. The reform measures include modifying eyewitness identification procedures, requiring police to videotape interrogations and confessions, and banning testimony by informants who will be rewarded for their cooperation. These procedures could nullify the vast majority of wrongful convictions.

Eyewitness testimony—either mistaken or perjured—is the leading cause of wrongful convictions in capital cases throughout the United States. In a recent study, the CWC examined eighty-six wrongful conviction cases since the death penalty was reinstituted in the mid-1970s. It found that forty-six (53.5 percent) had been predicated in whole or in part on eyewitness error. In thirty-three of those cases, the eyewitness testimony was the sole basis of conviction. The other significant factors producing wrongful convictions were: police and prosecutorial misconduct in the cases of seventeen defendants (19.8 percent); false testimony from jailhouse informants in ten cases (11.6 percent); so-called junk science—erroneous scientific evidence—in nine cases (10.5 percent); forced or coerced confessions in eight instances (9.3 percent); and various miscellaneous factors, including questionable circumstantial evidence and hearsay, in twenty-nine cases (33.7 percent).

The first documented case of wrongful conviction in the United States occurred in 1820. It was based on the mistaken presumption that a Vermont farmhand who disappeared had been murdered and, according to an account provided by Rob Warden, executive director of CWC, it involved junk science, a jailhouse informant freed in exchange for his perjured testimony, and two false confessions.

Russell Colvin

One day in 1812, Russell Colvin disappeared from his home in Manchester, Vermont, where he had worked on his father-in-law's farm along with his wife's two brothers, Jesse and Stephen Boorn. It was no secret that he and his brothers-in-law were not on the best of terms. The brothers had complained often and loudly that Colvin did not pull his weight and was taking advantage of their father's largesse. Few who knew the family were surprised that when Colvin didn't return, the Boorns were suspected of having had a hand in his disappearance. But it took the specter of divine intervention to seriously raise suspicions of homicide.

The missing persons case lay dormant for seven years until Amos Boorn, an uncle of the brothers, claimed that Colvin appeared at his bedside during a recurring dream. The ghost informed Amos that he had been slain but did not identify his killer. He did confide that his remains had been put into an old cellar hole in a potato field on the Boorn farm. The cellar hole was excavated and found to contain pieces of broken crockery, a button, a penknife, and a jackknife, but no body parts. Colvin's wife, Sally, identified the items as having belonged to her husband. It was, in a sense, in her interest to do so. Sally had given birth to a child more than nine months after Russell was gone from the scene. Under Vermont law, a child born to a married woman was presumed to be fathered by her husband, making Sally ineligible for state financial support; unless, of course, her husband was dead. She may not have understood at the time that her husband's demise would sharpen the focus of suspicion on her brothers.

Subsequent events kept the case under public scrutiny. Soon after the cellar hole had been searched, a mysterious fire destroyed the sheep barn on the Boorn property. A few days later, a dog unearthed several bone fragments beneath a nearby stump. Three local physicians said they were human bones. Seven years after he had vanished, it appeared clear to the local citizenry that Colvin had been murdered, his body buried and moved on several occasions, and the barn burned down to destroy evidence of the murder. On the basis of such speculation, Jesse Boorn was taken into custody and a warrant was issued for the arrest of Stephen, who had recently moved to New York.

In jail, Jesse shared a cell with a forger named Silas Merrill, who had a tale to tell the authorities. Merrill said that Jesse had admitted taking part in the murder after a visit from his father, Barney. As the story went, Jesse told him that during an argument, Stephen had knocked Colvin to the ground with a club. Barney then came by, and seeing that Colvin was still alive, slit his throat with Stephen's penknife. They buried the body in the cellar hole, then moved it to the barn, and finally to the stump area when the barn burned down. Merrill agreed to tell his story to a jury in exchange for his immediate release. It sounded like a good deal to State's Attorney Calvin Sheldon. Merrill was set free.

With a death sentence looming, Jesse decided to confess in order to minimize his own role in the crime while at the same time exculpating his father and placing the blame chiefly on his brother whom he doubtless believed to be outside the reach of Vermont's jurisdiction. However, when a Manchester constable visited Stephen in New York, he agreed to return in an effort to clear his name. Jesse immediately recanted, saying that he had falsely confessed in an attempt to save himself and his father from execution. Confession or not, the state's attorney chose to seek the death penalty.

During the trial, witnesses emerged to testify they had heard the Boorn brothers threaten to kill Colvin. Others recalled that after his disappearance, the brothers had said they knew that Colvin was dead. But there was one bit of new evidence that had served the defendants' interest. Before the trial started, the largest of the bones the dog had uncovered was compared with an actual human leg bone that had been preserved after an amputation, and the dissimilarities could not be ignored. The same three doctors who originally had deemed it to be a human bone now agreed it was of animal origin. But the damage had already been done. Were it not for the inaccurate identification of the bones, the brothers would not likely have been arrested, and the case would have continued to be little more than grist for the rumor mill.

The exclusion of the bone evidence now was of little consequence. The testimony offered at trial weighed heavily against the brothers. Stephen decided to follow his brother's lead. Hoping to slip the hangman's noose, he confessed that he had taken part in the killing but insisted that he acted in self-defense. It was to no avail. The jury quickly found the brothers guilty, and the three-judge panel sentenced them to death. In a specially convened session, the General Assembly of Vermont considered a plea for clemency. Jesse's sentence was commuted to life because he appeared to be less culpable. Stephen would be hanged.

The brothers had been convicted, as it were, on the basis of a tip provided by a ghost, the misidentification of a bone as being human, the trumped-up testimony of a jailhouse snitch, the seven-year-old recollections of some neighbors, and two false confessions. Nevertheless, justice sometimes finds a way of slipping back in through the cracks. If the spectral appearance of an unexpected visitor was, at least in part, responsible for the brothers' arrest, a confluence of events almost as unlikely would lead to their salvation.

On a late November day in 1819, an item in the *New York Evening Post* noting how divine intervention had helped bring Colvin's killers to justice was being read out loud by a guest in the lobby of a New York hotel. A traveler from New Jersey, Tabor Chadwick, overheard the story. Chadwick knew a man named Russell Colvin who often spoke of Vermont and who had worked the last few years as a farmhand in Dover, New Jersey. He immediately sent a letter to the *Post* and one to the Manchester postmaster. In each letter he described Colvin as "a man of rather small stature—round forehead—[who] speaks very fast, has two scars on his head, and appears to be between 30 and 40 years of age."

Chadwick received no response from Manchester, perhaps because the postmaster, Leonard Sergeant, also happened to be the junior prosecutor in the case. The *Post* published the letter on December 6, 1819. James Whelpley, a native of Manchester living in New York at the time, read it and went to Dover where he found Colvin alive and well but unwilling to return to Vermont. Apparently familiar with the case, Whelpley knew that Stephen's execution was scheduled for January 28, 1820. He enlisted the help of an attractive young woman to lure Colvin back to Manchester. She enticed him to accompany her to New York, but once there she abandoned him, and Whelpley found it necessary to devise a new scheme. The War of 1812 had left a British presence around New York, and Whelpley told Colvin, who now wanted to return to New Jersey, that British ships were offshore and they would have to take a circuitous route back to Dover. He then urged Colvin onto a stagecoach headed in the opposite direction. It was bound for Manchester.

They arrived on December 22, 1819. Having heard of his impending arrival, a crowd of Colvin's former neighbors, including local officials, were waiting to greet him, no doubt interested to see if another ghost might be on the loose. Having convinced the authorities that it was indeed the original Colvin who emerged from the stagecoach, the Boorn brothers were released. They had served seven years in prison; Stephen had come within a month of being hanged.

The first death-penalty exoneration in United States history had little overall effect. It was looked upon as a glitch in a criminal justice system that otherwise functioned pretty well. But as the years went by it became apparent that the glitches were part of the system. Corrections were made, new laws were passed aimed at protecting the innocent from wrongful conviction, but each refinement turned a brighter light on the heart of the problem: it was not possible to achieve a high degree of certainty in a system that depended so heavily on the imperfections of human response and perceptions. Despite forensic advances such as the use of fingerprinting in the latter part of the nineteenth century, the judging of guilt and innocence remained more an art than a science.

A significant shift in that balance occurred not that long ago with the awareness that DNA, which is in effect a molecular fingerprint, can be used to provide dead-certain evidence of a suspect's innocence. Beginning with the first DNA exoneration in 1989, the scientific technique of DNA comparison has been used to free dozens of innocent persons, many of them from death row. The first section of this book will describe some of those cases. The following six parts will examine the major causes of wrongful conviction: eyewitness error, corrupt practices, jailhouse informants, false confessions, junk science, and lack of evidence. Needless to say, every case of DNA exoneration fits neatly in one or more of the other categories. It is being treated separately because it has had the effect of transforming the manner in which guilt and innocence is judged. Perhaps more critically, it has elevated public consciousness of the dangers inherent in an inexact system that almost certainly has sent dozens, perhaps scores, possibly hundreds of innocent people to their deaths.

Almost all of the cases that follow concern the exoneration of prisoners who have been freed from death row. A handful of other cases are included because they have in some way prompted changes in the criminal justice system or influenced attitudes, particularly regarding capital punishment. Every case is an illustration of the grim consequences that ensue when the legal mechanism has gone awry. Freeing innocent people from death row is no indication that the system really works. It shows only that it is badly broken and in serious need of repair.

Part I

DNA: SCIENTIFIC CERTAINTY

In a legal system frayed by error and uncertainty, the advent of forensic DNA testing is often referred to as a magic bullet. The use of DNA technology can provide scientific proof, beyond any question, of a suspect's guilt or innocence. It has begun to revolutionize the criminal justice system in much the same way that the discovery of fingerprinting did more than a century ago. Although a fingerprint is no less unique than a DNA sample, fingerprints are more easily concealed. DNA is contained in blood, semen, saliva, hair follicles, and skin cells, all of which are more difficult to remove from a crime scene.

First identified as the molecule of heredity, DNA has been part of the scientific tableau since the sixties. It was used initially to resolve a few paternity and immigration cases. A British geneticist at the University of Leicester, Alec Jeffreys, who pioneered its application, estimated that the odds against two people other than identical twins sharing the same DNA profile are billions to one.

It was not for several decades that advances in technology made it possible to analyze and match samples quickly and economically enough for DNA fingerprinting to be used in the justice system. That happened for the first time in England in 1986. It was introduced in American courts a year later by a biochemist named Edward Blake, but it did not make its way into popular use until the mid-nineties. Since then, more than eighty wrongly convicted people have been exonerated by DNA evidence, at least a dozen of them freed from death row. It is estimated that DNA fingerprinting has resulted in as many as 25 percent of suspects charged with crimes being released from custody before going to trial.

Perhaps the principal effect of DNA testing is that it has brought to light the glaring inefficiencies of a system that convicts innocent people by the hundreds and sentences a substantial number of them to death. It is no longer possible to believe with any assurance that if a person is convicted he is probably guilty, that if he is sent to his death he no doubt deserves to die. That has all changed now. The reasoning is elementary: If DNA has established with scientific certainty that more than a dozen innocent people have been sentenced to death, can one harbor the belief that similar mistakes were not made in cases where DNA evidence was unavailable? Supporters of capital punishment are now obliged to live with the uneasy suspicion that innocent people are being sent to their deaths.

Curiously, the case that spawned the revolution in attitude toward the criminal justice system was not a capital case. The first DNA exoneration in the United States involved a rape that never took place. The conviction was the product of perjured testimony, prosecutorial misconduct, and defense strategies that backfired. The wrongly convicted man spent the better part of

2

twelve years in prison, but the price he paid was not entirely forfeited. It opened the door to freedom for countless others who had fallen victim to the system.

Gary Dotson
Illinois

Gary Dotson was the victim of a hoax. He was convicted of raping a young woman who was never in fact assaulted, in a trial that rested almost entirely on the false testimony of a police forensic scientist. Ironically, it was old-fashioned blood typing that was used to convict him and breakthrough DNA blood typing that finally set him free.

The web of events in which Dotson became trapped began on the night of July 9, 1977. A police patrol officer noticed a young woman standing alongside a road near a shopping mall in Homewood, Illinois, a suburb of Chicago. It was late at night and she looked disheveled and appeared to be distressed. The officer asked if she was all right. The woman identified herself as Cathleen Crowell. She was sixteen years old and worked as a cashier and cook in a fast-food chain restaurant in the mall. Then she related the following tale:

After leaving work, she was walking across the mall parking lot when a car with three young men in it pulled up alongside her. Two of the men grabbed her and threw her into the rear seat. One of the men climbed in the back, tore her clothes off, raped her, and scratched several letters onto her midsection with a broken beer bottle.

3

The officer took her to a hospital where a rape examination revealed what appeared to be a seminal stain on her panties. Several pubic hairs and a vaginal smear were taken as evidence. A drawing was made of the marks on her abdomen. The letters were illegible and appeared to be shaped in an unusual cross-hatched pattern.

From Crowell's description, a police sketch artist developed a likeness of the man she said attacked her. What emerged was a drawing of a young white male with long stringy hair. She did not mention his having any facial hair. When police showed her a mug book she identified Gary Dotson, a twenty-two-year-old high-school dropout who had had minor brushes with the law in the past. The police arrested Dotson at his nearby home in a working-class suburb where he lived with his mother and sister. Although Dotson had a full mustache that could not have been grown in the five days since the alleged attack, Crowell nonetheless picked him out in a police lineup.

Dotson went on trial for rape in May 1979. There were two chief witnesses for the prosecution. Crowell, who appeared to be a model student at her local high school, where she studied Russian and was a member of the junior varsity swimming team, identified Dotson with total conviction, saying, "There is no mistaking that face." The other key witness was Timothy Dixon, a state police forensic scientist who had been assigned to the case. It was Dixon's testimony regarding blood types that probably clinched the case against Dotson, adding scientific near certainty to Crowell's eyewitness identification. The problem was that Crowell was lying and Dixon was offering information that was at best incomplete, at worst intentionally misleading.

4

Dixon told the court that type B blood antigens had been found in the stain in Crowell's panties and that Dotson was a B-type secretor, placing him in a 10 percent minority in the white male population. Of course 10 percent of the white male population would still provide a substantial number of other suspects, but even those percentages were misleading. Type O blood contains the same antigens as type B, and taken together they account for two-thirds of the white male population. Furthermore, Crowell herself had B-type blood so it could have been her own secretions that produced the stain. The prosecuting attorney, Raymond Garza, also appeared intent on deceiving the jury. In his summation he stated that several pubic hairs taken from the victim matched Dotson's, although at that time it was technically impossible to make that determination. He also described Crowell as a sixteen-year-old virgin, which she was not.

Dotson's defense, based on eyewitness misidentification, rested entirely on the alibi provided by four of his friends who testified they were with him at the time Crowell claimed to have been raped. The prosecutor called them liars, and the jury apparently agreed. They found Dotson guilty; he was sentenced to twenty-five to fifty years. His appeal was denied three years later and to all appearances the case was concluded. In fact, it would follow a long and circuitous route that led finally to Dotson's exoneration.

The first turn came in 1985 when Crowell became stricken by conscience. She had married a high-school classmate, David Webb, three years earlier. They had moved to New Hampshire and joined the Pilgrim Baptist Church, and Cathleen, now known as Cathleen Crowell Webb, confessed to her pastor, the

Reverend Carl Nannini. She told him that she had fabricated the story eight years earlier because she was concerned that she might have become pregnant during a sexual encounter the previous day with her boyfriend, David Bierne. The rape story was intended as a cover-up in the event her fears were realized. She said she inflicted the superficial wounds on her body and tore her clothing to lend credence to her story.

Pastor Nannini retained an attorney, John McLario, who contacted the Cook County State's Attorney's Office. When the prosecutors appeared uninterested, he notified a Chicago television station, which broke the story on March 22, 1985. Warren Lupel, a commercial attorney, agreed to represent Dotson as a favor to a client who knew Dotson's mother. Lupel petitioned the court to set aside the conviction, and the trial judge, Richard Samuels, ordered Dotson's release on $100,000 bond on April 4, pending a hearing the following week. Dotson, who had already spent six years in prison, had reason to be optimistic even beyond Webb's recanting. A new report, prepared by the chief forensic serologist of the Illinois State Police seemed to corroborate her confession. It acknowledged that Dixon's blood-type testimony was flawed and that the semen could have come from O-type secretors, among whom was David Bierne. But Dotson's run of luck did not last long. It ended at the hearing on April 11.

Unaccustomed as he was to criminal proceedings, Warren Lupel committed a tactical error when he called a defense witness who had not testified at the previous trial. The witness was Dotson's closest friend, Bill Julian, who was one of the four friends who provided his alibi. Earlier, the other witnesses had stated that one of the girls had been driving the car on the night in question. Now, Julian said he was the driver. When the discrepancy was noted, the other witnesses agreed that they originally had lied about the driver because Julian was driving with a suspended license. Although the explanation was plausible enough and the driver's identity did not go to the heart of the matter, the credibility of the defense seemed to be shaken. Judge Samuels, unmoved by the new forensic evidence and Webb's recantation, declared that the woman's trial testimony seemed more credible than her revised story. He revoked the bond and sent Dotson back to prison, but his odyssey through the criminal justice system was far from over.

With public sentiment clearly running in Dotson's favor, Governor James R. Thompson granted Lupel's petition for clemency. The three-day hearing attracted media representatives from far and near, and Dotson's and Webb's testimony was carried live on local television stations. Dotson was, in effect, given a split decision. His clemency petition was denied by the governor, but Thompson commuted his sentence to time served. Dotson was released on parole.

Freedom did not necessarily nourish Dotson's lifestyle. He had taken to drinking beer regularly and in large quantities. It was not unusual for him to have a six-pack for breakfast and to continue drinking throughout the day. He had not found work and had no steady means of support. He signed several book and movie contracts but never followed through on any of them. Webb, in an apparent act of penance, gave Dotson $17,500, which she had received as an advance from a publisher of religious books. It would not take Dotson long to dispose of it. One of his most devoted drinking companions was a twenty-one-year-old bartender named Camille Dardanes, who had befriended him during his hearings. Now, with a hefty stake in hand, he and Dardanes went off to Las Vegas and married. On their return to Illinois, they bought two cars and rented and furnished an apartment. Two months later they were broke. Evicted from their apartment, they moved in with Dotson's mother. Camille found work as a waitress, but Gary remained unemployed.

In January 1987, Camille gave birth to a daughter. Gary tried to turn the corner by joining Alcoholics Anonymous, but his attempt at rehabilitation didn't last long. The drinking resumed and the fabric of their lives began to unravel. On a Sunday evening in August, driving home from a day in the park, Gary and Camille quarreled and Gary slapped her. He then took their eight-month-old daughter and bolted from the car. Camille chased after them and flagged down a cruising police car. She told the officers that her husband was a convicted felon and had taken their baby. She said he had struck her, and she wanted to press charges. From that point on, things began to spin out of control. Gary was arrested, charged with domestic battery, and held without bond since the offense might have violated the terms of his parole.

During the proceedings that followed, Gary found a new advocate. Civia Tamarkin, a journalist who wrote for *People* magazine, had interviewed Gary for an article and was convinced that he was innocent of the rape charge. She found him a new attorney, one who was steeped in criminal law and well acquainted with the workings of the legal machinery in and around Chicago. He was Thomas M. Breen, a former assistant state's attorney in Cook County, and he set to work immediately. Camille, despite her initial wish to press charges, decided she would not cooperate with the prosecution, and the domestic battery case against Gary was dropped. He was not yet in the clear, however.

Dotson indeed was found to be in violation of parole, and the Illinois Department of Corrections invoked a "parole hold" on him, requiring that he be held in custody pending a hearing before the Illinois Prisoner Review Board. Although the hearing appeared to go well, the board repealed his parole and reinstated his original sentence. Dotson now faced an additional sixteen years of prison time.

Breen was not happy with the turn of events. He did not think Dotson's parole should have been revoked for a domestic spat in which his wife no longer wished to press charges. Even his parole officer, Phillip Magee, seemed to agree. In his report to the review board he said: "His [Dotson's] violation neither indicated criminal orientation, nor does he appear to otherwise represent a serious threat to public safety." Breen was further irritated because the review board never notified him directly of its decision; he learned it from a reporter who was covering the case. Now, desperately seeking a pivot that might turn things in Dotson's favor, the attorney found one where one might least have expected it.

In the October 26, 1987, issue of *Newsweek* magazine, Breen came across an article entitled "Leaving Holmes in the Dust." The writer, Sharon Begley, reported that DNA technology would make it possible to connect a suspect to a crime and, conversely, could exonerate a suspect who was innocent.

Investigating further, Breen learned that DNA had not yet been used in a criminal case. Since Dotson's conviction now rested almost entirely on blood evidence, Breen saw the new scientific technique as made to order. He filed a motion with Judge Richard J. Fitzgerald of the Criminal Division of the Cook County Circuit Court, asking that DNA testing be used in the Dotson case. The assistant state's attorney, J. Scott Arthur, offered no objection. Governor Thompson also approved and asked Alec Jeffreys, the British geneticist and pioneer in DNA fingerprinting, to conduct the test.

With DNA technology still in its infancy, Jeffreys was initially unable to obtain a conclusive result. The sample had degraded over the years and the evidence had become stale. Governor Thompson, who seemed determined to bring the case to a conclusion, decided to take the testing a step farther. In California, the forensic scientist Edward Blake had been pushing DNA techniques to their limits. Thompson ordered that Webb's panties be sent to Blake along with fresh blood samples from both Dotson and David Bierne.

On August 15, 1988, Blake informed Thompson, the prosecutors, and Breen that the test had positively excluded Dotson and identified Bierne as the source of the semen. A day later, Breen asked the governor to grant Dotson unconditional clemency on the grounds of actual innocence. But Thompson was hesitant. He said he would not act on the clemency petition until he received a recommendation from the prisoner review board. In the meantime, Dotson was housed involuntarily in a residential center for alcohol and substance abusers. Nine months passed without any action being taken, and Breen filed a new petition for postconviction relief. On August 14, almost a year after results of DNA testing eliminated Dotson as a suspect, Judge Fitzgerald granted the motion. The State's Attorney's Office immediately announced that the charges against Dotson would be dropped.

The first case of DNA exoneration in the United States was now in the books, and the lid was pried open on a new era in the American penal system. Five years later, in 1993, DNA was used for the first time to free a man who had served time on death row.

Kirk Bloodsworth
Maryland

On July 25, 1984, nine-year-old Dawn Venice Hamilton went to play outside her cousins' apartment near Golden Ring Mall in the Rosedale section just outside of Baltimore. When she failed to return, her aunt called the police. A few hours later she was found dead in a nearby wooded area. She had been beaten with a rock, sexually assaulted, and strangled. A sneaker had made an impression on her neck and a stick was inserted in her vagina. Her underwear was found hanging from a tree. A chunk of cinder block, believed to be the murder weapon, was found near her head. Two boys who had been fishing in the vicinity told police they had seen Dawn enter the woods with a man who had curly blond hair. Three other residents of the apartment complex also claimed to have seen a blond, curly-haired man in the area on the day of the crime. A composite sketch was drawn up and given to newspapers and television stations.

Kirk Bloodsworth, a twenty-three-year-old ex-marine, worked at the Golden Ring Mall, but he was off on the day of the murder. He and his wife had been having marital problems, and he had followed her from their Cambridge, Maryland, home to the Middle River area of Baltimore County in an effort to patch things up. A week later, he decided the marriage could not be saved, and he left without telling her. His wife called the police to file a missing persons report. The name rang a bell. Not much earlier, the police had received an anonymous call saying the composite sketch resembled a man named Kirk.

When Bloodsworth returned to Cambridge a few days later, he was questioned by the police. One of the boys who had been fishing said Bloodsworth looked like the man he had seen, even though his hair was red rather than blond. Bloodsworth told the police that he had left Cambridge because his marriage was troubled and he wanted the comfort of being with friends. He said he had notified his mother-in-law that he was leaving and did not understand why his wife had filed a missing persons report. He also noted that while the suspect was described as about six feet five inches, thin, and blond, he was only about six feet tall, rather burly, and had bright red hair. He said he had never seen Dawn Hamilton. Nonetheless Bloodsworth, who had no previous record, was arrested and charged with sexual assault, rape, and first-degree murder.

There was no physical evidence linking him to the crime. The FBI, which was involved in the investigation, had the girl's panties examined and determined there was nothing there that would either help or hurt the state's case. The sole basis for Bloodsworth's arrest was the identification by five eyewitnesses, none of whom had ever seen him in the presence of the girl. The trial turned on degrees of credibility. It was the word of the state's witnesses that placed him near the crime scene against the testimony of the defendant's friends who said they were with him at the time of the murder. The jury believed the prosecution's witnesses. Bloodsworth was found guilty and sentenced to death.

In 1986, Bloodsworth's attorney filed an appeal contending that the police had had other suspects, including one who more closely resembled the composite sketch, and another man who had helped search for the missing girl and had found her underpants hanging from the tree. It was information, the defense maintained, that should have been revealed during the trial. The Maryland Court of Appeals agreed. Bloodsworth's conviction was overturned in July 1986 because the police had withheld evidence. He was tried again in April 1987 and again was convicted. This time he was sentenced to two consecutive life terms instead of death.

After having spent two and a half years isolated on death row, Bloodsworth was imprisoned with the general population. It was a mixed blessing. Though life on death row was depressing and bleak, Bloodsworth found that living among the general run of prisoners could be even tougher, since child molesters were disdained by even the toughest of convicts.

Bloodsworth continued to press his appeals with a new, court-appointed attorney, Robert E. Morin. He passed the time writing poetry and reading books by the hundreds. One of the books, *The Blooding,* by Joseph Wambaugh, a former Los Angeles cop, described how British police used DNA to solve murders in the Yorkshire area. He discussed the matter with Morin. Dawn's panties had contained a semen stain smaller than a dime. Morin recalled that the FBI had already tested the panties and could gather no useful evidence from the stain. But that was more than five years earlier, and DNA technology had been advancing quickly.

In April 1992, Morin sent the victim's panties and shorts as well as the stick that had been inserted in her vagina to Edward Blake in California. Blake, who had intervened in Dotson's behalf, was by now recognized as the father of forensic DNA testing in the United States. He headed the only private lab, Forensic Science Associates (FSA), that was then conducting DNA tests for criminal justice purposes. The samples were still fresh. The evidence had been locked up and preserved. The stain had been air-dried, and DNA can remain in dried samples of body fluids for years. Morin paid the $10,000 testing fee, as Bloodsworth's family had exhausted their life savings financing his defense. It took a year for the results to be returned. On May 17, 1993, the lab issued its report. It concluded that Bloodsworth's blood samples did not match any of the evidence it had tested. However, the lab also requested a fresh sample of Bloodsworth's blood for retesting to resolve questions about proper labeling on the original sample. On June 3, FSA issued a second report stating that its original findings were replicated: Bloodsworth could not be responsible for the stain on the victim's underwear. A few weeks later, the FBI conducted its own test of the evidence and came to the same conclusion.

Three months later, on June 28, 1993, Bloodsworth walked free. After another three months, Maryland governor William Donald Schaefer issued a full pardon. The state paid Bloodsworth

$300,000 for lost income, based on the estimate that he would have earned approximately $30,000 a year from the time of his arrest to his release.

Bloodsworth now lives with his second wife in Cambridge, a rustic town on Maryland's Eastern Shore, where he works as a crab and commercial fisherman. He works hard and lives simply. He never turns down a request to tell his story, in the hope that if the public is aware of the hazards of wrongful conviction, other innocent lives can be spared. The Dawn Hamilton murder-and-rape case remains open in Maryland.

Bloodsworth was the first man sentenced to death who was cleared as a result of DNA evidence. Since then, between 1995 and 2002, a dozen other men were released from death row on the basis of similar tests.

Rolando Cruz and Alejandro Hernandez
Illinois

Not everyone was immediately convinced of the infallibility of DNA testing. The most serious doubters often were police and prosecutors, and that did not bode well for suspects in their jurisdictions. Two such suspects—Rolando Cruz and Alejandro Hernandez—spent ten years, much of it on death row, in an Illinois prison while four police officers and three former prosecutors played fast and loose with the criminal justice system. They were unimpressed that DNA evidence had excluded the pair from having been involved in the crime with which they were charged.

The crime was a heinous one. It was the kidnapping, rape, and murder of a ten-year-old girl, Jeanine Nicarico, in DuPage County, Illinois, in 1983. The police questioned Hernandez, who was borderline mentally retarded and was inclined toward fantasy, based on a tip from an anonymous caller. Hernandez, who was nineteen years old, told them that he and some of his friends, including Cruz, who was twenty, knew something about the crime. They apparently were enticed by a $10,000 reward that had been offered for information leading to an arrest. Police officers told Hernandez and Cruz they would be considered heroes in the community if they helped solve the murder. Neither was able to provide any information that was not already public knowledge. However, police said that when Cruz was questioned he offered details of the crime that he told them came to him in a vision. No record was made of those statements, and Cruz later denied making them.

In January 1984, the district attorney announced that his office had insufficient evidence to bring charges against any suspect. The community, which was outraged by the brutality of the crime, was becoming impatient. Six weeks later, Cruz and Hernandez were charged with raping and murdering the young girl. The lead detective in the case, who had insisted all along that the two suspects were not the murderers, resigned in protest, saying that the state was proceeding against innocent men.

Nevertheless, Cruz and Hernandez were tried and convicted on perjured government testimony and questionable courtroom decisions. Cruz's alleged dream visions were admitted into evidence on the basis of the testimony of sheriff's detectives although there was no written or visual record of Cruz having made the statements. In Hernandez's case, an officer who claimed that the defendant had incriminated himself during interrogation, admitted that he had not documented those remarks until almost four years after the questioning. Other officers said they never took notes or maintained that their notes had been lost or destroyed. Cruz and Hernandez were sentenced to death.

They were not on death row very long before fortune turned in their direction. A repeat sex offender and convicted murderer, Brian Dugan, confessed to the crime for which they were convicted. He also admitted to five other crimes—two rape-murders and three rapes. His confession included many details of the crime that only the perpetrator could know. A number of his other crimes were similar in nature to the rape and murder of Jeanine. In addition, several witnesses corroborated Dugan's confession. They testified that he had committed the crimes by himself.

In 1988, the Illinois Supreme Court overturned the convictions and death sentences on the grounds that the defendants should have had separate trials. Two years later, Cruz and Hernandez were each retried, and again they were convicted. Their second trials were as tainted as their first. Dugan's confession was never offered in evidence because it was concealed from the defense team. It would not be disclosed for more than four years. A former cellmate of Cruz's who, in exchange for a four-month reduction in his sentence, had testified in the original trial that Cruz had admitted committing the murder, refused to testify at the second trial, stating that his story had been invented. Robert Turner, another death-row inmate with Cruz, testified against him. He said Cruz had confessed to committing the murder with Hernandez and Dugan. However, two other death-row inmates told the court that Turner had said he was going to set up Cruz using law books that described the crime. The prosecution told the jury that Turner had been offered nothing in return for his testimony, but nine months later one of the prosecutors spoke in his behalf at a resentencing hearing.

In 1990, a volunteer legal team headed by Lawrence C. Marshall, who was affiliated with the Center on Wrongful Convictions, agreed to represent Cruz on appeal. A divided Illinois Supreme Court granted Cruz another new trial because evidence regarding Dugan's confession had been excluded by the trial judge. In the meantime, the role of DNA technology as used in the Bloodsworth case came to the attention of the defense, and a test was ordered. The results were conclusive: Cruz and Hernandez were excluded as possible rapists of Jeanine Nicarico. The sample matched Dugan's DNA. But despite all evidence of their innocence, the state insisted on pressing the case against Cruz and Hernandez. The prosecutor, in the face of what now was regarded as scientific certainty, declared, "The DNA results . . . do not in any way negate Cruz's involvement in the Nicarico crime." The state decided to proceed with a third trial.

In 1992, Assistant Attorney General Mary Brigid Kenney wrote a memorandum identifying numerous errors made in the prosecution of Cruz and urged that they be acknowledged to the court. The memo concluded: "I cannot, in good conscience, allow my name to appear on a brief asking . . . to affirm his conviction." State Attorney General Roland Burris responded by removing Kenney from the case, and she responded by resigning. In her resignation letter, she wrote: "I was being asked to help execute an innocent man. Unfortunately, you [the attorney general] have seen fit to ignore the evidence in this case."

For the new trials, the team of four defense attorneys, which included Marshall, opted for a bench trial, which made the judge, rather than a jury, the finder of fact. Interviews with jurors from the previous trials indicated that many of them had been "caught up in the emotion that surrounds a crime of this kind," Marshall found. During Cruz's trial, a police officer admitted having lied under oath. He said he had fabricated Cruz's initial statement about seeing the crime scene in a vision. After hearing all the prosecution evidence, the judge directed a verdict of not guilty. Still, prosecutors seemed intent upon retrying Hernandez, whose conviction had also been overturned, but they dropped the charges on the eve of the trial. Cruz was set free in November 1995, Hernandez a month later.

Shortly after the two were released, a special prosecutor was appointed to investigate whether police and prosecutors had violated the law in pursuing their case against Hernandez and Cruz. A grand jury later indicted four sheriff's deputies and three former prosecutors, a group that became known as the DuPage 7, on charges of perjury and official misconduct. Although they were acquitted of the charges, DuPage County later agreed to pay $3.5 million to settle civil rights claims filed in federal court by Cruz, Hernandez, and Stephen Buckley, a third defendant who had been implicated. The district attorney who prosecuted Cruz later became Illinois attorney general.

Another prosecutor in the case is now a judge. Brian Dugan remains imprisoned for a number of other rapes and murders, but he has not been charged with the murder of Jeanine Nicarico.

Frank Lee Smith
Florida

DNA testing had come into its own by the year 2000 when it was used to clear Frank Lee Smith of the rape and murder of eight-year-old Shandra Whitehead in Fort Lauderdale, Florida. But it was of no help to Smith. After spending fourteen years on death row, he died of pancreatic cancer while awaiting execution in the electric chair ten months before he was found to be innocent.

At approximately eleven o'clock on the night of April 14, 1985, Shandra Whitehead was raped, sodomized, and beaten severely with a blunt instrument during an attack in her home. She died nine days later from the injuries. The victim's mother identified Smith as the man she saw leaning into an open window and then fleeing as she returned home at about eleven-thirty on the night of the crime. Two other witnesses also identified Smith. Chiquita Lowe and Gerald Davis, both nineteen, reported seeing a scraggly-haired, confused-looking black man with a droopy eye in the neighborhood at the time of the murder. The two teens helped police develop a composite sketch of the man they saw. Members of Lowe's family said they saw the man in the sketch standing outside their home some days after the crime, trying to sell a television set.

Although none of the eyewitnesses had gotten a good look at Smith, police could not have asked for a more likely suspect. A thirty-eight-year-old former convict, he was out on parole after serving fifteen years for manslaughter and a murder he committed as a teenager. Smith was arrested and charged with the Whitehead girl's murder.

As the case proceeded to trial, Lowe began to feel uncertain about the accuracy of her testimony. She later revealed her doubts on PBS network's *Frontline* television program in a film entitled *Requiem for Frank Lee Smith.* "When I went into the courtroom and seen him," she said, "he was too skinny, too tall, and he did not have the droopy eye." Lowe nevertheless confirmed her identification at the trial. "I was pressured by my family," she explained, "people that's in my neighborhood, and the police officer. They kept telling me that I'm the only one that seen that man that night." Despite her misgivings, Lowe was the key witness, and based largely on her testimony, Smith was convicted and sentenced to death.

Not long after the trial, Jeff Walsh, an investigator for the defense team, discovered that a number of rapes and murders of young black women had occurred in Whitehead's neighborhood during the same time period as the attack on Shandra. A man by the name of Eddie Lee Mosley was a suspect in a number of those cases. Mosley was a man that police had kept in their sights for some time. In fact, two policemen had begun to discern a pattern between local murders and Mosley's releases from prison or mental hospitals.

Police officer Kevin Allen told *Frontline*: "When [Mosley is] incarcerated there are no unsolved rape/murders of black females in northwest Fort Lauderdale," but "immediately upon his release or within thirty days, we find a black female [murdered] at the rate of one a month until he is incarcerated again. And that history . . . repeated itself consistently."

Walsh soon learned that Mosley, who was then in a state psychiatric hospital, was on the loose at the time Shandra Whitehead was murdered. He also discovered that Mosley knew the girl; he was her mother's cousin. What impressed Walsh even more was that Mosley's mug shot looked strikingly like the police sketch, complete with drooping eye. When Walsh showed the mug shot to Lowe, she did not hesitate. She said Mosley was definitely the man she saw the night of the murder. She signed a sworn affidavit attesting to her incorrect identification of Smith.

Walsh and the defense team thought they had a sure thing when they went before the Florida Supreme Court to ask for a new trial. They did not count on police offering testimony that was at odds with the account they had given at the trial and apparently was aimed at discrediting the word of a shaken and tentative Lowe.

Local authorities began the demolition of Lowe's credibility by contending that they had shown her Mosley's photo at the time of the investigation. The lead detective, Richard Scheff, had previously testified that Lowe had looked at two lineups and had identified Smith each time. Now, he insisted that Lowe had been shown a third lineup in which Mosley was included, but she had not picked him out as the man she saw at the murder scene. The court denied Smith's motion for a new trial. It also denied several motions for DNA testing. Smith was sent back to death row to await execution. However, cancer got to him before the executioner. He died in February 2000.

After Smith's death, DNA tests performed in relation to two other cases linked Mosley, still in custody, to murders for which an innocent man had been convicted. Smith's DNA was tested posthumously. No match was found with samples from the Shandra Whitehead case. The test confirmed that she had been raped and murdered by Eddie Lee Mosley.

With the test results in, the governor of Florida appointed a special counsel to investigate accusations that Detective Scheff had lied on the witness stand. Scheff was subsequently reassigned.

Ronald Keith Williamson
Oklahoma

Ron Williamson spent nine years in a death-row cell in the state penitentiary in McAlester, Oklahoma, for the rape and murder of a young woman in 1982. He was convicted in 1987, largely on the basis of state-of-the-art tests on hair and semen samples found at the scene of the crime. He was freed in 1999 after DNA from those same samples were found not to match his own.

When Debra Sue Carter, a twenty-two-year-old waitress, was found raped and strangled in her apartment in Ada, Oklahoma, Williamson was a target of easy opportunity for the police. Once a star high-school baseball player, good enough to be drafted by the Oakland A's organization before an injury ended his career, he was now, in his late twenties, something of an outsider in the small town where he had grown up. He had been hospitalized for mental problems on more than one occasion, he had a police record, and a few women reported that he had bothered them in the past. Five years after the Carter murder, Williamson and another man, Dennis Fritz, were arrested and charged with the crime. The evidence presented at trial consisted of the presumed matching hair samples and the testimony of a jailhouse informant. Williamson was sentenced to death; Fritz was given a life term.

In prison, Williamson became friendly with another condemned man, Greg Wilhoit, who occupied the cell across the hall. After a while, the two men became convinced of each other's innocence. Wilhoit's appeal was being handled by a public defender, Mark Barrett, who believed Wilhoit's conviction was the result of incompetent counsel. "His lawyer was the town drunk by the time of Wilhoit's trial," Barrett said, "enough of a town drunk that he had wet himself in some courtrooms [and] thrown up in the judge's chambers." Eventually, Barrett won a new trial and an acquittal for his client.

Having learned about Williamson's case from Wilhoit, Barrett found reason to believe that he too had been victimized by ineffective representation. His lawyer had never tried a capital case and had refused to be left alone with his client. He had failed to investigate and present to the jury the fact that another man had confessed to the crime of which Williamson was convicted. Barrett took his appeal to federal court, but time was becoming a factor. Williamson's sister had already received a letter from the prison describing the correct procedure for claiming his body. In 1997, five days before he was scheduled to be executed, the court overturned the verdict on the grounds of

incompetent counsel. A new trial was held, and Williamson and
Fritz were again convicted, on the same evidence that had been
offered at their first trial. But Barrett was now on a mission.

Two years later, he and his cocounsel, the DNA expert Barry
Scheck, submitted for DNA testing the same samples that had
been used to convict the two men. Mary Long, a criminologist
for the Oklahoma State Bureau of Investigation, testified that
the hair and semen specimens did not match those of either man.
They did, however, match a third man's DNA. He was Glen
Gore, who was the suspect not mentioned by the defense at
Williamson's first trial, and the jailhouse witness who had testified that he had seen the two defendants at the crime scene on
the night of the murder. Gore, who was serving a sentence at the
Lexington Correctional Center, escaped from the facility on
April 14, 1999, the day before Williamson and Fritz were set
free. He surrendered to authorities six days later.

Williamson received no reparations from the state, other than
the standard $50 check given to all inmates who are destitute
upon release. He lives in a group home in Oklahoma City and
earns extra income playing the guitar in coffeehouses. He continues to suffer from bipolar disorder and has been hospitalized
for treatment.

Ronald Jones
Illinois

Although DNA testing was in common use by 1994—it played
a prominent part in the media event that was the trial of O. J.

Simpson—a Cook County circuit court judge declined to authorize it for a man who had been sentenced to death chiefly on the strength of a disputed confession.

The victim was a twenty-eight-year-old mother of three who was raped and murdered in an abandoned motel on the South Side of Chicago in 1985. Charged with committing the crime was Ronald Jones, a thirty-four-year-old alcoholic who lived in the neighborhood and who at the time was being questioned as a suspect in another rape case for which he denied responsibility. Two Chicago detectives, Steven Hood and John Markham, obtained a signed confession from Jones for the rape/murder. They insisted the confession was voluntary, but Jones contended that he was beaten into confessing. At his trial in 1989, Jones testified that Hood hit him in the head several times with an object that resembled a blackjack. Also according to the defendant, Markham told Hood, "Don't hit him like this because he will bruise," and then proceeded to punch Jones repeatedly in the midsection. Even as written, the confession seemed flawed because Jones is recorded as saying that the victim was a prostitute although she had no record of prostitution.

The other evidence presented by the prosecution was equally questionable. The victim of the alleged rape for which Jones originally was questioned was permitted to testify against him in order to establish a pattern, although he was never prosecuted for that crime. The only other significant piece of evidence was a witness who said she saw Jones panhandling from the victim around the time police think the murder occurred. There was no physical evidence placing him at the scene. Despite the fact that the signed confession said Jones had ejaculated and the prosecution contended that he was the source of the semen found on the victim, the state maintained at the trial that the quantity of semen that had been recovered was insufficient for a test to be made. Jones was convicted and Judge John E. Morrissey sentenced him to death.

Five years later, in 1994, an assistant Illinois appellate defender, Richard Cunningham, asked Morrissey to authorize a DNA test, since the technology was unavailable at the time of the trial. Morrissey denied the request. When the defense reminded the judge that the prosecution had argued at the start that the semen found on the victim belonged to Jones, the judge responded: "Save arguments like that for the press. They love it; I don't."

The judge's ruling was appealed to the Illinois Supreme Court, which reversed Morrissey and ordered the test. The DNA evidence proved conclusively that the semen found at the crime scene was not Jones's. With the prosecution still not satisfied, the case initially seemed headed for a retrial, but the state soon relented and the charges against Jones were dropped on May 17, 1999.

Earl Washington
Virginia

The mentally retarded often appear to be inviting targets in a flawed criminal justice system that seems at times to prefer a wrong conviction to none at all. They are overmatched in confrontation first with police eager for an arrest and then with conviction-hungry prosecutors. Nor can the public be counted an ally, for the mentally retarded are sometimes treated as disposable items who contribute little and will not be missed. They have been executed regularly, and in states like Texas quickly, after trials through which their lawyers slept at the defense table. The appeal process that followed was likely to be abbreviated because it was difficult to find a competent appellate attorney willing to invest the time needed to explore the prospect of his client's innocence. Not until the United States Supreme Court ruled in 2002 that the practice was cruel and unusual punishment, in violation of the Eighth Amendment, did the execution of the mentally retarded cease.

Earl Washington Jr. twice came perilously close to becoming a victim of the system. Mentally retarded, with an IQ of 69, Washington was nine days away from dying in Virginia's electric chair for a 1982 rape and murder he did not commit. In his early twenties and working as a farmhand, Washington had been arrested on an unrelated assault charge in 1983. Questioned by police, he was manipulated into confessing to the brutal attack on nineteen-year-old Rebecca Williams, who was raped and then stabbed thirty-eight times in her apartment in Culpeper, Virginia, on June 4, 1982. He also confessed to three other rapes, none of which he committed. Washington later recanted his statement. His lawyer contended that the confession was internally inconsistent with known facts in the case and more than likely the words of a man with subnormal intelligence who was "easily led" by police to confess. Despite the tainted confession and the absence of any other evidence, Washington was found guilty and sentenced to death.

Having been convicted of burglary and assault in the 1983 case and already serving time on two fifteen-year sentences, Washington was now transferred to death row. It was not intended to be a long visit. An execution date was set for September 5, 1985. Washington did not have an appeal attorney, and he was not capable of filing an appeal in his own behalf. Joseph Giarratano, a fellow death-row inmate whose sentence had been commuted to life imprisonment, brought Washington's situation to the attention of a federal judge. The judge put Giarratano in touch with Marie Deans, who was head of the since-defunct Virginia Coalition on Jails and Prisons. Deans was determined to find an appeal attorney who would take Washington's case. It was not easy. She was turned down by seventy-five lawyers before Eric M. Freedman, a New York attorney, agreed to intervene. He succeeded in obtaining a stay of execution nine days before Washington was scheduled to die.

Six years later, in a 1991 federal appeals court decision, a three-judge panel found that Washington's confession resulted from a two-day interrogation that contained "numerous factual errors," including the victim's race, her injury, and the location of her apartment. Nonetheless, the conviction was permitted to stand. By 1993, Washington's attorneys had reached the end of the line on their appeals. A request for a pardon was sent to Governor L. Douglas Wilder, who asked that a DNA test be performed before he ruled on the application. The test on semen samples found at the crime scene excluded Washington as a possible source, but the authorities were not ready to let him go. Prosecutors suggested that the semen belonged to an accomplice of Washington's, although the victim had said before she died that there was only one assailant. In December 1993, with his term near an end and a new execution date approaching, Governor Wilder commuted the sentence to life without the possibility of parole.

Seven more years passed before another glimmer of hope came Washington's way. In the summer of 2000, with more sophisticated DNA technology available, Governor Jim Gilmore ordered new tests to be made and a state police investigation into Washington's case. Though much of the semen taken from the victim's body had deteriorated, additional evidence was discovered. A blue blanket taken from the scene of the crime was tested for the first time, and the DNA found on it matched that of a previously convicted rapist. On October 2, Earl Washington was granted a full pardon. On February 12, 2001, he was finally freed after serving eighteen years in prison.

Charles Fain
Idaho

The case that sent Charles Fain to Idaho's death row for almost eighteen years was so weak, so badly managed, so willfully manipulated by the prosecution that the state's attorney general, Alan Lance, a conservative Republican, intervened on Fain's behalf and explained his actions publicly when the innocent man was finally released.

Fain was convicted of the kidnapping, rape, and murder of nine-year-old Daralyn Johnson on February 24, 1982. The girl was snatched off the street in Nampa, Idaho, a small town just west of Boise, while on her way to elementary school. Her body was thrown into a ditch near the Snake River and was not discovered for several days. The crime stunned the citizens of Nampa, and the pressure for a solution grew as each day passed without an arrest.

Seven months after the murder, the police picked up Fain for questioning. He was one of scores of men who were deemed suspects, and there seemed to be little evidence that pointed in his direction. He was a Vietnam veteran who had served with the 101st Airborne and was honorably discharged. Since leaving the service he had had difficulty holding a job and moved back and forth between Idaho and Oregon, but he had never been in trouble with the police. The only apparent reasons for treating him as a suspect were that he lived one block from the victim's house and his light-brown hair was similar in color to hairs found on the girl's body. About a month after the initial interrogation, the police brought him back and questioned him intensely for more than two hours. They asked him if he would take a polygraph test, and he agreed. A state examiner who viewed the test results concluded that Fain was telling the truth when he denied any involvement in the crime. The results were of no help to Fain.

A forensics expert with the FBI said that microscopic examination—the standard test at that time—indicated that three hairs found on Daralyn's body were a match for Fain's. That identification was the principal evidence the prosecution had at its disposal when they charged Fain with the murder. In court, the case against him was nailed down by two jailhouse informers who offered a lurid description of what Fain, then awaiting trial, allegedly told them about how he had raped and murdered the girl. One of the informers, Ricky Chilton, was facing 230 years on various charges when he gave his testimony. He was released three years later and said he had been pressured by the prosecution to testify.

As for the defendant's case, it was virtually nullified. Fain said he was at his father's house in Redmond, Oregon, at the time of the crime, but there was no one but his father to corroborate his alibi. The prosecution objected to introducing the lie-detector results into evidence, and the judge agreed to exclude it. Fain was sentenced to die in Idaho's death house.

D. Frederick Hoopes and Spencer McIntyre, two of the attorneys who worked tirelessly on Fain's defense, managed to keep the case alive on appeals, and in the spring of 2001 a DNA test was performed on the hairs that were used to convict him. When an initial round of testing proved favorable to Fain, Lance ordered that further testing be performed. The second round of tests was conducted in June at an independent laboratory in Virginia. Once again, the results indicated that the DNA found at the scene was not Fain's. Lance asked a federal court to throw out the conviction and give the state sixty days to decide whether it wished to retry the case. When it chose not to, Fain walked free on August 23, eleven days shy of his fifty-third birthday.

Lance, whose website describes him as a "staunch defender of Idaho's sovereignty" who has been honored "for his leadership as an advocate for crime victims," saw fit to explain his cause of action. He said:

We cannot know how much weight the jury gave to the

FBI agent's testimony. However, it is clear from this new evidence that the hairs were not Fain's. This fact raises the critical question: Would the jury have reached the same verdict had the jury known the hairs were not Fain's? It is the attorney general's duty to defend the decisions of Idaho juries and trial courts when challenged in the appellate courts. However, that duty is not ethically blind. As prosecutors we also have a duty to seek the truth and justice. We have a duty to do what is right.

It was a noble sentiment that was not necessarily shared by the prosecutor who tried the case or the trial judge. The prosecutor, Richard Harris, insisted that he still believed Fain to be guilty, based on the testimony of the two informers. Judge James Doolittle also said he had no doubt about Fain's guilt. "If I had the slightest doubt," he said, "I certainly would not have imposed the death penalty."

Doolittle's certainty, so far as defense attorney Hoopes was concerned, was precisely the point; it served to emphasize the dangers inherent in administering the death penalty. One's certainty in another man's guilt is never conclusive. "We just can't kill people who we are sure are guilty," Hoopes said.

Ray Krone

Arizona

When Ray Krone walked out of Arizona State Prison at Yuma on April 8, 2002, he became the one hundredth innocent person convicted of capital murder to be released from custody since 1973, according to the Death Penalty Information Center. Krone was freed by DNA evidence after being convicted twice and spending ten years in prison, including three years on death row. His was the twelfth DNA exoneration in the United States since 1993.

Krone was convicted of first-degree murder and kidnapping in the stabbing death of Kim Ancona, a thirty-six-year-old Phoenix cocktail waitress whose body was found in a local lounge on December 29, 1991. In an apparent frenzy to make an arrest, Phoenix police charged Krone with the crime two days later. He was assigned an attorney by the state. The evidence against him was circumstantial and he was convicted chiefly on the basis of expert testimony that bite marks found on the victim's breast matched Krone's distinctive dental pattern. During his trial, the press labeled him the "snaggletooth killer." The trial lasted about a week, and the jury returned a verdict of guilty after deliberating for two hours. The judge sentenced him to death.

Krone's parents, Carolyn and Jim Leming, retained a private attorney, Christopher J. Plourd, and in June 1995 the Arizona Supreme Court overturned the conviction and granted Krone a new trial at which DNA evidence would be introduced. Aware that the state's case hinged almost completely on what the prosecutor called Krone's "unique dentition," Krone's lawyer used his opening remarks to contend that the bite marks were not the defendant's and that saliva found on the victim provided a DNA pattern that excluded Krone. However, the DNA test was not entirely conclusive and the jury again found Krone guilty.

But Maricopa County Superior Court Judge James McDougall was unconvinced. Saying he had a list of troubling questions about the case and serious doubts about the "clear identity of the killer," he sentenced Krone to twenty-five years to life on the murder charge and an additional twenty-one years for kidnapping. Although he was moved off death row, the prospect of spending the rest of his life in prison for a crime he did not commit was of little comfort to Krone. He said he gave up hope when the jurors ignored what he thought to be overwhelming evidence and testimony in his favor. "[T]hat pretty much ruled out all the faith I had in truth and justice," he said later. Thirty-nine years old when he was sentenced for the second time, he would be seventy-five before he became eligible for release.

Once again, DNA technology came to the rescue. Alan Simpson, a member of Krone's defense team, had a new DNA test performed in 2002 on saliva found on the victim's tank top. The results not only cleared Krone as a possibility, but they were found to be a perfect match for Kenneth Phillips, who was serving time in the same prison for an unrelated sex crime and who had lived about six hundred yards from the bar where Ancona was killed. In addition, a dental expert said that Phillips could not be eliminated as the person who left the bite mark on the victim's breast. Krone was released four days after a police lab confirmed the DNA match with Phillips.

The futility of working within an inexact system that too often condemns innocent men was reflected in a statement made by Rick Romley, a Maricopa County prosecuting attorney. "What do we say to him?" Romley asked. "An injustice was done and we will try to do better. And we're sorry."

• • •

Eddie Joe Lloyd
Michigan

If Michigan were not one of twelve states without capital punishment, Eddie Joe Lloyd might well be dead now. Lloyd was
freed in August 2002 after spending seventeen years in six
prisons for the rape and murder of sixteen-year-old Michelle
Jackson in 1984. The basis for Lloyd's conviction was a confession he says police asked him to provide that was intended to set
a trap for the real killer.

Michelle Jackson, a high-school honor student, disappeared
early on the snowy morning of January 24, 1984, from a bus stop
near her home in Detroit. A search party comprised of her
neighbors found her body in an abandoned garage. She had been
strangled. More than eight months passed before police charged
Lloyd with the crime.

At the time of his arrest, Eddie Joe Lloyd was in a mental hospital, where he had been sent for psychological evaluation after
becoming involved in a violent dispute with a clerk in a welfare
office. When he read about the murder he contacted the police.
He told them he had some information about the crime. He
seemed to know quite a bit about the victim's clothing and her
condition when she was found. Most of it had appeared in the
press. There was one detail that had not seen print: A green
bottle had been used to sexually assault the girl. Lloyd told police
he had heard someone in a store mention something about a bottle.
It was enough to point a finger at Lloyd. He was interviewed three

times in the mental hospital. Finally, according to Lloyd, a Detroit detective told him he could help the police trap the real killer by confessing to the murder. He obliged by providing them with a six-page signed confession and an audiotape. The confession was released to the public, and a jury found him guilty after deliberating less than half an hour. While sentencing him to life in prison, Wayne County Circuit Court Judge Leonard Townsend said: "The sentence that the statute requires is inadequate. The only justifiable sentence, I would say, would be termination by extreme constriction."

Lloyd, who spent much of his time in prison doing biological and legal research on his own case, saw the codirector of the Innocence Project at the Cardozo School of Law in New York, Barry Scheck, discussing DNA evidence on a television talk show. He wrote to Scheck, who arranged for a DNA test that eliminated Lloyd as a possibility. In granting a joint request by prosecution and defense that Lloyd be released, Judge Townsend sounded matter-of-fact about Lloyd's plight. "Even though he might have lied about what he did," the judge said, "the fault falls on him. The fault lies with no one else."

Scheck thought otherwise. He told the press that the lead detective in the case, Thomas De Galan, should be criminally prosecuted. He also called for misconduct investigations into the roles played by William Rice, the sergeant who oversaw the case, and Timothy Kenny, the prosecutor, because they never pursued biological evidence available at the time that might have cleared Lloyd.

As for Lloyd, fifty-four years old upon his release, he expressed his gratitude that Michigan did not have the death penalty as well as his appreciation of DNA technology. "That's God's signature," he said. "God's signature is never a forgery."

According to statistics compiled by the Innocence Project, Lloyd was the 110th person to be exonerated by DNA evidence.

Part II

EYEWITNESS ERROR

The playfully cynical injunction that you should believe nothing you hear and only half of what you see has its purchase on truth in the criminal justice system. False eyewitness testimony is the principal cause of wrongful convictions in U.S. courts.

There are, of course, several types of eyewitness error, from simple cases of mistaken identification to perjured testimony. It is difficult to counter mistaken identification offered in good faith by a witness who actually saw the accused. But even when the sole intent of the witness is to abet the judicial process, eyewitness accounts have been found to be generally unreliable. The original identification is often made under unfavorable conditions: the witness was likely to be a good distance away from the accused who was possibly shrouded in darkness; the glimpse of the suspect was likely a fleeting one, perhaps no more than a second or two; observations made in extreme circumstances, when adrenaline is running high, tend to be untrustworthy.

When a defendant is convicted solely on the basis of such testimony, the possibility of error is exceptionally high.

While honest eyewitness testimony, offered freely, can nonetheless send innocent people to prison, testimony that is perjured or compelled can appear to a jury to be even more convincing, for it is apt to have been carefully crafted and well rehearsed. The eyewitness or firsthand evidence offered by criminal informants in exchange for considerations such as reduction of sentence or the imposition of lesser charges is always, at best, questionable. Jailhouse snitches in search of privilege, codefendants hoping to slip the noose themselves, or suspects looking to point the finger in other directions are all hazardous to the prospect of justice being done in a court of law. Equally hazardous is testimony prompted by agents of the prosecution—police or attorneys eager to nail down a conviction by squeezing a witness to alter, if not fabricate, the story they tell the jury.

The Center on Wrongful Convictions recently studied eighty-six cases in which defendants sentenced to death were exonerated on claims of actual innocence (rather than on the basis of judicial error or circumstances involving prosecutorial or police misconduct) since capital punishment was restored after being put on hold by the U.S. Supreme Court in 1972. Eyewitness testimony played a part in forty-six convictions and was the only evidence against thirty-three defendants. In thirty-two cases, only one eyewitness testified. The eyewitnesses were strangers to nineteen defendants, and in nine other cases they were acquainted with the defendant but not accomplices. Fifteen of the eyewitnesses were in some way accomplices of the accused, and they all had incentives to testify, ranging from full immunity to leniency in sentencing. In five cases, a nonaccomplice witness received consideration from the prosecution in a pending case. In four other instances, the false testimony appeared to have been motivated by a grudge, and in another the eyewitness and the defendant formed two sides of a love triangle.

The vulnerability of eyewitness testimony became the focus of national attention in 1998 when Anthony Porter was freed from Illinois's death row following an investigation into his case by Lawrence C. Marshall and David Protess, both law professors at Northwestern University Law School, and a cadre of journalism students at the university's Medill School of Journalism. Further investigations led to eight other innocent men on death row being released, and a nationwide drumbeat began calling into question the merits of a system of capital punishment that condemns innocent people to death. If a class of journalism students led by two law professors was so readily able to uncover the wrongful convictions and death sentences meted out to nine men, how many others awaiting execution might also be innocent? Indeed, Anthony Porter was just fifty hours away from being put to death. For how many others did time run out?

Anthony Porter
Illinois

The funeral arrangements had been made and Anthony Porter was counting down the hours of life he had left. He was scheduled to die in an Illinois death house on September 23, 1998. The stay of execution came two days earlier, but another five months would pass before he was released. He had spent more than fifteen years on death row.

The trouble began for Porter when two teenagers—Marilyn Green, nineteen, and Jerry Hilliard, eighteen, were shot to death in the bleachers overlooking a swimming pool on the South Side of Chicago late on an August night in 1982. William Taylor, who had been swimming in the pool at the time, was among those interviewed by police immediately after the shooting. Taylor first told them he had not seen who did the shooting, but at the station house he said he recalled seeing Porter running right after the shots were fired. Seventeen hours of questioning seemed to further sharpen Taylor's memory. He remembered, he told police, having seen Porter shoot the pair.

Porter, who was known to belong to a South Side street gang, was a likely enough suspect. There were others, perhaps even more likely. The mother of the female victim, Ofra Green, told the police that a man by the name of Alstory Simon had been engaged in a drug dispute with Hillard. She also reported seeing Simon and his wife, Inez Jackson, with the victims not long before they were killed. Questioned by police, the couple said they had not been in the park that night. A few days later, they moved to Milwaukee.

On no evidence other than Taylor's eyewitness account, Porter was charged with the double murder. His family opted to retain a private attorney rather than employ a public defender, believing it would give Porter a better chance of acquittal. It was a decision that might have cost Porter dearly. The lawyer, Akim Gursel, was to be paid $10,000 for his services. However, he never received the full payment and Gursel later said he cut short his investigation of the case due to lack of funds.

The trial, which began in September 1983, did not go well for the defendant. Gursel fell asleep at the defense table at least once, and the judge had to awaken him. The defense called only two alibi witnesses and a photographer who had taken aerial shots of the park in which the shooting took place. It took the jury nine hours to return a verdict of guilty.

With a possible death sentence on the table, Gursel waived Porter's right to have the jury decide the sentence and left it to the judge. Sentencing hearings in Illinois are carried out in three phases. During the first phase it is determined whether the convicted man is eligible for the death penalty; the second is devoted to a consideration of mitigating circumstances; and the third is for sentencing. After phase one, in which the judge decided Porter was eligible for execution, Gursel informed the judge, Robert L. Sklodowski, that one of the jurors attended the same church as Marilyn Green's mother. The juror had failed to disclose that bit of information during voir dire, and, armed with this revelation, Gursel now moved for a mistrial. As the jury had not yet been dismissed, Sklodowski questioned the juror about her relationship with the victim's mother and why she had not made it known to the court. The juror told the judge that she did not realize that she knew Ofra Green until the trial was under way, but that it made no difference to her. That satisfied the judge, and he denied the motion for a retrial. The next day, Sklodowski found nothing to mitigate his final judgment and sentenced Porter to death.

Gursel appealed the verdict to the Illinois Supreme Court on the grounds that Porter had been denied a fair trial before an impartial jury. In February 1986, the court denied the appeal by a vote of four to three, the majority noting that the relationship between the juror in question and the victim's mother did not appear close enough to warrant a mistrial.

Porter carried his case to the U.S. Supreme Court where he petitioned for a writ of certiorari, which would have ordered the state court to submit the case to the higher court for review. The petition was denied, with dissents from Justices Thurgood Marshall and William Brennan who wrote that the defendant should not have borne the burden of showing actual prejudice. The likelihood of bias should have been sufficient.

Porter then filed a postconviction petition claiming that he had not had the benefit of effective counsel since Gursel had not called four witnesses who might have cast suspicion on Alstory Simon and Inez Jackson, thereby raising reasonable doubt about Porter's guilt. When his request for relief was turned down, Porter petitioned for a federal writ of habeas corpus, which would have referred his case to a federal court to decide whether there were adequate grounds for his imprisonment. The U.S. District Court denied the request, and that decision was affirmed by the U.S. Court of Appeals for the Seventh Circuit.

Porter's case had been grinding through the judicial machinery for twelve years, but it now appeared that he had reached the end of the line. When the court of appeals handed down its decision, on March 23, 1998, his execution was set for December 23. The nine-month time period proved to be salvation for Porter.

A volunteer Chicago lawyer, Daniel R. Sanders, entered the

case and had Porter's IQ tested. It was measured at 51, which by all standards indicated that Porter was mentally retarded. Execution of the mentally retarded was legal in Illinois at the time, still several years before the U.S. Supreme Court ruled it unconstitutional. Nevertheless, with the execution date fast approaching, Larry Marshall and three other pro bono attorneys filed a last-minute petition with the state supreme court contending that Porter was incapable of comprehending the nature of his punishment and therefore should not be put to death. Two days before he was scheduled to die, the court granted a stay of execution and ordered the Cook County Circuit Court to hold a competency hearing to determine whether Porter was capable of understanding the consequence of his fate.

At this point, Northwestern University law professor David Protess and his students, along with Paul Ciolino, a private investigator, began their investigation. The first break came in December when William Taylor, whose eyewitness testimony had doomed Porter, recanted and told Ciolino and one of the students that he had not seen him commit the crime. He said in an affidavit that he had been pressured by the police to identify Porter as the killer. On January 29, 1999, Inez Jackson, now separated from her husband, gave him up. She told Protess, Ciolino, and two students that she had seen Alstory Simon shoot Green and Hilliard. Four days later, Simon gave Ciolino a videotaped confession in which he claimed to have killed Hilliard in self-defense during a disagreement over drug money. He said the shooting of Green had been accidental.

Porter was released from prison on a recognizance bond on February 5 and he was cleared of all charges a month later. In

September 1999, Alstory Simon pleaded guilty to two counts of second-degree murder. He was sentenced to thirty-seven and a half years in prison.

Porter's exoneration was the first of at least nine that resulted from investigations by Protess and his student team. The effects of their efforts have already been massive, and the likelihood is that they have just begun to be felt. In January 2000, one year after Porter walked free, Governor George Ryan imposed a moratorium on all executions. In October 2002, capital punishment was put on trial in Illinois. Clemency hearings, coordinated by the Center on Wrongful Convictions, were ordered for 142 of the 158 prisoners on death row. Experts on witness identification, false confessions, and other causes of wrongful conviction were flown in from California, New Mexico, and Texas. Some three hundred lawyers prepared briefs to be presented. A few months later, Governor Ryan would make headlines by emptying Illinois's death row.

Executing the mentally retarded had already been taken off the table by a U.S. Supreme Court decision in the spring of 2002 in which the majority noted that a shift in public attitude over the past decade or more had rendered executions of the retarded cruel and unusual punishment. Prompted by events in Illinois, other states have begun to examine the manner in which they apply capital punishment and the likelihood that it results in the execution of innocent people. It is not possible to estimate how many have been unjustly sent to their death. But the probability obviously increases as the total number of executions rises, and the imposition of the death penalty is a practice in which, annually and by far, Texas leads all other states.

• • •

Randall Dale Adams
Texas

Randall Dale Adams was sentenced to death for the murder of a Dallas police officer during a traffic stop on Thanksgiving weekend in 1976. The testimony that convicted him was offered by the actual killer and three eyewitnesses who appeared to be pulled from a hat without warning during the trial.

Adams, twenty-seven years old, had arrived in Dallas from his native Ohio early in November and had taken a job repairing wooden pallets, which are movable platforms used in factories for storing heavy materials. He felt he had made a pretty good start in his new venue, but things turned suddenly and unexpectedly for the worse when his car ran out of gas on Fort Worth Avenue on Saturday, November 27. Adams was walking along the avenue looking for help when he was offered a lift by sixteen-year-old David Ray Harris. Harris, who had known trouble in the past and was formally declared a juvenile delinquent in his hometown of Vidor, Texas, was driving a stolen car that contained a shotgun and a .22-caliber pistol he had taken from his father. Adams was grateful for the ride, and the two spent Saturday afternoon and evening together, drinking beer, smoking marijuana, and taking in a couple of soft-porn movies at a drive-in. Later that night, Harris dropped Adams off at the motel where the older man was staying.

Shortly past midnight, Harris was pulled over by Dallas police officers Robert Wood and Teresa Turko for driving with his headlights off. As Wood approached the car, the driver pulled a pistol from under the front seat and shot the officer five times, killing him. Turko fired at the car as it sped off. She did not get the license plate number, but she knew it was a blue car and was pretty certain the driver was alone.

Harris returned to Vidor, and in the next few days he burglarized a house and held up a convenience store using a rifle. He also bragged to friends that he had "offed a pig" in Dallas. Nine days after the shooting, Harris was arrested for stealing the blue car and was released into the custody of his parents. A few days later, police got wind of the statements he had made about killing a cop and brought him in for questioning. He first told police he had just been bragging in order to impress his friends, but he changed his story when police told him a ballistics test had established that the gun used to kill the police officer belonged to his father. Harris now confessed to being at the scene when the cop was shot, but said it was Adams, a hitchhiker he had picked up, who fired the shots.

Adams was arrested, and he immediately seemed to become the suspect of choice, although most existing evidence pointed in the direction of Harris. It was Harris who stole the car, the murder weapon was registered to his father, the shotgun found in the car was his, and he had a fairly long criminal record for a teenager. Adams, by contrast, had only a drunk-driving offense against him and a minor AWOL infraction while serving for three years in the army paratroopers. The prosecution's preference for Adams as a suspect might, however, have been motivated by other factors.

Dallas, like most other jurisdictions, tends to be tough on cop killers. But Dallas specifically, and Texas generally, seem to be tougher than most. In fact, the two weeks it took to apprehend Adams was a Dallas record; it was the first time in the city's history that more than two days was required to "solve" a case involving the murder of a police officer. It is also customary in Dallas to seek the severest penalty possible for cop killers, which in Texas is death. But Texas law does not permit the execution of offenders under seventeen, so Adams was eligible; Harris was not. Adams was indicted, and the trial began in April 1977.

Officer Turko testified that she had not gotten a good look at the killer, but that his hairstyle and color were the same as Adams's. Harris, of course, was the prosecution's chief witness, and he stuck to the story he had told the police. Adams, in turn, denied any complicity in the shooting and, with little evidence against him beyond the word of Harris, he had reason to feel optimistic about his chances for acquittal. But on the last day of testimony, a Friday, the prosecution produced three presumed eyewitnesses who said they were driving by the scene shortly before the murder, had noticed the car that had been stopped by the officers, and were able to identify Adams as being in the car. The first witness, Michael Rendell, testified that he had seen two people in the car and was able to identify Adams. The other two, Robert and Emily Miller, said they saw only one person in the car, and it was Adams. Under Texas law, the prosecution was not required to inform the defense of the existence of the three witnesses prior to their being called because they were summoned only to rebut Adams's testimony and would offer no new evidence. After the weekend, the defense asked to recall the surprise witnesses but was told they were no longer available. They seemed to have vanished as quickly and mysteriously as they had appeared.

The jury wasted little time in rendering a verdict of guilty. The issue of sentencing was yet to be considered. As a condition of imposing a death sentence, Texas law required the jury to determine that "beyond a reasonable doubt there was probability" that the offender would commit future acts of violence. It was a supposition that rarely created difficulties for the prosecution. Called to assure the jury of Adams's enduring menace was Dr. James Grigson, a psychiatrist who earned the designation of Dr. Death after testifying in more than one hundred cases that ended in death sentences. Grigson, along with Dr. John Holbrook, former chief of psychiatry for the Texas Department of Corrections, told the jury that Adams would remain an ongoing menace if he remained alive. The jury obliged by issuing a sentence of death.

Adams spent nearly two years on death row and was three days away from his scheduled execution, set for May 8, 1979, when a stay was ordered by U.S. Supreme Court Justice Lewis F. Powell. Powell noted that prospective jurors who had misgivings about the morality of the death penalty had been excluded from the jury even though they said they would abide by Texas law. By an eight-to-one decision, the court agreed with Powell and remanded the case for further proceedings. Initially, the court's ruling seemed to indicate that a new trial would be held. But Dallas district attorney Henry Wade (immortalized as the latter half of *Roe v. Wade*) decided that a new trial would be a waste of money. He therefore asked Governor Bill Clements to commute Adams's sentence to life in prison, and the governor complied. The Texas Court of Criminal Appeals upheld the action, asserting, "There is now no error in the case, and the judgment of conviction will be affirmed." Adams, though liberated from death row, was now preparing to spend the rest of his life in a Texas prison. But chance intervened in his favor. In an unpredictable turn of events, it was Dr. Death, with Hollywood in his future, who inadvertently came to his rescue.

In March 1985, a young filmmaker and former private detective named Errol Morris came to Dallas to work on a documentary about Dr. Grigson. The film was intended to examine how a psychiatrist can determine whether a person would probably commit other violent crimes unless executed. Morris had no intention of questioning the guilt of the defendants. However, when he met Adams, there was something in the prisoner's manner that led Morris to think he was an unlikely killer. He decided to take a closer look. He read the transcript of the trial, and the suspicion grew that Adams might be innocent. Morris then compared notes with Randy Schaffer, a volunteer Houston lawyer who had been working on the case since 1982. Among other things, Morris learned that while Adams languished in prison, David Ray Harris had been compiling a criminal record of some magnitude.

Not long after Adams's conviction, Harris enlisted in the army. Stationed in Germany, he was court-martialed on charges of burglary and sentenced to eight months in prison in Leavenworth, Kansas. Five months after his dishonorable discharge from the army, he was sentenced to six and a half years in California for kidnapping, armed robbery, and burglary. He was paroled four years later, in 1984, just past his twenty-fourth birthday. Back in Texas a year later, Harris broke into an apartment in Beaumont and tried to abduct a young woman from her bed. When her boyfriend came to her aid, there was an exchange of gunfire in which Harris was wounded and the other man shot dead. Harris was convicted of murder and sentenced to death.

As Morris pressed his investigation, he became increasingly certain that the state had convicted the wrong man. He discovered that Officer Turko had made her identification about the killer's hair while under hypnosis in the prosecution's effort to mine deeper for evidence. That testimony clashed with her original claim that she had not seen the killer. Morris and Schaffer also found that robbery charges against the daughter of Emily Miller, one of the eyewitnesses, had been dropped when she agreed to identify Adams as the killer. She initially had described the shooter as black or Mexican; Adams was Caucasian. Morris also was told that Mrs. Miller had picked another man out of the police lineup but switched to Adams with the prompting of the police officer in charge of the lineup. On the basis of such revelations, Adams was granted a hearing for a retrial. At the hearing, testimony was offered that the other two surprise eyewitnesses also had lied and, to clinch the case, David Harris confessed that he was the killer. He told the judge: "Twelve years ago, I was a kid, you know, and I'm not a kid anymore, and I realize I've been responsible for a great injustice."

Adams was granted the right to a new trial, but on March 23, 1989, Dallas district attorney John Vance, who had succeeded Wade, dropped all charges. After his release, Adams commented on the criminal justice system in an interview with *Texas Monthly* magazine:

In the beginning, I blamed David. But David did not have the power to arrest me, indict me, and sentence me to die. The problem is larger than David Harris. Our criminal justice system, on paper, is the best in the world. But we're human, and so we make mistakes. If you execute and execute and execute, at some point you will execute an innocent man.

Ricardo Aldape Guerra
Texas

Ricardo Aldape Guerra spent fifteen years on death row in Harris County, one of the toughest prisons in Texas, for the 1982 murder of a Houston police officer. Guerra's only crime, it later appeared, was being an undocumented Mexican immigrant who was in the wrong place at the wrong time.

All the physical evidence in the case pointed to another man, who was killed in a shootout with police a few minutes after the officer was shot. The slain policeman's service revolver was found on the body of the other suspect, but the prosecution maintained that Guerra could have placed it there. The principal testimony against Guerra was the eyewitness identification by the ten-year-old son of a bystander who was killed in the shootout.

The Texas Court of Criminal Appeals affirmed both the conviction and the death sentence. But Guerra's fortune took a sudden turn when a pro bono team from the law firm of Vinson & Elkins joined his defense. The firm spent more than $3 million in time and expenses on the case and eventually managed to get Guerra freed on a writ of habeas corpus.

Nineteen years old at the time of the crime, Guerra was a Mexican national who had recently arrived in Houston. In granting the writ, the U.S. District Court found that the prosecution had intimidated witnesses, conducted a deceptive lineup, hidden exculpatory evidence, and injected false evidence into the trial. In addition, the court found that the trial was tainted with appeals to ethnic prejudice and anti-immigrant bias from the start. During voir dire, the prosecution repeatedly emphasized Guerra's alien status, telling the jury that it could be considered at the punishment phase in determining whether Guerra would continue to commit violent acts that would constitute a threat to society. Even in its brief contesting the petition for habeas corpus, the state continued to insist that the "inferences that the jury might be able to draw from that fact [Guerra's immigration status] could legitimately shed light on whether a death sentence was appropriate." The court concluded that the prosecutor's references invited the jury to sentence the defendant based not on his acts but on his national origin.

In granting the writ, the federal judge ruled that Guerra should either be retried within thirty days or released, stating that the actions of the police and prosecutors were "intentional, were done in bad faith, and are outrageous." The district court's ruling was upheld, and the Houston district attorney dropped all charges against Guerra in 1997.

Guerra's exoneration raised doubts about the guilt of many who have been executed in Texas since the death penalty was reactivated a little over twenty-five years ago. Between 1976 and 2002, 783 people were executed nationwide, 273 of them in Texas. During that time, there were slightly more than 700 inmates on Texas's death row. So approximately 2 out of every 5 convicts sentenced to death in Texas have been executed. In California, by contrast, only 10 of more than 600 death row inmates have been put to death during that time.

But if Texas is the nation's undisputed capital of capital punishment, Florida is the clear champion when it comes to sending innocent people to death row. More than 20 percent of death-row prisoners who have been exonerated throughout the country were tried and sentenced in Florida. In fact, the manner in which the state applies the death penalty was an issue in Florida's 2002 campaign for attorney general. State senator Locke Burt, the Republican candidate for the office, challenged a study that found that sixteen of twenty-three people sent to death row were innocent of the charges. All sixteen had been exonerated, but Burt contended that exoneration did not establish their innocence. Though the study did not address the issue, statistics indicate that it is a lot easier for an innocent man to be sentenced to death if he is black and the victim is white. Of the sixteen men mistakenly sent to death row in Florida, only five were Caucasian.

Delbert Tibbs
Florida

Few victims of the capital justice system have roused public support the way Delbert Tibbs did when he was sentenced to death in 1974 for killing a hitchhiker and raping the man's sixteen-year-old traveling companion. Tibbs, a young black theology student, was celebrated in song by Pete Seeger and Joan Baez and was made a cause célèbre by the 1960s black activist Angela Davis.

Tibbs's travails began innocently enough when he was hitchhiking his way from Florida back to his Chicago home earlier that year. Nearing Leesburg, he was stopped by a Highway Patrol trooper who said he fit the description of a man who was wanted in Fort Myers. The officer questioned Tibbs and, satisfied that he was not the man they were looking for, let him go. Before releasing him, however, he photographed Tibbs with a Polaroid camera.

A few days later, on February 3, two white hitchhikers, Terry Milroy and Cynthia Nadeau, were picked up by a black man driving a green truck just south of Fort Myers. Milroy was on his way to a job in the Florida Keys and Nadeau was a teenage runaway from Rhode Island. As Cynthia later told it, after a brief ride the driver pulled off the road into a vacant field and stopped the truck. He asked Milroy to come out and help him with something. When Nadeau followed, she saw the driver pointing a gun at Milroy. The driver ordered her to undress, then shot Milroy and raped her.

Police showed her the Polaroid photo of Tibbs, and Nadeau identified him as the man who had raped her and shot Milroy, although he did not fit her original description of the killer. A regional search by police found Tibbs hitchhiking in Mississippi. He was brought back to Fort Myers, and Nadeau picked him out of a police lineup.

Tibbs was tried before an all-white jury. Nadeau's testimony was the guts of the prosecution's case, and it was woefully weak. There were too many questions that had no answers and virtually nothing that would support Nadeau's story. No physical evidence was offered, the murder weapon had not been found, and no witnesses could place Tibbs anywhere near Fort Myers at the time of the crime. Then there was the matter of the truck that was central to Nadeau's account. Where was the truck and how did it figure in the odyssey of a man who apparently had spent much of the past week hitchhiking from Florida to Mississippi? If he had access to the truck, why was he thumbing rides along the highway? The only corroboration of Nadeau's story was delivered by Tibbs's cellmate, who testified that Tibbs had confessed to him while awaiting trial.

Tibbs structured his defense around what appeared to be an airtight alibi: he was in Daytona Beach on February 2 and 3, in Leesburg on the sixth and Ocala on the seventh—each location a long distance from Fort Myers—and he had the documentation to prove it. The defense also sought to impeach Nadeau's testimony, noting that at age sixteen she was already a heavy drug user and had admitted to getting high on marijuana shortly before the crime was committed. It was of no avail. The trial was over in less than three days; the verdict was in an hour and a half later: Tibbs was found guilty of murder and rape. The jury recommended death as the penalty for the murder, and a life sentence was added for the rape.

The appeal process began, and so did the drumbeat of protest and support that came from up north. Tibbs was, after all, not a likely suspect for the random murder and rape of a pair of wayward hitchhikers. He was well educated, an aspiring poet, a veteran of the civil rights struggles of the sixties, and when arrested he was in the midst of a coast-to-coast journey "to experience firsthand the woes and wonders of the world," as a newspaper reporter put it. When he returned, he had planned to finish studying for his degree at the Chicago Theological Seminary.

The basis for Tibbs's appeal to the Florida Supreme Court was that there was insufficient evidence to place him at the scene of the crime. Florida law requires close scrutiny of the victim's testimony if she is the only witness for the prosecution. (The jail-house snitch, himself a convicted rapist, had already admitted that his testimony was false and was given in the hope of receiving consideration in return.) In reviewing the trial court's record, the judges found several weaknesses in Nadeau's story: all available evidence other than the witness's testimony seemed to place Tibbs far from the scene at the time of the crime; a car and helicopter search of the area failed to locate the green truck; the gun was never found and Tibbs had no car keys in his possession when he was picked up; Tibbs had been stopped by police more than once as he hitchhiked his way north, he cooperated each time, and none of the officers who questioned him found cause to suspect his credibility; finally, since the crime took place at night and Nadeau had been high on marijuana, her ability to identify her attacker was diminished. The state supreme court reversed the conviction and ordered a new trial.

The question then raised was whether a new trial would subject Tibbs to double jeopardy, which is prohibited by the Fifth Amendment. Tibbs filed a motion to dismiss the indictment on those grounds. The trial court agreed that retrying the case would violate the defendant's Fifth Amendment protection. The state took the case to the Florida Court of Appeals, which ruled that double jeopardy would not apply since the reversal of the conviction was based on the *weight* of the evidence presented, not its *insufficiency*. Had the court decided that the evidence offered, even if unchallenged, was not sufficient to support a conviction, the case against Tibbs would have been dismissed. The legal proceedings moved through the judicial machinery for five years. In June 1982, when the U.S. Supreme Court affirmed the decision of the court of appeals, it appeared Tibbs was headed for a new trial.

Two months later, however, the state decided not to retry Tibbs. The prosecution's case had, in the past five years, evaporated. Cynthia Nadeau had become a confirmed drug addict, making her useless as a witness, and there was no other evidence to be presented to a jury. What's more, James Long, who had prosecuted the case, announced that the original investigation had been "tainted from the beginning" and that if there was a retrial he would testify for the defense.

Since his release, Tibbs has campaigned actively against the death penalty, giving public lectures and testifying at legislative hearings. "It's quite easy," he tells listeners, "to build a case against an innocent man."

William Jent and Earnest Miller
Florida

William Jent and Earnest Miller, half brothers, came within sixteen hours of being executed for raping and bludgeoning to death an unidentified woman during a drunken bash at a railroad trestle on the Lacoochee River in Pasco County, Florida, on a July night in 1979. The twenty-year-old woman, initially known only as Tammy, had been beaten to death, and her badly burned body was found in a nearby game preserve. Jent, twenty-eight, and Miller, twenty-three, were convicted largely on the testimony of three purported eyewitnesses who had been at the party.

At trial, the defense maintained that the witnesses' testimony could not be trusted because they were drunk and high on drugs at the time of the crime. Nonetheless, Jent and Miller, who were tried before separate juries but with the same judge presiding, were both convicted. In an unusual twist, the two men, though similarly charged, were given different sentences. The jury in Jent's case recommended the death penalty. Miller's jury deemed the mitigating circumstances to outweigh the aggravating circumstances and suggested a term of life in prison. However, under Florida capital sentencing procedure, the jury's decision is only advisory. The actual sentence is determined by the trial judge, and in this instance the trial judge, obviously an advocate of equal justice, sentenced Miller to death as well.

The Florida Supreme Court affirmed the convictions in 1981, and in 1983 the pair came perilously close to execution before receiving a stay from a federal judge because the prosecution had withheld exculpatory information. The news soon got even better for Jent and Miller. In 1986, the victim was finally identified. Her name was Linda Gale Bradshaw, and a reexamination of the autopsy indicated that death had occurred at a different time than the eyewitnesses had attested. Jent and Miller both had airtight alibis for the actual time of the murder. It also was discovered that a former boyfriend of the victim had been convicted in Georgia of committing a similar crime.

In 1987, a federal district court concluded that prosecutors had indeed withheld evidence and acted with a "callous and deliberate disregard of the fundamental principles of truth and fairness," and ordered a retrial. Still, the state refused to drop the charges. In January 1988, a deal was struck. State Attorney James T. Russell agreed to set Jent and Miller free on time served in exchange for pleas of guilty to second-degree murder. The brothers repudiated their pleas upon leaving prison. Two of the three presumed witnesses then recanted their testimony, saying they had been coerced by sheriff's officers to fabricate the story they told the jury. In 1991, the Pasco County Sheriff's Office paid Jent and Miller $65,000 to settle a wrongful-arrest suit.

Bradley Scott
Florida

On an October afternoon in 1978, twelve-year-old Linda Pikuritz left her home in Port Charlotte, Florida, on her bicycle. She was seen riding around the neighborhood and in the vicinity of a local convenience store. When she failed to return home by nine o'clock that evening, her sister, Deborah Bianchi, filed a missing persons report with the Charlotte County Sheriff's Department. At eleven that night, authorities received a report of a brush fire about three miles from the convenience store. Linda Pikuritz's body was found at the scene of the blaze. An autopsy indicated that she had been set afire while still alive. The cause of death was smoke inhalation. There was no evidence of sexual assault or any other injuries inconsistent with those produced by fire. Several of Linda's personal items were found at the site, including a shell necklace. Her bicycle was discovered the following day in the brush just off the road.

Bradley Scott soon became a prime suspect. He was being investigated for an assault on a sixteen- or seventeen-year-old girl a few months later, and police wanted to know his whereabouts on the night the Pikuritz girl was murdered. He told them he was shopping in the Sarasota Mall, about fifty miles from the crime scene, and he was able to document it. His wife produced receipts with the date, time, and store where they had shopped and brought with her the items they had purchased, including a suede jacket from Foxmoor Casuals. Scott also agreed to take a polygraph test, which he assumed he passed, since he was released from custody without further comment. Scott had every reason to believe he was in the clear.

More than seven years later, he was indicted for the girl's murder and sentenced to death. The case against him was based entirely on the eyewitness accounts of people who had seen Scott and Linda together, although no one could place him near the scene of the crime or provide a motive for the murder. He had reportedly been seen talking to the girl from his car near the convenience store and again later in the store's parking lot. Their conversation appeared to be friendly. A classmate of Linda's testified that she and Linda had met Scott at the store many times prior to the night of the crime, and he had occasionally bought them beer and smoked marijuana with them. Other acquaintances of Linda offered the same type of testimony.

The forensic evidence that was dug up seven years later was at best flimsy. The state produced hair samples taken from Scott's car about a year after the murder and four months after Scott had sold the vehicle to a used-car dealer. They were compared with two hairs from a wool cap that belonged to the victim, and the state claimed a match although another forensic expert said identification was impossible based on so small a sample. A small seashell also was found in Scott's car, which the prosecution said could have come from Linda's necklace. On just such evidence, Scott was convicted of first-degree murder and sentenced to death in 1988.

Three years later, years Scott spent on death row, the Florida Supreme Court unanimously vacated the conviction and ordered the trial court to enter an order of acquittal. The court's decision was based on an "unjustified" delay in bringing the case and the insufficient nature of the evidence, noting that the eyewitness accounts had been riddled with inconsistencies and shortcomings. The decision stated: "We find that the circumstantial evidence presented by the prosecution could only create a suspicion that Scott committed this murder. Suspicions cannot be a basis for a criminal conviction. Our law requires proof beyond a reasonable doubt and a fair trial for a defendant."

Joseph Nahume Green
Florida

If an award were given for the man sentenced to death on the least compelling evidence, Joseph Nahume Green would be on the short list. Green was convicted of the murder of the society editor of the local newspaper in Starke, Florida, on the presumed identification of a single eyewitness who was intoxicated on the night of the crime, memory-impaired, and, with an IQ of 67, borderline retarded.

Judy Miscally was using a public pay phone on the night of December 8, 1992, when she was approached by a man who demanded money. When she refused and screamed, the man shot her and fled the scene. In a dying statement, Miscally described her assailant as a skinny black man in his mid-twenties and described the gun as a small, semiautomatic pistol. Three people said they witnessed the incident. Two said they were unable to make an identification. The third, Lonnie Thompson, told police the killer was a white man wearing brown pants. After further questioning, however, he picked Joseph Green, who is black, out of a police lineup that included no one but Green. Green produced three witnesses who said they were with him at the time of the crime. He was nonetheless convicted of first-degree murder and sentenced to death.

In late 1996, the Florida Supreme Court struck down the conviction, saying that it had hinged "delicately and entirely" on the "inconsistent and contradictory" account of a lone eyewitness. The court ordered that if Green were to be retried, the trial must be held in a different venue. The case was moved to Gainesville, where a judge ruled that Thompson was unreliable and incompetent to testify. Without Thompson's testimony, the state was left with no case to present to a jury and the charges were dropped. Green was released in 1999, and the state was given until March 2000 to retry him. It did not file for retrial, and Green was acquitted on March

16. He had spent seven years in a Florida prison, three and a half of them in the state's chamber for the condemned. During that time, eight of his fellow inmates were put to death in the electric chair.

Perry Cobb and Darby Tillis
Illinois

Illinois is second to Florida in the number of death-row exonerations, with a total of thirteen since 1973. Of course that number includes the inmates who were freed as a result of Professor Protess's work which led to the Medill School of Journalism investigation in 1998. More than two decades earlier, Perry Cobb and Darby Tillis were among the first to see their death sentences reversed in Illinois. It was no simple proceeding. It took three jury trials to convict them of a double murder and two additional trials to set them free.

Early on the morning of November 13, 1977, Melvin Kanter and Charles Guccion were shot to death during an armed robbery at a hotdog stand on the North Side of Chicago. Three weeks later, Cobb and Tillis were arrested when a professed witness, Phyllis Santini, went to the police and said she had heard Cobb and Tillis discussing the robbery. Police investigated and found a watch taken from one of the victims in Cobb's room. Cobb said he bought the watch for $10 from Santini's boyfriend, Johnny Brown. The accused both insisted they were innocent.

The first two trials resulted in hung juries. Cobb and Tillis, both black, were convicted by an all-white jury and sentenced to death in a third trial that raised questions of racial bias. The prosecution used peremptory challenges to dismiss thirty-six of thirty-eight black jurors; the other two were dismissed for cause. An eyewitness, Arthur Shields, who tended bar across the street from the scene of the murder, had testified at the first two trials that he had seen two black men standing inside the door of the hotdog stand at about the time the crime was committed, but he was unable to identify them. He also had told two police officers on the night after the crime was committed that Tillis was a regular customer of his and not one of the men he had seen the previous night. At the third trial, however, he identified Cobb and Tillis as those men. Under cross-examination, Shields admitted having previously said that he had not seen the two men's faces very well and that he thought all blacks looked alike in photographs.

Some rulings of the trial judge, Thomas Maloney, also were suspect. Maloney refused to allow two defense witnesses to take the stand. Patricia Usmani was prepared to testify that in June 1978 Santini told her that she had assisted Johnny Brown in committing the crime. Carol Griffin would have testified that Santini said she expected to receive a reward for taking the stand against Tillis and Cobb. She was in fact given $1,200. The Illinois Supreme Court reversed the conviction in 1983 on the grounds of judicial error. The state prepared to try the two men for a fourth time.

After the reversal, Rob Warden, currently executive director of the Center on Wrongful Convictions, wrote a detailed account of the case for *Chicago Lawyer* magazine. The article was read by Michael Falconer, a recent graduate of DePaul University College of Law. Before entering law school, Falconer had spent a summer working in a factory where Santini also worked. He said she had confided to him that she and her boyfriend had committed the robbery and murder. Falconer, an assistant state attorney by the time of the fourth trial, testified on behalf of Cobb and Tillis, but once more the jury was hung. Finally, at a bench trial in 1987, the two won an acquittal. They had been tried more times than anyone in the history of the United States and had spent more than a decade in prison, including four years on death row. Brown and Santini have never been charged.

After their release, Cobb became a janitor for an apartment building on the South Side of Chicago. "I used to be a singer," he said, "but this nightmare destroyed my confidence. It's like being shell-shocked, and I can't stand up in front of people anymore." Tillis became an ordained Protestant minister and established an inner-city youth organization in Chicago.

Judge Maloney was convicted in 1993 on charges of federal corruption, including sharing in a $100,000 bribe to acquit three reputed New York gangsters of murder and taking a $10,000 bribe to acquit two alleged Chicago street-gang members of two killings. Maloney was said to have returned the latter bribe when he learned that he was being investigated by the FBI. That investigation resulted in Maloney's becoming the first Cook County judge ever convicted of taking bribes in capital cases. During Maloney's trial, federal prosecutors charged that the judge had often been biased against defendants who had not bribed him in order to divert suspicion that might have been raised by his acquittals.

•   •   •

Joseph Burrows
Illinois

Joseph Burrows was convicted and sentenced to death for the murder and robbery of an eighty-eight-year-old retired farmer in Iroquois County, Illinois, largely on the testimony of the actual killer. The victim, William Dulan, was found dead from bullet wounds in his home on November 8, 1988. Hours later, Gayle Potter, a cocaine addict, was arrested when she tried to cash a $4,050 check in Dulan's name at the Iroquois Farmer's Bank. Potter admitted taking part in the crime, but she also named two accomplices—Burrows, who she said was the triggerman, and Ralph Frye, a mildly retarded friend of Burrows.

According to Potter, Burrows was the enforcer for a drug dealer and was sent to collect money she owed from a drug deal. As she did not have the money, she was told to borrow it from Dulan, for whom Potter's mother had done housework and who had loaned her money in the past. Potter, Burrows, and Frye went to Dulan's home in Sheldon, Illinois, and asked him to write a check. When he refused, Burrows pulled a gun, and as the two men struggled Dulan was shot in the head. Potter started screaming, and Burrows struck her, drawing blood. The next day, Burrows and the drug dealer came to the trailer where Potter lived and handed her a check for $4,050 signed by William Dulan. That was her story. Frye corroborated it. The only physical evidence was some of Potter's blood, which was found at the scene, and the gun, which was registered to her.

As for Burrows, four witnesses placed him sixty miles away from the scene at the time of the crime. It took two trials to convict him. The first ended in a hung jury; the second brought a verdict of guilty and a sentence of death. Potter was sentenced to thirty years and Frye to twenty-seven in exchange for their testimony.

The journey to Burrows's exoneration began in 1992 with an investigation of the case by Peter Rooney, a reporter for the Champaign-Urbana *News-Gazette*. Frye, who had an IQ of 67, told Rooney that the police had coerced the confession from him and intimidated him into naming Burrows as the shooter. After the story appeared, Burrows's pro bono lawyers, Kathleen Zelner and Michael Hemstreet, discovered a letter in which Potter asked a friend to testify falsely to corroborate her story. Shown the letter, Potter admitted that she had acted alone, killing Dulan while attempting to rob him for drug money. She said she had implicated Burrows because she believed, incorrectly, that he had burglarized her trailer.

On a petition for postconviction relief, the trial court granted Burrows a new trial, but the prosecution dropped the charges. Frye's murder conviction was vacated, and he was sentenced to ten years for perjury. After his release, in 1994, Burrows went to work for a landscaping company. On his left forearm is a tattoo from his time spent on death row. It reads: "Die Free."

Steven Smith
Illinois

Convicted of shooting to death an off-duty prison official outside a bar on the South Side of Chicago in 1985, Steven Smith was the eleventh death-row inmate set free in Illinois between 1987 and 1999. During that time, the state freed as many inmates from death row as it had executed since reinstating the death penalty in 1977.

The victim of the 1985 murder was Virdeen Willis Jr., an assistant warden at the Illinois penitentiary in Pontiac. Smith had been drinking in the bar shortly before Willis was slain. He was arrested after being identified by a woman named Debrah Caraway, who said she witnessed the killing from across the street. Her testimony was the only evidence against Smith, but he was as obvious a suspect as police could hope for. He had been convicted of murder twice before.

In 1964, at the age of sixteen, he had pleaded guilty to a murder during a street robbery on Chicago's South Side. Five years later, he was convicted in the killing of a reputed member of a rival gang and sentenced to forty years in prison. He was paroled after serving a little more than seven years when it appeared that the murder was committed by Smith's brother, Charles Lee Smith, who was never charged with the crime. As a motive for killing Willis, the prosecution surmised that Smith was a member of the King Cobras, a well-known Chicago street gang, and the slaying was in reprisal for the harsh line Willis had taken against gang members in Illinois prisons.

Still and all, Caraway's identification of Smith strained credibility for a number of reasons. She acknowledged that she had been smoking crack cocaine on the night of the murder. She said she saw Willis leave the bar alone and light a cigarette and that Smith followed, also alone, and fired the fatal shot. But other witnesses testified that Willis was with two other people—a friend and a cousin—when he was shot, and neither of Willis's companions could identify Smith as the shooter. Also, the bartender, among others, testified that although Smith had been in the bar on the same evening as Willis, Smith had left with two friends while Willis and his companions remained. Caraway's credibility was further compromised when it was learned that her sister had been taken in for questioning in the case and her sister's boyfriend, Pervis (Pepper) Bell, was an alternative suspect.

Despite the weakness of the state's case, Smith was convicted and sentenced to death not once, but twice. The first conviction was reversed for prosecutorial misconduct. The prosecutor pinned much of his closing argument on Smith's street-gang association, which was suspected but never proven. At his second trial, in 1996, Smith was again convicted and this time sent to death row. However, on appeal three years later, the Illinois Supreme Court again reversed the trial court, ruling that Caraway's testimony was less credible than the contradictory testimony of the other witnesses.

While setting Smith free, the court specifically stated that its decision was not a finding that Smith was innocent, just that the state had failed to prove its case. The court's opinion, written by Justice James Heiple, said:

> While there are those who may criticize courts for turning criminals loose, co zens receive those rights which are applicable equally to every citizen who may find himself charged with a crime, whatever the crime and whatever the circumstances.
>
> When the state cannot meet its burden of proof, the defendant must go free. . . . It is no help to speculate that

the defendant may have killed the victim. No citizen would be safe from prosecution under such a standard.

Larry Hicks
Indiana

Larry Hicks, scheduled to be executed for a double murder, was snatched from Indiana's electric chair with help from two unlikely sources: the warden of the prison where he was being held and the Playboy Foundation.

Hicks, a seventeen-year-old from the deep ghetto of Gary, Indiana, had been convicted of stabbing two men to death during a party at the apartment of a neighbor in February 1978. The case against him consisted chiefly of the testimony of two women who said they had seen him arguing with the victims and waving a knife. His execution was two weeks away when the prison warden persuaded two lawyers to take a closer look at his case.

There was, after all, nothing in the defendant's background to suggest he was a likely murder suspect. He had never been in trouble with the law; he did not drink alcohol or use drugs. Although he had dropped out of high school, he was still trying to earn his diploma by taking evening courses while working part-time wherever he could find work. Those who had employed him described Hicks as an honest and hard worker. He was known in his neighborhood as Black Jesus, a young man respected for his cheerful, unselfish nature.

The lawyers who took his case, Nile Stanton and Kevin

McShane, obtained a stay and in the process of their investigation discovered that the public defender (PD) assigned to Hicks's case: (1) was not even aware his client faced the death penalty until a week before the trial; (2) failed to investigate Hicks's alibi that he was not present at the time the murders took place; (3) failed to interview the witnesses who said they had seen him commit the crime; (4) failed to examine the dark red stains on his jeans, which the prosecution termed blood but which were found to be, as the defendant had claimed, bits of rust from old barbells he kept in his basement; (5) failed to examine the knife the state said was used to stab the two men; and (6) failed totally to prepare for the one-and-a-half-day-long trial that resulted in his client's being sentenced to death.

After a new trial was granted, Stanton and McShane hired an investigator with funds provided by the Playboy Foundation, and slowly the truth began to emerge. The murders did not occur at midnight, as the prosecution had claimed, but at around five in the morning, when Hicks was at home. That information was contained in the coroner's report, which the PD apparently had not consulted. Forensic analysis determined that the knife the state said was the murder weapon could not have inflicted the fatal wounds; only a knife with a much longer and narrower blade could have been used.

At Hicks's second trial, in 1980, Stanton chose to employ an unorthodox strategy. In his opening statement, he told the jury that although, as the judge had told them, the burden of proof was on the state to prove guilt beyond a reasonable doubt while the defense was obliged to prove nothing, he would go the state one better; he would accept the burden of proof and conclusively establish that the defendant was absolutely innocent. And he did. Both eyewitnesses recanted their testimony, and Hicks was acquitted after spending more than two years on death row.

Eric Clemmons
Missouri

Eric Clemmons saved his life by fighting his own fight while awaiting execution on Missouri's death row. Clemmons was sentenced to death for the fatal stabbing of another inmate while serving a fifty-year sentence on a previous murder conviction.

Clemmons was arrested in 1982 for killing a man in St. Louis during a fight. Clemmons tells the story in his own words on an Internet website in which he seeks public support for his efforts to gain his freedom.

"In 1982," he says, "two men followed my younger brother, Stanley, home from work. In the block on which we lived, they proceeded to rob Stanley. Friends and I were nearby. When Stanley cried out for help, we ran to his aid and a fight ensued. Unfortunately, one of the robbers later died from blows sustained during the fight. . . . I turned myself in and have been locked up since!"

Clemmons's situation soon grew worse. In 1987, he was charged with stabbing to death a fellow inmate, Henry Johnson, in the dark yard of a Jefferson City prison. A prison guard testified that he saw Clemmons stab Johnson. It also was noted that Clemmons had a smear of blood on his sweatshirt and some blood spots on his hat. He told police he received the stains when

Johnson ran into him after being stabbed by another man. The only other evidence against him came from Captain A. M. Gross, who testified by deposition that Clemmons had told him, "I guess they got me." Gross's statement was permitted into the record without cross-examination.

Three other inmates told a different story. They said that another prisoner, Fred Bagby, was the one who stabbed Johnson. Unfortunately for Clemmons, Bagby himself was stabbed to death three months later. The prosecution contended that Bagby was chosen as a foil because he was conveniently dead. Clemmons was found guilty and sentenced to death.

While on death row, he began acquainting himself with the legal system. His early appeals, which were denied, did not raise the critical issue that Gross was never cross-examined. Clemmons's prospects brightened when a guard brought him papers and a message from another inmate. Included was a prison memo written by Gross. It said that Gross was told immediately after the attack that it was Bagby who killed Johnson.

In his final federal appeal, Clemmons raised the two key points: Gross had not been cross-examined and his memo had not been introduced into evidence. The judge ruled that neither point could be sustained on appeal since they had not been raised earlier. Clemmons phoned his mother in Potosi, Missouri, and told her to arrange for his funeral. At the same time, he played what he believed to be his last card. He got himself a new attorney, Cheryl Pilate of Kansas City, who was reputed to be sympathetic to victims of the criminal justice system.

Pilate filed for a rehearing before the same three judges who had denied Clemmons's previous appeal. She argued that although his appeals lawyers had not raised the key issues, Clemmons had done everything he could to preserve them, even filing them himself. In 1997, ten years after he was convicted, the same three federal judges reversed themselves. They agreed that Clemmons had raised the issues in his own filings and that his rights had been violated. He was granted a new trial. The state decided to ask for life without parole rather than death.

Pilate and her partner, Charles Rogers, turned up a wealth of new evidence, including a letter from Johnson to a prison guard, dated the day prior to his murder, saying that he had been in a fight with Bagby but that he was not worried about death threats. An expert witness testified that the blood on Clemmons's sweatshirt and hat was consistent with what might be expected if a bloody man had run into him; it did not exhibit the splatter effect that would come directly from a stab wound. After just three hours of deliberation, the jury found Clemmons not guilty. It was the first time since Missouri reinstated the death penalty in 1977 that a condemned prisoner was acquitted at a retrial.

In an account of the case published in the *Kansas City Star,* reporter Joe Lambe quotes the defense lawyers as saying that the acquittal shows that Missouri faces the same problems that confronted Illinois before it instituted its moratorium on the death penalty. "These cases march through the system [in] assembly-line fashion," Pilate said. "Sometimes an innocent person is executed."

Missouri attorney general Jay Nixon, whose office fought against Clemmons's retrial for years, saw it differently. It indicated to him that Missouri did not need a moratorium. "It proves the system works," he said. "We have never executed anyone near innocent since I have been attorney general." The system, one might think, worked a lot better for Nixon than it did for Clemmons, who spent eleven years in a death-house cell demonstrating for Nixon the smooth working of the system.

Defense attorneys said it was probable that at least a few of the forty-one people Missouri executed in the previous twenty-three years were innocent. Unlike Illinois, said Kansas City defense lawyer Sean O'Brien, no one did much about it. "We bury our mistakes."

Shareef Cousin

Louisiana

Shareef Cousin had as solid an alibi as a murder suspect could hope for. He was playing in a league basketball game at the time of the crime, and there was a videotape to prove it. Yet he was sentenced to death on the uncertain identification of three eyewitnesses.

Sixteen years old at the time, Cousin was convicted of murdering Michael Gerardi as he and his date left a restaurant in New Orleans's French Quarter at about 10 P.M. on a fall night in 1995. The game in which Cousin was playing had started at 9:30. The case against Cousin gave every suggestion of having been fabricated by prosecutors and police to railroad a suspect they knew was innocent.

The prosecution's most telling witness was Connie Babin, Gerardi's date on the night of the murder. Three days after the crime took place, she told police during a taped interview, "It was dark, and I did not have my contacts nor my glasses, so I'm coming at this at a disadvantage." But the jury never heard that remark. She apparently overcame her disadvantage as time passed, because at the trial she testified that she was "one hundred percent, absolutely sure" that Cousin was the killer. The other two eyewitnesses had tentatively identified Cousin from a police photo spread and testified only that he looked like the killer. There was no physical evidence tying Cousin to the murder.

His alibi appeared to be airtight, but the videotape of the game was altered to indicate that it had ended at 9:30 instead of its having begun at that time. Three of Cousin's teammates came to the trial to testify that they were playing basketball when the murder was committed, but defense lawyers were unable to find them in the hallway when they were called. Prosecutors had brought them across the street to wait in the DA's office.

Though he was still a juvenile, Cousin was tried as an adult and sent to death row. Three years later, in 1999, the Louisiana Supreme Court remanded the case based on prosecutorial and police misconduct, including improper argument at trial and failure to disclose the existence of exculpatory witnesses.

Gary Beeman
Ohio

Gary Beeman was convicted and sentenced to death on the testimony of a man who had recently escaped from prison and who had told other witnesses that he was the actual killer. The witness, Clair Liuzzo, had escaped from an Ohio penitentiary shortly before the 1977 murder of a man in Ashtabula County. Liuzzo claimed he saw Beeman with the victim at about the time the crime was committed and saw him again a while later with blood on his clothes. He also said Beeman told him he had killed the man.

On appeal, the Ohio Supreme Court reversed the conviction because the trial judge had not allowed the defense to call witnesses who had heard Liuzzo admit that he had committed the murder and was framing Beeman. At the retrial, in 1979, five witnesses testified to that effect, and Beeman was acquitted.

Charles Ray Giddens
Oklahoma

It took an all-white Oklahoma jury only fifteen minutes to convict Charles Ray Giddens, an eighteen-year-old black man, of murdering a grocery store cashier in 1978. The basis for the conviction and death sentence was the eyewitness testimony of a man named Johnnie Gray, who said he had accompanied Giddens to the scene of the crime. Police initially had arrested Gray for committing the murder but never charged him.

The Oklahoma Court of Criminal Appeals reversed the conviction in 1981, holding that Gray's testimony was "replete with conflicts." The court maintained that the uncorroborated testimony of a witness with much to gain from the conviction of another man was insufficient evidence and could not support a conviction. Since there was no other evidence against him, Giddens was set free. A year later, the court ruled that retrying him would violate the prohibition against double jeopardy.

Lawyer Johnson
Massachusetts

The circumstances that sent Lawyer Johnson to death row were not unlike those experienced by Giddens. He, too, was a black man convicted by an all-white jury chiefly on the testimony of a witness who later was identified as the real killer. Unlike the case of Giddens, however, Johnson's conviction and his death sentence came not in the South, but in Massachusetts, one of the most liberal states in the country.

The victim, James Christian, was shot to death in 1971, and Johnson was identified as the killer by a man named Kenny Myers. Myers had initially accused someone else of the slaying, but that person had a solid alibi—he was in prison at the time. Myers then fingered Johnson, who was convicted of first-degree murder and sentenced to death. As events played out, it became clear that Myers had every reason to provide the police with a killer.

In 1974, the state supreme court reversed Johnson's conviction because the defense had not been given sufficient latitude to cross-examine witnesses. Johnson was retried and again convicted on the basis of Myers's testimony. This time he was sentenced to life in prison.

In 1982, Johnson was granted yet another trial after Dawnielle

Montiero, who was ten years old at the time of the murder, came forward and told the police she had seen Myers shoot Christian. Montiero said she had tried to give that information to the authorities nine years earlier, but that she was not taken seriously because of her age.

Johnson was released at the age of twenty-nine, after spending ten years in prison, three of them on death row.

Timothy Hennis
North Carolina

In 1986, U.S. Army Staff Sergeant Timothy Hennis was convicted of raping and murdering Kathryn Eastburn and stabbing her two children to death in their Fayetteville, North Carolina, home. An eyewitness testified that he had seen Hennis in the Eastburns' driveway at about the time of the crime. He said Hennis was wearing a black beret and a Members Only jacket and was carrying a black bag. The only other direct evidence offered by the prosecution was the testimony of another witness, a bank employee, who said she saw a man who resembled the defendant use what turned out to be the victim's ATM card shortly after the murders. Hennis was convicted and sentenced to die in North Carolina's gas chamber.

Two years later, he was granted a new trial by the state supreme court because the judge had permitted the prosecution to show the jury gruesome photos of the victims' bodies, which were projected on a large screen directly above the head of the defendant. The court found the slide show to be inflammatory and reversed the conviction. In rendering its decision, the court also described the first witness's testimony as "tenuous" and the second's as "extremely tentative."

At the new trial, in 1989, Hennis's lawyer, Gerald Beaver, called as a witness a neighbor of the Eastburns who bore a close resemblance to Hennis. He testified that he often walked the neighborhood at night wearing similar clothing, and it was clear that he could easily have been taken for the defendant. In addition, the witness who had placed Hennis at the scene of the crime said he had been pressured by the prosecution into making an identification even though he was not certain it was Hennis he had seen. As for the bank employee, ATM receipts established that the person who used the victim's card had done so before the employee had arrived at work. The jury found Hennis not guilty.

Part III

CORRUPT PRACTICES AND

MISCONDUCT

Those who do the arithmetic attest that eyewitness error accounts for more than half the wrongful convictions in the United States. If the identifications of jailhouse snitches are added to the mix, the total would be nearly two-thirds. But while false eyewitness testimony may be the proximate cause in most cases where the wrong man is sent to the death house, it is rarely sufficient to get a conviction. Corrupt practices, usually prosecutorial misconduct, are present in almost every instance, greasing the rails on which hundreds of innocent people are sent to death's door. Misidentifications are not always the honest mistakes of well-meaning citizens doing their civic duty. They are prompted by police eager for an arrest, orchestrated by prosecutors hungry for a conviction, nourished by judges who owe their seats to a public that has not outgrown its wistful reverie of frontier justice.

The corrupt practices of those who run the machinery of justice are not the aberrations of an otherwise sound system. They have been woven into the fabric of a social structure that often appears to presume guilt rather than innocence. The ideal of justice that once favored our best instincts has been turned against itself. The great fear of a politician or prosecutor is not that an innocent man may be convicted but that a guilty one might walk free. For which candidate seeking public office today will be ready to chance the prospect of being called soft on crime?

By most educated estimates, about 10 percent of the inhabitants of death row or inmates serving life sentences are innocent. They were put where they are by a combination of such corrupt practices as: police perjury, which has become so commonplace that defense attorneys often refer to testimony by police as "perjumony"; the false testimony offered by those who themselves are in trouble with the law—sometimes suspects, often already incarcerated—who receive favors in return for their fabrications; prosecutors who withhold evidence that might benefit the defense; incompetent or overworked defense lawyers, some of whom have been known to sleep through their clients' trials while presenting virtually no defense at all; and confessions that have been prompted or coerced from suspects who have little or no understanding of how the law works.

When a defendant is acquitted on the basis of such misconduct, there invariably ensues a public outcry that a guilty man may have been turned loose on a technicality. But in truth there are no technicalities, only laws designed to protect the innocent that have been skirted or twisted by those whose power has corrupted the system badly, but not yet absolutely.

• • •

The Ford Heights 4

Illinois

The case that became known as the Ford Heights 4 was a textbook example of corrupt practices involving prosecutorial and police misconduct, false eyewitness identification, the perjured testimony of a jailhouse snitch, and junk science that validated an inconclusive match of both blood and hair samples. The result was the wrongful conviction of four men, all black, two of whom received death sentences, the other two given respective terms of life and seventy-five years.

Their long night's journey through the criminal justice system began at around 2:30 A.M. on May 12, 1978. A newly engaged couple, Lawrence Lionberg and Carol Schmal, were abducted from a gas station in the virtually all-white Chicago suburb of Homewood, Illinois, where Lionberg was working the overnight shift. They were driven to an abandoned town house in the predominantly black section of East Chicago Heights, which later became known as Ford Heights. Schmal was raped, and she and Lionberg were shot in the back of the head. The Ford Heights 4—Dennis Williams, Verneal Jimerson, Kenneth Adams, and Willie Rainge—were arrested a few days later.

The appearance of prosecutorial bias was evident from the start, with the selection of the jury. The seventeenth potential juror called for voir dire was Leroy Posey, a pump operator from Chicago's South Side. After answering the routine questions, Posey, who had noticed that black candidates were being regularly stricken with peremptory challenges by the prosecution, asked permission to speak. "It's obvious the state's attorneys want an all-white jury," he said. "They don't want me here." Posey was excused. The trial jury consisted of eleven whites and one black woman.

The star witness for the prosecution was Charles McCraney, who lived near the murder scene. He testified that at around three o'clock on the morning the couple disappeared he saw six to eight people—among them Williams, Rainge, and Adams—enter the abandoned town house. A second witness, David Jackson, who was doing time in the Cook County jail where Williams and Rainge were being held after their arrest, said he heard the two talking about how they had killed a man and "taken" sex from a woman. As neither witness was able to identify Jimerson, the charges against him were dropped but, as it turned out, only temporarily.

In some respects, the most critical "witness" in the case was a seventeen-year-old woman who saw nothing and never testified. Paula Gray, illiterate and mildly retarded, lived near the crime scene and was questioned by police shortly after the murders. Gray had quite a story to offer. She told the police and later a grand jury that she had actually witnessed the rape and murders. She said, in fact, that she provided light for the assailants in the town house by holding a disposable cigarette lighter while Schmal was raped seven times. However, Gray soon recanted her statements and refused to testify at the trial. She was then charged as an accomplice, convicted, and sentenced to fifty years.

The physical evidence presented by the prosecution was as weak as the eyewitness testimony. The type-O blood from one of the victims was the most common type and therefore an unreliable indicator even if a match was made. Yet less reliable was the examination of three hairs found in Williams's car. Unlike fingerprints, a person's hair type is not unique (except as a repository for DNA, a technology unavailable in 1978). Even under a microscope, the most certain conclusion a scientist can reach is that two hairs *could* have come from the same person. The forensic expert who testified about the hair samples said that two of the hairs found in the car were "similar" to Carol Schmal's and the third was "similar" to Lionberg's. However, the prosecutors continually substituted the word *matched* for *similar* during the balance of the trial, a designation that went unchallenged by the defense.

In 1983, Williams, who had been on death row for four years, won a new trial as a result of the ineffective assistance of counsel. Looking to buttress their case, prosecutors offered to cut a deal with Gray, and she was more than ready to accept. She agreed to revert to her original testimony that she had witnessed the crime and this time would implicate Jimerson as well as Williams. Gray insisted that she had not been offered anything in exchange for her testimony. But shortly after the conclusion of the trial, some of the charges against her were dropped and, with about forty years of her sentence remaining to be served, she was released from prison on two years' probation. Both Williams and Jimerson were convicted and sentenced to death.

The Ford Heights 4 case subsequently came under the scrutiny of the Medill Journalism School investigative team, headed by Professor Protess. They enlisted the pro bono help of Mark Ter Molen, of the Chicago law firm of Mayer, Brown & Platt. Among the team's discoveries was a file showing that five days after the crime, a witness had told police he had seen four men flee the scene of the crime. He identified all four by name, and none of the names was Williams, Jimerson, Rainge, or

Adams. One of them was Arthur (Red) Robinson, who would later be identified as one of the actual killers.

As the students continued their probe, other instances of misconduct were uncovered, and the case started making its way back into the judicial machinery. In 1995, the Illinois Supreme Court unanimously reversed Jimerson's conviction because the prosecution had allowed Gray to testify falsely about the deal she had made. Although the prosecutors never admitted striking the bargain, the judges noted that in reaching their decision they "are not required to suspend common sense." Jimerson was released on bond.

In 1996, DNA tests showed that none of the Ford Heights 4 was involved in the murders. The DNA provided a match with Robinson, who confessed and named his three accomplices. One had since died of a drug overdose; another was serving time on a murder charge. He and the remaining two were convicted and sentenced to life.

Jimerson, Williams, Rainge, and Adams were exonerated and set free. Jimerson had spent eleven years on death row; the others each were imprisoned for eighteen years. Three of the attorneys who represented them have since had their licenses to practice law revoked or suspended for other reasons. The Ford Heights 4 were awarded $36 million by Cook County to settle civil rights claims. It was the largest civil-rights settlement in U.S. history. Williams died on March 20, 2003, of undisclosed causes. He was forty-six years old.

• • •

Thomas Gladish, Richard Greer, Ronald Keine, and Clarence Smith
New Mexico

What the *Detroit News* called "one of the most extensive criminal investigations in American journalistic history" uncovered police corruption that included the attempted bribery of a key witness whose testimony put four innocent men on death row for seventeen months. The witness, the investigation showed, had been told what to say in her pretrial statements and threatened with perjury if she did not repeat her fabricated story during the trial.

Thomas Gladish, Richard Greer, Ronald Keine, and Clarence Smith, all members of a California motorcycle club called the Vagos, were arrested on a robbery charge in Oklahoma City in March 1974. It was just the beginning and, as it turned out, the least of their troubles. Several weeks earlier, a young man had been brutally murdered in a motel room in Albuquerque, New Mexico. His mutilated body was found in a gully a few days later. The victim was identified as William Velten, a student at the University of New Mexico. Velten was known to be a homosexual, and pathologists speculated that he might have been attacked by a group of homosexuals who came to town and left quickly, perhaps on motorcycles.

When Albuquerque police learned that a band of bikers had been arrested in Oklahoma City, they obtained photos of the suspects and began showing them, along with a photo of the victim, in neighborhood gay bars and motels. A part-time maid in one of the motels, Judy Weyer, said she recognized the men. She subsequently spun a tale that included murder, kidnapping, sodomy, and rape. New Mexico police went to Oklahoma to investigate further. After being questioned, four of the bikers were booked on murder charges and brought back to Albuquerque.

Weyer told her story to the jury, and two other prosecution witnesses, a father and son, testified that they had seen the bikers in Albuquerque on the day of the murder. To counter that testimony, the defendants produced a succession of receipts for gas and other purchases that they made on stolen credit cards, to support their claim that they were in California when the crime was committed. The jury was not persuaded. It took fifteen hours to convict the four and ticket them for New Mexico's gas chamber.

The *Detroit News* became interested in the case when it learned that three of the defendants and the victim all originally came from the Detroit area. Veteran crime reporters were assigned to the story, and their primary target was Judy Weyer. To all appearances, Weyer's initial identification, though mistaken, was made in good faith. The embellishments, on the other hand, she said were fashioned and coaxed out of her by the police. She told the reporters that the chief of detectives promised to pay her way through secretarial school if she repeated in court what she had said, under coaching, when she was questioned prior to the trial. If she did not comply, he said, she would do five years in prison for perjury.

The newspaper published its findings in a series of articles that formed the basis of the defendants' appeal, but the appeal process was never concluded. Nearly a year and a half after their conviction, Kerry Rodney Lee, a young drifter who worked as an informant for the Drug Enforcement Administration, walked into a South Carolina police station and confessed to the killings in Albuquerque. Homosexuality had nothing to do with it, he said. It was a drug quarrel that triggered the murder.

A police investigation supported Lee's story. The murder weapon, a gun that was found near the site where the victim's body was discovered, was found to have been stolen from the father of a young woman Lee had dated. The girl said that Lee told her that he had killed a man and that she had seen him splattered with blood on the morning after the crime. To clinch the case, a tow-truck operator identified Lee as the man whose car he had pulled out of the gully just hours after the murder. Two months later, all charges against the four men wrongly convicted were dropped and they were set free.

Earl Charles
Georgia

Earl Charles was sentenced to death on the perjured testimony of a corrupt cop. He was freed because of the dedicated precision of an honest cop and the unflagging efforts of a mother who believed that ultimately the truth would prevail.

Charles was convicted of shooting to death a Savannah, Georgia, furniture store owner and his son during a robbery late one October afternoon in 1974. Max Rosenstein and his wife, Myra, both in their seventies, along with their son, Fred, and the bookkeeper, Bessie Corcelius, were the only ones in the store when two young black men entered. After pretending to make a purchase, one of the men brandished a pistol and announced a stickup. The Rosensteins resisted. Max attempted to scoop up money from the cash register and get it into a safe and was shot in the head. Myra was hit in the face with a tape dispenser and fell to the floor bleeding. Fred was shot when he went to her aid. Bessie Corcelius hid under a desk and was still there when the men fled with the money.

The two survivors, Myra and Bessie, spent hours looking at police mug shots but were unable to identify the killers. Among the mug shots they rejected was a five-year-old photo of Earl Charles. Now twenty-one years old, Charles had been convicted of burglary and shoplifting while in his teens and had spent fourteen months in custody. A few days later, police showed the women a more recent photo of Charles, but they still did not recognize him. In yet another attempt to get an identification, Detective F. W. Wade visited Bessie at her home with another batch of photos. When she was unable to point anyone out, Wade told her it was not important because he was ready to make an arrest. On November 15, Charles was picked up in New Port Richey, Florida. A month later, he was extradited and returned to Savannah where he was charged with the double murder.

Charles had left Georgia in early September, more than a month before the crime was committed. Together with his neighbor Michael Williams and Williams's girlfriend, Charles had driven to Tampa, Florida, looking for work. He and Williams took jobs at a gasoline service station. The station manager, Robert Zachery, was wary about leaving his new hired hands to man the station unsupervised, and he asked his friend,

Deputy Sheriff Lemon Harvey, to look in on them from time to time. Harvey agreed and dutifully kept notes on his visits to the station. Barely two weeks after the men had begun work, the station was robbed of about $1,000. Zachery was uncomfortable with the story they told of the holdup, and he fired them both. Charles soon found a job as a handyman for a company that managed apartment buildings, but more trouble was just around the corner.

On November 15, Charles and Williams were driving north from Tampa with two other acquaintances, Raymond Ash and James Nixon. They stopped for lunch in New Port Richey. Once inside the restaurant, Nixon went back outside, saying he wanted to retrieve something from the car. The other three finished lunch before he returned. When they went to the parking lot, they found Nixon being held at gunpoint by the owner of a nearby store who said she had caught him taking money from the till.

All four men were taken to the police station, and when their names were fed into the computer, it was discovered that Charles and Williams were wanted in Georgia for murder, armed robbery, aggravated assault, and fleeing across state lines to avoid prosecution. Myra Rosenstein and Bessie Corcelius came to Florida, in the company of Detective Wade, to identify the suspects at an extradition hearing on December 19. Both picked Charles out of a police lineup and identified him as the gunman, though Mrs. Rosenstein acknowledged that Charles looked different from the man who shot her husband. He was nonetheless returned to Georgia for prosecution; the state said it would seek the death penalty.

Testifying against Charles, in addition to Mrs. Rosenstein and Mrs. Corcelius, were Detective Wade and James Nixon. Nixon, who had been arrested on a robbery charge, said that while he and Charles were in jail, Charles bragged to him about shooting "a man and a little boy" in a Savannah furniture store. The "little boy" apparently was forty-two-year-old Fred Rosenstein, who Nixon doubtless had heard described as the elder Rosenstein's son. Wade testified that when he interrogated Zachery, the service station owner, he was told that Charles had not been at work on the day of the murders.

The case for the defense appeared to give Charles an unimpeachable alibi. Zachery, who had fired Charles, voluntarily drove to Savannah at his own expense to testify that Charles was working at the station on the day of the murders. His story was documented by time cards and payment vouchers, but was ignored by the jury. They found Charles guilty. The trial judge, who later acknowledged doubts about the defendant's guilt, sentenced him to die in the electric chair.

At this point, Charles needed an advocate who believed in his innocence and who was prepared to work tirelessly in his behalf, and he had one. It was his mother, Flossie Mae. Mrs. Charles understood that the one man who knew for a fact that her son was innocent was Robert Zachery. She called the service station owner repeatedly, soliciting his help. Zachery, who had returned home after his testimony, was astonished that Charles had been found guilty, but could think of nothing else to do. His friend Lemon Harvey, the deputy sheriff, came to his rescue. Harvey had checked up on Charles and Williams regularly when they were working at the station and had kept a detailed diary of his daily rounds. He checked the entries and discovered that he had seen the two men at work on the day of the murders. He notified Zachery who called Mrs. Charles who called Earl's attorney. Lemon was interviewed by lawyers for both the defense and the prosecution. The case against Charles began to unravel.

Nixon recanted his testimony, saying that Wade had coached him and promised him he would be released in exchange for testifying, but Wade had not kept his end of the deal. Wade was further implicated for having withheld exculpatory evidence and coaching eyewitnesses. It also seemed certain that he had perjured himself at the trial. The district attorney said he would not oppose a motion for a new trial and, if granted, he would not retry the case. The judge responded by vacating the conviction, and Charles was released after spending more than three years in prison awaiting execution.

The following year, with the help of the Southern Poverty Law Center, Charles filed suit against the city of Savannah and Detective Wade. Claiming false imprisonment and malicious arrest, the suit alleged that Wade had coerced false eyewitness identifications, manipulated Nixon into committing perjury, withheld exculpatory evidence, and committed perjury himself. In October 1983, four years after the suit was filed and three years after it was thrown out of federal district court, the Fifth Circuit Court of Appeals reversed the lower court. The claim against the city was denied, but Wade was assessed $417,000 in damages. Since Wade had few assets that could be offered in payment, the city agreed to pay $75,000 in his behalf, and all litigation was dropped.

Though Charles was vindicated, the ten-year ordeal took its

toll. He felt that people still doubted his innocence. "It's a scar that's been placed on me," he told a newspaper reporter, "and I have to live with it." But, as it turned out, not for very long. In March 1991, the *Atlanta Constitution* reported that Earl Charles had "walked into the path of an oncoming car" in Cobb County, Georgia. It was an apparent suicide.

Jerry Banks

Georgia

"Southern justice in capital murder trials is more like a random flip of the coin than a delicate balancing of the scales. Who will live and who will die is decided not just by the nature of the crime committed but by the skills of the defense lawyer appointed by the court. And in the nation's Death Belt, that lawyer too often is ill-trained, unprepared and grossly underpaid."

That quote opened a special report on the quality of defense attorneys in capital cases, published in the *National Law Journal* in 1990, and referenced by Michael L. Radelet, Hugo Adam Bedau, and Constance E. Putnam in their 1992 book *In Spite of Innocence*.

The case of Jerry Banks illustrated the travesty of Southern justice while eerily reprising the devastation that the state of Georgia visited upon Earl Charles. Banks was twice convicted and condemned to die for a double murder that occurred just weeks after the crime for which Charles was convicted. Like Charles, Banks was arrested on scant evidence, railroaded by corrupt police practices, and denied justice at every turn. He eventually was exonerated and awarded a ludicrously nominal sum by way of compensation for five years spent on death row. Also like Charles, Banks, a black man who lived at the edge of poverty, finally resolved matters by taking his own life.

Banks was rabbit hunting in a wooded area south of Atlanta in early November 1974 when he came upon two bodies partially covered by a red bedspread. Banks hurried down to the road, flagged down a motorist, and told him to call the police. The police discovered that the victims, both white, were Marvin W. King, a thirty-eight-year-old high-school band instructor, and Melanie Ann Hartsfield, a former student of King's. Each had been hit with two shotgun blasts, one in the back and one in the head. Two red shotgun shells were found nearby. Banks, who had been hunting with a shotgun, said he had not fired his weapon that day. Police twice tested his gun and believed they had found a match. About a month later, a third shell was found near the crime site, and Banks was arrested and charged with murder. The legal machinery moved swiftly. Less than two months after his arrest, Banks was convicted and sentenced to death.

Banks had little money, but he put together enough to retain a local attorney, Hudson John Myers. Myers said he was hired for what amounted to "a mess of collard greens." He performed as if collard greens were too high a fee. He failed to call key witnesses who could have corroborated Banks's account of where he was at the time the crime was committed and others who had spotted more likely suspects in the area shortly before the murders. Equally important, Myers had failed to find the motorist who called the police at Banks's request. Banks was convicted on an entirely improbable scenario, highlighted by the fact that the state never suggested a motive for the crime. The jury was thus obliged to consider that Banks had killed two people for no apparent reason, then asked someone to notify police of the crime, waited for them to arrive, and eagerly handed over the murder weapon.

Not long after the trial, the so-called mystery caller, Andrew Eberhardt, called the trial judge and told him that he had identified himself when he reported the crime and that he had been questioned by the police. In September 1975, the Georgia Supreme Court reversed the conviction because information regarding the motorist was withheld from the defense. It did Banks no immediate good. Myers presented even less of a case at the retrial than he did the first time. Eberhardt was the only witness called, and his testimony was not nearly enough to convince the jury. Banks again was convicted on two counts of murder and returned to death row.

Ironically, evidence that would eventually contribute to Banks's acquittal was used to justify the death penalty. Banks had a single-barrel shotgun that had to be reloaded after each shot, a maneuver that would have taken at least five seconds. That should have raised doubts in the minds of the jury since witnesses who heard the shots said they came in rapid succession. Instead, it was turned to the advantage of the prosecution. The jury was told that the delay in reloading three times intensified the anxiety experienced by whoever was the second victim. In the words of the Georgia statute, this made the second slaying "outrageously and wantonly vile, horrible, and inhuman" and justified imposing the ultimate sanction.

Banks's life was saved by a chance meeting with a public defender at the Henry County jail. Alex Crumbley was visiting with some of his clients, Banks's fellow inmates, when Banks asked for a small favor. He had not heard from his lawyer in a long time, and Banks wondered whether Crumbley could inquire whether Myers was still on the case. He was not. Crumbley soon learned that Myers was not on anyone's case. He was in the process of being disbarred because of his incompetent representation of other clients. In the process of his inquiries, Crumbley had become convinced of Banks's innocence and began working his case pro bono. But in 1978, he was appointed a judge and could no longer represent Banks. Determined to press on, Crumbley enlisted a legal team that consisted of A. J. "Buddy" Welch Jr., Stephen P. Harrison, and Crumbley's younger brother, Wade, who had recently graduated from Georgia Law School.

Their first initiative resulted in failure. Both the superior court and the Georgia Supreme Court denied a request for a new trial based on ineffective assistance of counsel. Undeterred, Banks's new legal cadre pushed forward with their investigation. They found no fewer than nine witnesses who had not been called whose testimony would have served the defendant's cause. Seven people, including Paul Collier, the police chief of Stockbridge, had heard four shots in rapid succession that could not have been fired from Banks's twelve-gauge, single-barrel shotgun. Together with the mayor of Stockbridge, Collier later visited the murder site and found two green shotgun casings that did not match Banks's weapon. In addition, two witnesses said they had seen a white man brandishing a shotgun near the scene of the crime minutes after the shots were fired.

Despite the imposing array of new evidence, the trial judge denied a request for a new trial. This time, however, the superior court reversed and ordered a third trial for Banks. Six months passed while the prosecution prepared its case. But Welch, Harrison, and Crumbley made a new discovery that turned the proceedings around. They learned that the shell casings originally found at the scene had almost certainly been planted.

Philip S. Howard, the lead investigator in the case, was found to have a less than enviable record as a police officer. Howard, in fact, had a history of falsifying evidence. He had resigned from one police force and been fired from another, was convicted of forgery, and, most tellingly, had "tampered with and manipulated evidence involving [shotgun] shells" in another case. Now it appeared that he had done it again in an effort to convict Banks. Howard said he had found the shell casings matching Banks's gun the day before it was taken for test firings. However, credible new evidence, including the statement of a former county commissioner, indicated that the gun was tested before the shells were found. The likelihood grew that Howard had taken the test shells and planted them in the woods. Confronted with these findings, the district attorney conceded that the shotgun shells, the only evidence tying Banks to the crime, "lack[ed] sufficient legal credibility to be believed." All charges against him were dropped.

Three days before Christmas 1980, Banks returned home to his wife and three children. But his homecoming was not all one might have hoped for. He found that five years of separation were difficult to breach. He and his wife had grown apart, and she wanted a divorce and custody of the children. Three days before the divorce was to become final, on March 29, 1981, Banks shot his wife with a .38-caliber pistol, then shot himself in the chest. He died instantly. His wife died of the gunshot wounds six weeks later.

The Banks children sued the Harris County Sheriff's Department for $12 million. They were awarded $150,000. The *Atlanta Constitution* called the settlement "blood money." The editorial continued: "No amount of money could every really make up for what the system—all of us included—did to Jerry Banks and his family. But $150,000 doesn't even begin to address the level of damages, the lasting pain. In fact, it comes closer to being an insult."

Clifford Henry Bowen
Oklahoma

Clifford Henry Bowen was a victim of good-faith mistaken identity and an overly zealous Oklahoma City district attorney who had shown little inclination to play by the rules.

Bowen was no one's candidate for Man of the Year. He was a potbellied, fifty-year-old professional poker player with a history of burglary. But he was not a killer. Yet he was sentenced to death for the execution-style murders of three men sharing a poolside table at an Oklahoma City motel at about two in the morning on July 6, 1980. Bowen, the state charged, approached the table, drew a .45-caliber automatic loaded with silver-tipped, hollow-point bullets, and shot the victims at point-blank range.

The prosecution pinned its case on the testimony of two eye-witnesses who identified Bowen as the stranger wearing a red cap they saw standing around the concession machines near the pool area sometime between 12:15 and 1:30 that morning. One of the witnesses claimed to have seen him through a window more than eighty-five feet away. The other witness was believed to have required hypnosis to recall what she had seen, although that bit of information was never presented to the jury. Bowen, for his part, had twelve witnesses who testified that he was at a rodeo in Tyler, Texas, three hundred miles away, until about midnight that night.

Prosecuting the case was Oklahoma County's district attorney, Robert Macy. Nicknamed "Cowboy Bob," Macy was in the tradition of Wild West frontiersmen who dished out justice as they saw it and asked questions later. He was a favorite with the public in Oklahoma County, where he had put fifty-three defendants on death row. Former U.S. attorney general William Barr called him a "true patriot."

But there was another side to Macy. Ken Armstrong, a legal affairs writer for the Oklahoma *Tribune,* wrote in a 1999 article that state and federal appellate rulings have repeatedly condemned Macy's methods. "Here's what they have found," Armstrong wrote: "Macy has cheated. He has lied. He has bullied. Even when a man's life is at stake, Macy has spurned the rules of a fair trial, concealing evidence, misrepresenting evidence, or launching into abusive, improper arguments that had nothing to do with the evidence."

In some of Macy's other cases, a federal judge said he had engaged in "blatant misrepresentation" while convincing a jury to sentence a man to death; the state appellate court rebuked Macy for employing a host of "improper tactics" in his argument to the jury. Macy clearly had a way with juries, and his timing was often impeccable. At Bowen's trial, he waited until closing argument, when the defense had had its final say, to advance a theory that would circumvent Bowen's midnight alibi. He could have made it from Tyler, Texas, to Oklahoma City in about two hours if he had taken a private jet from the rodeo grounds to the downtown airport in Oklahoma City. No such evidence had been offered during the trial, and for good reason. The airstrip in Texas had been abandoned, and neither airport would have been able to accommodate the kind of jet needed for that fast a flight. The jury apparently swallowed it whole. Bowen was convicted and sentenced to death.

Two years after Bowen took residence on death row, a South Carolina police detective came to Bowen's lawyer with a stunning piece of news. He had uncovered compelling evidence that the three men at poolside had been killed by a small-town South Carolina police lieutenant. The lieutenant, Lee Crowe, bore a strong resemblance to Bowen—both had respectable paunches and salt-and-pepper hair. Crowe had been known to carry a .45 with silver-tipped, hollow-point bullets. He also had something Bowen did not have—a motive. The lieutenant's fiancée had been married to Ray Peters, one of the three men killed. Peters was also said to have threatened his ex-wife, and on at least one occasion he had struck her.

What's more, Crowe had been under investigation by South

Carolina police as a suspected hit man. He was known to be in Oklahoma at the time of the murders and returned to South Carolina later that day. It was also learned that Crowe had once before dated a woman who was being harassed by a former lover. That ex-boyfriend had been shot five times in the head. All of the information regarding Crowe had been known by the prosecution before Bowen was tried, but they did not share it with Bowen's attorneys. Macy later contended that he believed the Oklahoma City police investigation had eliminated Crowe as a suspect. He also said he would have turned over the evidence if the defense attorney had requested it. The U.S. Court of Appeals for the Tenth Circuit saw it differently. The court ruled in 1986 that the evidence that was concealed was so critical that it cast "grave doubt" on Bowen's guilt and should have been disclosed on the initiative of the prosecution. Bowen's conviction was overturned.

Five months later, Macy was reelected with 80 percent of the vote. In 1987, he was named the state's outstanding district attorney, cited for his "exemplary professionalism in the exercise of prosecutorial duties." A few years later, his fellow prosecutors elected him president of the National District Attorneys Association.

Bowen died in 1996, ten years after being set free.

Clarence Lee Brandley
Texas

Race often plays a part in wrongful arrests and convictions, particularly in the South, but rarely is it as blatant a factor as it was in the case of Clarence Lee Brandley. A custodian at Conroe High School in Conroe, Texas, Brandley was sentenced to death for raping and strangling the sixteen-year-old manager of the visiting Bellville High volleyball team on August 23, 1980. There was virtually no evidence linking Brandley to the crime, but his being black seemed to be reason enough to convict him.

The victim, Cheryl Fergeson, was found dead after the game in a loft above the school auditorium. Fergeson, who was white, would have entered her junior year in the fall. The two custodians who had found the body, Brandley and Henry (Icky) Peace, were questioned and fingerprinted. They gave blood and hair samples. They both passed lie-detector tests. But none of that seemed to matter. The investigation had been shaped on the day of the murder. According to Peace, the officer conducting the interrogation had said, "One of you two is going to hang for this." Then he turned to Brandley and added, "Since you're the nigger, you're elected."

With the new school year about to begin and parents threatening to keep their children home unless the killer was caught, the authorities knew they needed a quick arrest. The list of suspects was short. Three other custodians—Gary Acreman, Sam Martinez, and John Sessum—provided alibis for one another. There seemed to be no place else to go, and Brandley, after all, had already been elected. Texas Ranger Wesley Styles, who was put in charge of the investigation, arrested him on a charge of capital murder.

The state had little to offer by way of proof except for the statements of the other custodians, all of whom were white, which at the very best obliquely placed Brandley near the crime scene that afternoon. Acreman, Martinez, and Sessum related stories so similar in detail that the defense claimed they had been coached by the police. In any event, it was difficult to deny that they each had a stake in the outcome. In individual statements, they said they had seen Cheryl enter a girls' rest room near the gym and, a short time later, Brandley approached with an armful of toilet paper. They said they warned Brandley that a girl was in the facility, and he said he was going to the boys' rest room. They did not see him again for about forty-five minutes until the search for the missing girl began. In his statement, Peace also turned the focus of suspicion toward Brandley. He said that when he told Brandley he had not found the girl in the loft, Brandley went with him to search more thoroughly. When they found the body, Peace said Brandley calmly checked for a pulse and then notified the authorities. In addition, all four said that only Brandley had keys to the auditorium.

Just five days after the crime was committed, Brandley found himself testifying before an all-white grand jury. His version of events differed slightly from those presented by his fellow custodians. He admitted disappearing for about thirty minutes, not forty-five, but said he was smoking a cigarette and listening to the radio. He also testified that there were others who had master keys that could be used to open the auditorium. All the same, the grand jury returned an indictment, and Brandley went on trial in December 1980, again before an all-white jury.

What little physical evidence existed seemed to favor the defendant. A fresh blood spot had been found on the victim's blouse that was of a type different from both hers and Brandley's. Sperm that had been recovered from Cheryl's body had been destroyed, presumably before it was tested. The remnants of the prosecution's case that remained proved to be conclusive enough for eleven jurors. The twelfth, William Srack, was unconvinced, and Srack held his ground despite being assailed by the other jurors as a "nigger lover" during deliberations. When the trial was over, Srack was the target of threats and harassing phone calls, some of which were monitored by the police. But the jury was hung and a retrial was scheduled for February 1981.

At the second trial, yet again heard by an all-white jury, an original prosecution witness was dropped and a new one was added. John Sessum apparently was no longer willing to echo the story told by his three colleagues. He was threatened with a charge of perjury but stood fast. The state's new witness was a junior at the school, Danny Taylor, who had worked with the custodial staff briefly during the summer. Taylor testified that one day, as they watched a group of white female students pass by, Brandley had commented, "If I got one of them alone, ain't no tellin' what I might do."

In an attempt to add some meat to the bones of its case, the state called the Harris County medical examiner who verified that a belt belonging to Brandley was consistent with the injuries inflicted by the instrument that was used to strangle the victim. In his closing argument, the district attorney offered the information that Brandley had a second job at a funeral home and suggested that he might be a necrophiliac and had raped Cheryl after she was dead. The defense's objection that the remark was inflammatory, was overruled. This time there was no holdout. The jury returned a verdict of guilty and recommended the death penalty. The judge obliged.

Eleven months later, as they were preparing his appeal, Brandley's attorneys discovered that a good bit of evidence that the state had used at trial had mysteriously disappeared while in the custody of the prosecution. A total of 166 of the 309 exhibits that had been introduced could no longer be found. These included hairs taken from Cheryl's body that matched neither Brandley's nor her own. Also missing were photos of Brandley taken on the day of the crime that showed he was not wearing the belt that was suggested to be the murder weapon.

The Texas Court of Criminal Appeals was unimpressed. It affirmed the conviction and death sentence. "No reasonable hypothesis is presented by the evidence to even *suggest* that someone other than [Brandley] committed the crime," the court ruled. Brandley's execution date was set for January 17, 1986. However, the defense succeeded in getting a delay. A petition for a writ of habeas corpus, claiming that the lost evidence had deprived Brandley of a fair trial, was granted, and a hearing was scheduled for the summer. The six-month delay saved Brandley's life, for his luck was about to change.

A young woman by the name of Brenda Medina, who lived in the neighboring town of Cut 'n' Shoot, Texas, saw the case being discussed on a television broadcast. She told a neighbor that she had not heard about the case before, and added that her former boyfriend, James Dexter Robinson, had told her in 1980 that he had committed such a crime. The neighbor urged her to tell a lawyer, and the lawyer told her to take her story to the district attorney. The DA concluded that Medina was unreliable, and thus he was under no obligation to share the information with Brandley's lawyers. The attorney Medina had consulted did not agree. He notified the defense, and an evidentiary hearing was ordered, with District Court Judge Ernest A. Coker presiding.

John Sessum, the custodian who had not testified at the second trial, now took the stand and recanted his earlier testimony. He also implicated Gary Acreman. He said he had seen Acreman follow Cheryl up a staircase and then heard her scream, "No" and "Don't." Later that day, he said, Acreman had warned him that there would be trouble if he said anything about the incident. Nonetheless, Sessum chose to inform Texas Ranger Styles. It was a poor choice. Styles told him they already had their man and threatened him with arrest if he did not support Acreman's story. With Acreman now beginning to look like a suspect, his father-in-law, Edward Payne, did not help his son-in-law's position. He testified that Acreman had told him where the victim's clothes were hidden on the night of the murder, which was two days before they were found.

When Medina took the stand, she stated flatly that Robinson had confessed to the murder. A former custodian at Conroe High who had been fired about a month earlier, Robinson told her he was leaving town for a while because he had killed a girl and hidden her body. Medina said she did not believe him and thought nothing more about it until Brandley's case came to her attention years later. Robinson also appeared at the hearing. He testified that he had invented the story he told Medina because she was pregnant and was hassling him, and he wanted to frighten her into leaving him alone. Despite what appeared to be overwhelming new evidence in his favor, Brandley's request for a new trial was denied. On December 22, 1986, the Texas Court of Criminal Appeals upheld that decision. In February, a new execution date was set—March 26, 1987.

But by that time, the case had drawn wide national attention. Civil rights activists had raised $80,000 to finance further legal action. A protest demonstration in Conroe drew more than one thousand marchers. A "Free Clarence Brandley" coalition was formed. Amnesty International entered the fray. James McCloskey, of Centurion Ministries in Princeton, New Jersey, agreed to take the case. A former seminary student before he became an attorney, McCloskey had made a career of seeking to win freedom for innocent prisoners.

Working with a private investigator, McCloskey was able to get Acreman to give an updated version of the events on videotape. Acreman said that Robinson alone had abducted and killed Cheryl. He said he saw Robinson drop her clothes in the Dumpster where they were found. Acreman later recanted his videotaped statement, but by that time events were moving in Brandley's direction. Two new witnesses surfaced who said they heard Acreman say that Brandley did not kill the girl. He said he knew who the killer was but would never tell. Only six days before the scheduled execution, Judge Coker ordered a stay.

In September 1987, a new evidentiary hearing was held. Presiding was Special State District Judge Perry Pickett, seventy-one years old and with a time-honored reputation for being scrupulously fair. The key witnesses, including Acreman, Robinson, and Styles, offered testimony that seemed to discredit one another rather than implicate Brandley. Robinson and Acreman emerged as serious suspects. Styles was depicted as a bullying racist. On October 9, Judge Pickett concluded the hearing with a statement that rang with indignation about the manner in which the case was conducted. He said: "The litany of events graphically described by the witnesses, some of it chilling and shocking, leads me to the conclusion [that] the pervasive shadow of darkness has obscured the light of fundamental decency and human rights." He continued with an indictment of how the prosecution was conducted, declaring that the state had "wholly ignored any evidence or lead to evidence that might prove inconsistent with their premature conclusion that Brand-ley had committed the murder. The conclusion is inescapable that the investigation was conducted not to solve the crime, but to convict Brandley." The judge recommended that the Texas Court of Criminal Appeals grant Brandley a new trial. Then he went a step further: "The testimony . . . unequivocally establishes that Gary Acreman and James Dexter Robinson are prime suspects and probably were responsible for the death of Cheryl Dee Fergeson."

The court sat on the case for fourteen months while Brandley languished in prison. On December 13, 1989, a sharply divided court accepted Judge Pickett's recommendation and ordered a retrial. The prosecution, in its relentless insistence on Brandley's guilt, announced it would appeal to the U.S. Supreme Court. Free on bail after spending nine years on death row, Brandley waited another ten months for a final disposition of his case. On October 1, the Supreme Court denied the state's request for certiorari and Brandley's ten-year ordeal was finally over. No disciplinary action was ever taken against the officials who played a role in his conviction.

Patrick Croy
California

On rare occasions, being a member of a racial minority can be to the advantage of the defendant. It worked that way for Patrick Croy who was given the death penalty for the murder of a police officer in Yreka, California, in 1979.

There was never any question that Croy, a Native American, had killed the policeman. Croy's defense was that he was drunk when the officer came on the scene and was concerned that he might be arrested for being intoxicated in public, as he was on probation at the time. The jury did not buy his story, and Croy was convicted and sentenced to death. The California Supreme Court overturned the conviction because the jury had been improperly instructed.

At his retrial, Croy mounted an entirely different defense. He maintained he had shot the cop in self-defense and that the officer had shot first. But the heart of his case was that Yreka was a racist community, and being of Native American background he had a reasonable fear that the police officer intended to kill him. Croy's testimony appeared to be entirely unconvincing, tentative, and rehearsed. He admitted that he had consumed an "impressive amount of liquor and marijuana" before the confrontation with the police. He also admitted lying at his first trial because he did not think he could win on the merits of his case.

The defense depicted the second trial as a political proceeding rather than one concerning guilt or innocence. According to his attorney, the case was about Croy's "symbolic value as an aggrieved Indian," and he presented a cultural defense based on his Native American heritage. Croy was acquitted, though it was never established that he was actually innocent. Years later, he was living in Arizona in the witness protection program.

Jay C. Smith
Pennsylvania

Being freed from prison, even from death row, does not imply the actual innocence of the convict. As innocent people are often found guilty, the guilty are sometimes acquitted for reasons that have little to do with whether they did or did not commit the crime. Unless the real killer is found and convicted, the actual guilt or innocence of the person released remains the property of speculation.

Such was the case with Jay C. Smith, who was freed from Pennsylvania's death row in 1992 after being convicted of the 1979 murder of a woman and her two children in a case memorialized by a best-selling book and a TV miniseries. Smith, a former high school principal, and William S. Bradfield Jr. were convicted in 1986 of conspiring to kill Susan Reinert, whose nude and battered body was found in the trunk of an abandoned car in the parking lot of a Swatara Township motel. The bodies of the two children, ages ten and eleven, were never found. Bradfield and Reinert, both English teachers in the Upper Merion School District, were engaged to be married, and he was the beneficiary of her $750,000 life insurance policy. Smith, who was convicted largely on Bradfield's testimony, received a triple death sentence. Bradfield was given three sentences of life in state prison.

Right from the start, there seemed to be something off-register in the state's case. Pete Shellem and Laird Leask, who covered the story for the local newspaper, the *Patriot-News,* reported almost annual revelations of new or suppressed evidence. The big break came in March 1992 when a box removed from the attic of State Trooper Jack Holtz, the lead investigator, was found to contain evidence that would finally lead to Smith's exoneration. The most critical piece of evidence found in the box was a comb marked with the name of Smith's army reserve unit. During the trial, prosecutors introduced an identical comb that they said was found under Reinert's body in the trunk of the car. That comb was labeled as a trial exhibit; the comb found in the box was not. Furthermore, the comb submitted at the trial should have been sealed with other evidence in the Attorney General's Office. It seemed clear that Smith had been convicted, at least in part, on the basis of fabricated evidence.

Also found in the box was a letter from the crime writer Joseph Wambaugh, which indicated he had offered Holtz's late partner, Sergeant Joseph Van Nort, $50,000 for information before any arrests were made. A postscript to the letter read: "Since I would start the leg work [on the book] immediately we should be very careful about being seen together for the sake of your job. As far as witnesses would know, I received all my information from news stories and anonymous tips."

A week later, Shellem and Leask reported that they had obtained documents showing that Wambaugh, whose book *Echoes in the Darkness,* became a best-seller, paid Holtz at least $45,000 the same year that Smith was convicted. Records also indicated that Holtz, a twenty-three-year veteran of the state police, purchased a Porsche 944 and a resort home in North Carolina the year after the trial while earning an annual salary of about $35,000. State police regulations prohibited investigators from accepting outside money for police work without the approval of the commissioner.

The box also contained dated notebooks numbered one through twenty-three, except that number thirteen was missing. Smith's lawyer, William C. Costopoulos, contended that the missing notebook covered a period when Holtz was dealing with a jailhouse informant named Raymond Martray who testified he had heard Smith admit to having committed the murders. Elsewhere, according to Costopoulos, Holtz claimed that Bradfield told him he had acted alone. The attorney filed papers asking Judge Robert L. Walker to put all the evidence in the case in the care of a court-appointed custodian. He also asked the judge to order the prosecution to explain why the evidence was not made available to the defense.

Costopoulos's suspicions about his client's conviction were first aroused when it was discovered that rubber evidence-lifters containing sand, presumably taken from Reinert's feet, were found in an evidence locker near the end of the trial. The presence of the sand was not made known to the defense until more than a year later. It supported the defense's contention that Reinert was killed at the Jersey shore by Bradfield. Other evidence indicated that Bradfield too had been at the beach, while Smith had been elsewhere. It was later discovered that the police and prosecutors had known all along that the sand was in the evidence locker but concealed it from the defense.

In 1989, Smith was granted a new trial on the grounds that

the trial court allowed inadmissible hearsay testimony to be presented. Costopoulos seized upon the ruling to try to win freedom for his client by invoking the double-jeopardy clause in the Pennsylvania constitution. In an unusual reading of the law, the attorney claimed that it would violate Smith's civil rights to subject him to a second trial on the same charge since it was the state, by its own misconduct, that had caused the verdict of the original trial to be reversed. As a rule, double jeopardy—trying a suspect twice on the same charge—is the refuge for those who have been acquitted at trial, preventing them from being tried again if new evidence surfaces. But in Smith's case, the court ruled that the prosecution's conduct had been so outrageous that subjecting the defendant to a new trial would indeed amount to double jeopardy under the state constitution.

Smith was set free, with much fanfare and a degree of protest, on September 18, 1992. Interestingly, the court based its decision on the secret deal with the jailhouse informant and the sand evidence that was concealed from the defense. No mention was made of the evidence found in Trooper Holtz's attic, and no charges were brought against any of the state officials in the case. William Bradfield continued serving his sentence in the Graterford state prison.

Troy Lee Jones
California

The question of guilt or innocence had little to do with murder charges being dropped against Troy Lee Jones in 1996. In fact, the California Supreme Court, in vacating Jones's conviction, noted that the evidence, though not overwhelming, suggested that Jones was guilty. It nonetheless felt compelled to overturn the conviction because Jones's defense was deemed ineffective.

Jones was sentenced to death in 1982 for fatally shooting Carolyn Grayson in order to prevent her from implicating him in the murder of an elderly woman, Janet Benner. Grayson had told Jones's brother Marlow that she had seen Jones strangle the old lady. She also told her daughter Sauda that Jones had killed Mrs. Benner. In addition, Jones's sister testified that she overheard a conversation in which Jones seemed to suggest to their mother that he should have killed Grayson when he murdered the older woman. She also said her brother was involved in a family plot to kill Grayson.

A neighbor of Grayson's testified that she witnessed a violent altercation between Grayson and Jones in which she assured him that she would not reveal his involvement in Benner's murder but that he still continued to threaten her. Grayson's body was found in a field the day after she was said to have left with Jones for Oakland.

In short, the prosecution's case included testimony that Jones was observed threatening Carolyn Grayson with a tire iron a few weeks before she was shot to death, that he and his family had plotted to poison her, that he confided to his brother that if he didn't kill Grayson she would send him to the gas chamber, that he told his brother he needed to establish an alibi for the evening Grayson was murdered, and that Grayson told her daughter she was going out with Jones on the night she was killed.

Jones served fourteen years on death row while he appealed

his conviction. Finally, in 1996, the court ruled that he should have a new trial because he had been inadequately defended. The court found that his defense attorney failed to conduct an adequate pretrial investigation, interview possible witnesses, obtain a relevant police report, or seek pretrial investigative funds. It also noted that the attorney elicited damaging testimony against his own client while cross-examining a witness. The state dropped the charges rather than retry the case because more than a decade after the original trial, the witnesses and evidence were no longer available.

Carl Lawson
Illinois

On July 27, 1989, eight-year-old Terrence Jones was found murdered in his home in East St. Louis, Illinois. It did not take the police very long to arrest Carl Lawson, who had recently ended a romantic relationship with the boy's mother, Pam Burts. The state based its case on the forensic evidence that his Pro Wing sneakers were consistent with bloody shoe prints found at the crime scene.

Lawson, who continued to live with Burts even after their breakup, did not deny that the shoe prints might have been his. But if they were, they would have been made when he arrived at the home after the boy's body was discovered. The Pro Wing sneakers were a popular model worn by young men in that neighborhood and, for added measure, seven other bloody shoe prints, clearly not made by Lawson, were found at the scene.

The prosecution's most effective weapon was the lawyer chosen for Lawson's defense. William Brandon, the assistant public defender who was handling Lawson's case, had recently switched sides. He previously was an assistant state's attorney and had served in that capacity at Lawson's arraignment.

As the shoe prints and fingerprints on a beer bottle and matchbook were the only physical evidence the state possessed, it would have been in Lawson's interest to have them examined and tested by an independent expert. However, he did not have the means to hire someone, and Judge Michael O'Malley denied his *pro se* request for funds to be used for that purpose. Lawson was convicted by a St. Clair County jury and sentenced to death.

On appeal, the Illinois Supreme Court reversed the conviction, citing the conflict inherent in Lawson's being defended by an attorney who had represented the state earlier in the case. "[W]e find," the court ruled, "that under the circumstances here, where defendant's court-appointed defense counsel also previously served in the same criminal proceeding as the prosecuting assistant state's attorney, a possible conflict of interest existed." In remanding the case for retrial, the court also noted that the trial court had been in error when it denied resources for hiring forensic experts.

By the time Lawson's appeal was upheld, a new suspect had emerged and doubt had been cast on the prosecution's reliance on the shoe-print evidence. Still, Lawson was tried twice more. The first retrial ended in a hung jury although eleven of the twelve jurors favored acquittal. At the second retrial, a year later, Lawson was found not guilty when it was revealed for the first time that the blood had been wet when the child's body was found and so the shoe prints could have been made by anyone in the crowd that gathered at the scene before the police arrived.

Lawson was freed on December 12, 1996. The alternative suspect died without ever being investigated. Lawson moved to Missouri but, according to the Center on Wrongful Convictions, he has not had an easy time of it. "It's hard," he said. "Not very many people want to hire a man who's been on death row." On August 1, 2002, Governor George Ryan pardoned Lawson based on actual innocence.

William Nieves
Pennsylvania

William Nieves, a thirty-four-year-old small-time drug dealer, was looking for a way to start a new life. He had been taking classes for about two weeks at the Community College of Philadelphia when he was picked up for questioning in connection with the 1992 murder of Eric McAiley. Nine months had passed since the December 22 slaying, and while Nieves admitted knowing the victim (it was alleged that McAiley had sold drugs for Nieves), he could not provide police with an alibi for the night of the crime.

Nieves had been identified by an eyewitness who had been unable to identify him at the start of the investigation. A police officer, who said he saw a bearded Hispanic man drive away from the crime scene in a Cadillac, interviewed people who were there that night, but none could offer a detailed description of the killer. Nine months later, one of the people the officer had interviewed came forward and said she had seen Nieves step out of a Cadillac and shoot the victim. The suspicion was that McAiley was shot following a dispute over a drug debt.

Nieves was reluctant to use a court-appointed attorney. He chose instead to retain a lawyer, Thomas Ciccone Jr., who had represented him on a few minor charges in the eighties. The decision raised two problems for Nieves: first, he didn't have the money to pay Ciccone's fee; second, Ciccone had never before tried a capital case. Ciccone asked for $10,000 but eventually agreed to work for one-fourth that amount. Nieves sold his Chevy Jeep for $2,000, and his mother, who was living on Social Security, scraped together an additional $500. Nieves felt that Ciccone was "very nice about it, very understanding," and by all accounts he gave it his best effort. But his inexperience showed, and it cost Nieves dearly.

The eyewitness who testified against him, a thirty-four-year-old prostitute and crack-cocaine user, had offered conflicting accounts of what she had seen from the very beginning. She initially identified two thin black men as the killers, then said it was a husky Hispanic man. Nieves was Hispanic but in no way could he be considered husky. Ciccone offered little by way of defense. He called no witnesses and mistakenly advised Nieves not to testify in his own behalf, because if he took the stand, the district attorney would be able to question him about his prior record. The trial lasted only two days in July 1994, and the jury found Nieves guilty of murder in the first degree. No mitigating evidence was presented at the sentencing phase, and without mitigation, Pennsylvania law mandated the death penalty.

Once he was moved to death row in the Pittsburgh State Correctional Institution, Nieves began to research his own case and discovered that he been given ineffective and incorrect counsel. Chiefly, he had been deprived of the right to testify for himself in open court. A former prosecutor, John McMahon Jr., agreed to represent Nieves on appeal. "William Nieves's first trial was not presented in the way it should have been presented," McMahon said, "and that's wrong when someone is being sentenced to death."

In 1997, the original trial judge granted Nieves a retrial, but the prosecutor contested the judge's decision, and three more years passed before the Pennsylvania Supreme Court upheld Nieves's right to a new trial, on February 17, 2000. As the defense prepared to try the case again, it became evident why the prosecution fought so hard to prevent it. The prosecutor had withheld critical evidence that would have aided Nieves in his basic defense of misidentification. Documents that never came to light included a statement by an FBI informant that gave the police names of people who might have been involved in the crime as well as a new eyewitness. The eyewitness, who was the boyfriend of the victim's sister, testified in the retrial that he told the detectives investigating the case that they had the wrong man. He was told that his information was of no use and was escorted out by police.

Nieves was found not guilty on October 20, 2000. He was released three days later, after serving six years on death row. After his release, Nieves began traveling about the country, telling his story, working as the community organizer with the Pennsylvania Abolitionists Against the Death Penalty.

• • •

Michael Graham and Albert Burrell
Louisiana

In the world of crime and penology, the name Angola has the same forbidding ring of finality that Alcatraz and Sing Sing had generations ago. Officially named Louisiana State Penitentiary, Angola is known as one of the toughest, dead-end destinations in the country. Its death-row cells, measuring six-by-nine feet, more closely resemble the cages used to house animals at a zoo, except that those cages are usually more spacious. It was in such cells that Michael Graham and Albert Burrell spent twenty-three hours a day every day for thirteen years for a crime they did not commit after a trial in which the state presented no credible evidence.

Graham and Burrell were charged with shooting to death an elderly couple, William and Callie Frost, in their home in Union Parish, Louisiana, on August 31, 1986. The only evidence against them was the testimony of two witnesses, neither of whom could put the suspects anywhere near the scene at the time of the crime. The first, Burrell's ex-wife, Janet, triggered the investigation with a call to Sheriff Larry Averitt. She told the officer that she had met with Burrell on a deserted road the night of the murder and found a wallet on the car seat. It contained William Frost's identification documents but no money. Burrell then took out his own wallet, she said, and counted out twenty-seven $100 bills and told her he had killed the Frosts. The second witness was a jailhouse snitch named Olan Wayne Brantley who said he heard both Burrell and Graham confess to the murders while they were being held. There was no other evidence of any kind. Yet Burrell and Graham were convicted in separate trials and both were sent to Angola's death house.

With death in the electric chair drawing nearer and revelations continuing to surface nationally that many death-row inhabitants did not belong there, the cases of Burrell and Graham attracted the attention of a number of criminal attorneys. Nick Trenticosta, a New Orleans lawyer, took on Burrell's appeal free of charge and added to the defense team Chuck Lloyd, an attorney from Burrell's hometown of Minneapolis. The burden of seeking to clear Graham was assumed pro bono by Michele Fournet.

Working independently, the two lawyers learned fairly soon that the state had had no case worth presenting. Burrell, who was mentally retarded and unable to read or write, was clearly incapable of assisting in his own defense and should not have been forced to stand trial. They also discovered that the testimony of the state's two witnesses was worthless.

Burrell's wife admitted that she had made up the story hoping that if Burrell were arrested she could gain sole custody of their son. She signed an affidavit stating, "What I told the police was not true." The testimony of the jailhouse snitch, Olan Wayne Brantley, was found to be no more reliable. Brantley, it was learned, had a reputation for falsely implicating others in crimes they knew nothing about. In at least two previous cases, he testified that he had overheard the suspects confess. A law-enforcement official acknowledged that Brantley was known as Lyin' Wayne. Brantley's behavior could be better understood in light of the fact that he had a history of mental illness. Although it was never revealed to the defense, he had admitted at his own trial that he had spent time in several mental hospitals where he was treated for manic depression. He also said he had written more bad checks than he could keep track of. On top of it all, Brantley had made a plea deal on unrelated charges he was facing, and the defense was never told of it.

In March 2000, District Judge Cynthia Woodard threw out the convictions and sentences and ordered a new trial. Judge Woodard cited the incidents of prosecutorial misconduct and also noted that Dan Grady, one of the prosecutors, had said the case against Burrell and Graham was "so weak that [it] should never have been brought to the grand jury." Prosecutors for the Attorney General's Office, which assumed control of the case when the Union Parish district attorney voluntarily withdrew, said they found a "total lack of credible evidence" connecting the men with the crimes.

On December 27, 2000, the State Attorney General's Office filed documents with the state district court in Union Parish dismissing all charges against the men. In making the announcement, Pam Laborde said, "We have no physical evidence in this case, and that has been the problem from the start." The attorney general reopened the investigation of the shootings, noting there was a "very real possibility that someone else committed the murders."

After the charges against Burrell and Graham were dropped, a DNA test showed that blood taken from the doorjamb of the Frosts' home belonged to the victims. There was still no physical evidence that put Burrell or Graham at the scene. The trial attorneys appointed to represent Burrell were later disbarred for other reasons and sent to federal prison. The former sheriff of Union Parish also received a prison term on charges that he stole from his office. According to Michele Fournet, Graham's lawyer, the kind of prosecutorial misconduct found in the case was not unusual. "It is a problem inherent in the criminal justice system," she said.

When they were released from prison, Burrell and Graham were each given a denim jacket several sizes too large and the standard $10 check the state tenders for transportation. Burrell was picked up by his stepsister in a pickup truck and taken to her small ranch in East Texas. Graham, who worked as a roofer before going to prison, headed for his mother's home in Roanoke, Virginia. His ticket home on a Greyhound bus was paid for by his attorney. It cost $127. As for the $10 the state gave him, Graham told a reporter for the *New York Times* that he thought about framing it, but decided to put it to better use. When the bus made a stop in Atlanta, he cashed it and gave it to a panhandler.

Joaquin Martinez
Florida

The case of Joaquin Martinez was no ordinary legal proceeding. It attracted the attention of the pope, the king of Spain, and the Spanish government. Martinez, a Spanish national, was convicted in 1997 of murdering a young couple—Douglas Lawson and his girlfriend, Sherrie McCoy-Ward—in their home in Clair

Mel, just east of Tampa, Florida. When he was sentenced to death, Martinez became a cause célèbre in the Spanish media in Miami and in Spain, which does not have the death penalty. The convicted man's mother, Sara Martinez, met with King Juan Carlos and asked him to intervene. Spanish prime minister José María Aznar spoke out in Martinez's behalf. Pope John Paul II appealed for his life to be spared. Hundreds of thousands of dollars was raised to pay for his defense on appeal and, as it turned out, for a new trial.

Lawson had been shot several times with a 9mm pistol. McCoy-Ward was shot and stabbed more than twenty times as she ran to the front door to try to escape. There was little that linked Martinez to the crime except that he and Lawson had once worked together at a warehouse. It was Martinez's ex-wife, Sloane, who implicated him.

When police searched the crime scene they found a phone list that included a pager number for someone named Joe. They called the number several times and left messages. Finally, Sloane returned the call and explained to police that she had Martinez's pager. She said that she had suspicions that her ex-husband might have committed the murders. Cooperating with the authorities, Sloane secretly recorded a conversation with Martinez at her home, during which he was said to have made "several remarks that could be interpreted as incriminating." The tape of the conversation, which was barely audible, was allowed in as evidence. Martinez's girlfriend testified that he had gone out on the night of the murders and returned with a swollen lip and scraped knuckles, looking as though he had been in a fight. With no clear-cut motive for the crime, the prosecution contended that

Martinez had gone to the victims' house to buy marijuana. It was not much of a motive, and the prosecution's entire case seemed to rest on the testimony of a woman the defense portrayed as a vengeful ex-wife and on a tape that was at best suggestive.

Nonetheless, Martinez was convicted and in the end might have been executed were it not for the misstatement of one of the state's witnesses. Under direct examination, a police detective told the jury that he thought the defendant was guilty. The prosecutor repeated the statement in his closing argument. Because of the improper statements, the Florida Supreme Court overturned the conviction and sentence and ordered a new trial.

The state's case was even weaker the second time around. A critical blow to the prosecution came when Circuit Court Judge J. Rogers Padgett ruled that the taped conversation between Martinez and his ex-wife was inaudible and therefore could not be introduced as evidence. Furthermore, the transcript of the tape, which had been used for clarification during the first trial, was excluded when it was revealed that it had been prepared by Lawson's father, who was the evidence manager for the Hillsborough County Sheriff's Office. The pool of witnesses also had shrunk during the four years since the first trial. One witness had died, another now refused to cooperate, and the prosecution's star, Sloane Martinez, had changed her story to the point where it was of little use to the state.

It took the jury just two hours to acquit Martinez. The verdict was broadcast live in Spain. The Spanish prime minister welcomed the news, saying, "I'm very happy that this Spaniard was declared not guilty. I've always been against the death penalty and I always will be."

• • •

Juan Roberto Melendez
Florida

Juan Roberto Melendez, born in Brooklyn and raised in Puerto Rico, was sent to Florida's death row in 1984 for the murder of a beauty school owner who was found shot to death in his Auburndale school on September 13, 1983. His appeals were denied and the sentence upheld, but Melendez continued to protest his innocence, and in 1988 he secured the services of an important ally. His case was taken by the Capital Collateral Representative (CCR), a public defender for those who have been sentenced to death in the northern region of Florida. CCR intervenes after the death sentence and conviction have been affirmed on direct appeal.

According to Rosa Greenbaum, who assumed responsibility for the Melendez case in 2000, "The next stage is referred to as postconviction and, unlike direct-appeal attorneys, we are allowed to bring up nonrecord violations such as the withholding of exculpatory evidence and newly discovered evidence." Greenbaum found such evidence to be in no short supply, and much of it had been withheld by the state. She also discovered that the testimony of the prosecution's two key witnesses lacked any vestige of credibility.

The beauty school owner, Delbert Baker, had been shot three times, his throat had been cut, and the expensive gold jewelry he was wearing had been taken. Early in 1984, a man by the name of David Falcon contacted Florida law-enforcement officials and said he knew who killed Baker. Melendez's defense team gave the following account of the events that ensued, as reported by Bill Berkowitz on the WorkingForChange website:

Falcon aspired to become a confidential informant for local law enforcement officials and he also held a personal grudge against Juan [Melendez]. Falcon claimed Juan had confessed to the killing, but he did not know basic details such as where the crime had occurred. Falcon also implicated . . . John Berrien [who] was picked up and, after being threatened with the death penalty, told multiple stories riddled with inconsistencies and inaccuracies. Berrien finally wove a tale that was acceptable to authorities, saying he had driven Juan to the beauty school around the time of the killing.

According to Berrien, Juan had been armed with a .38-caliber firearm that day and later described jewelry he'd taken in the robbery. Berrien also claimed [that] his cousin, George Berrien, had gone into the school with Juan that day. No weapon or jewelry was ever recovered. No physical evidence was found in Berrien's car, in which Juan and George had allegedly made their escape from the blood-deluged crime scene. George Berrien denied his cousin's story, testified on behalf of Juan's defense, and this supposed co-perpetrator was never even charged. John Berrien was sentenced to two years of house arrest as an accessory to first-degree murder after the fact.

Falcon and Berrien were the key witnesses for the state when

Melendez went on trial in September 1984. Melendez's only defense was that there was no physical evidence linking him to the crime and a girlfriend who testified that she was with him at the time. The jury chose to believe the two prosecution witnesses. Melendez was convicted and sentenced to death.

Some critical evidence in Melendez's favor had surfaced about a month before the trial, but the defense was unable to use it. Another man, Vernon James, had confessed to being implicated in the murder, and a tape-recorded confession was made in the presence of Melendez's investigator and attorney. In his statement, James admitted "he had been at the beauty school when Baker was murdered by two other men and . . . that Melendez had not been anywhere near the scene of the crime." Despite the existence of the tape, James invoked his Fifth Amendment right against self-incrimination when he was called to the witness stand. The taped statement then was considered to be hearsay evidence and was never shown to the judge or jury. It was, however, turned up by Rosa Greenbaum, and it became the cornerstone of her appeal that finally led to Melendez's conviction being reversed.

Greenbaum contacted the trial defense investigator, Cody Smith, and the defense attorney, Roger Alcott. They eventually found the transcript of the tape. The state attorney, Hardy Pickard, said he had been in possession of the transcript since the original trial. The defense also produced a dozen witnesses at two separate hearings who testified that James had made incriminating statements to them regarding his involvement in the murder and had indicated again and again that the wrong man was convicted of the crime.

Circuit Court Judge Barbara Fleischer, who heard the appeal, also found that John Berrien's trial testimony repeatedly contradicted the sworn statement he had given to the prosecutor during an interview and that the prosecutor had failed to disclose the out-of-court statement to either the defense or the jury. In addition, the judge determined that the state had misled the jury when it said Falcon had nothing to gain by testifying. In fact, charges that Falcon had broken into a residence had been dropped in exchange for his testimony.

In overturning the conviction, Judge Fleischer noted that the evidence that was withheld supports the defense's theory that another man committed the murder. She said that if the state wanted to keep Melendez in prison it must try him again and pointed out that the new evidence "seriously damaged" the state's case. Indeed it did. Berrien had lost all credibility, and Falcon and James had both died during the seventeen years Melendez spent on death row. The state agreed to drop the charges, and Melendez was finally released.

In summing up, Rosa Greenbaum said:

The important thing to remember is that this outcome does not show that the system works, as death penalty supporters might claim. If not for a courageous judge, witnesses who selflessly showed up and told the truth, the simple dumb luck of locating the taped confession of Vernon James after all these years, and the surprising fact that James told lots of people what he'd done, this story would likely have a very different ending.

• • •

Thomas H. Kimbell Jr.
Pennsylvania

The crime was a particularly brutal one. Four members of a family in Lawrence County, Pennsylvania—a woman, her two young daughters, and her niece—were found dead in the woman's mobile home on the afternoon of June 15, 1994. They were stabbed many times and their throats slashed. Thomas H. Kimbell Jr., who lived near the scene, was an early suspect, although he appeared to have no clear motive. More than two years later, Kimbell was arrested and charged with the murders of Bonnie Dryfuse; her daughters Jacqueline, seven, and Heather, four; and her five-year-old niece, Stephanie Herko. Prosecutors portrayed the forty-year-old Kimbell as a onetime crack addict who had become violent when he was caught lurking around the family's trailer on the night of the murder.

There was no physical evidence that Kimbell had ever entered the mobile home, but several witnesses said they had seen him in the vicinity shortly before the murders were committed. In addition, three jailhouse informants testified that Kimbell told them he had killed four people. On the basis of such evidence, Kimbell was convicted and sentenced to die. Two years later, the conviction was overturned because of the contradictory testimony offered by one of the defense witnesses.

The witness was Marilyn Herko, the mother of one of the victims and the sister of Tom Dryfuse, Bonnie's husband. Herko, who was called by the defense, testified that she was on the phone with her sister-in-law shortly after two o'clock on the afternoon of the murders. At 2:20, Dryfuse ended the call, saying, "I got to go; somebody just pulled up in the driveway." That statement differed from an earlier one Herko had given to police in which Dryfuse said that it was her husband, Tom, who was pulling into the driveway. That would have placed Tom Dryfuse at the scene within an hour of the murders. Yet Tom had testified that he had spent the day with his father and did not return home until past three o'clock, when he found the bodies and called police. Kimbell's defense lawyer, Thomas W. Leslie, tried to question the witness about her earlier statement, but the prosecutor objected, saying Leslie could not impeach his own witness. Judge Glenn McCracken Jr. sustained the objection.

In 2000, two years after he had been sent to death row, the Pennsylvania Supreme Court granted Kimbell a new trial, ruling that the trial court wrongfully excluded testimony that might have created doubt about the defendant's guilt. The court said there was "a significant difference" between Herko's versions of what Bonnie Dryfuse said to her. "Defense counsel's inability to cross-examine Herko regarding the statement" deprived him of the opportunity to establish that the husband "was at the scene of the murders during the time he claimed to be elsewhere. . . . This obviously worked to the benefit of the prosecution," the court concluded.

At the retrial, both versions were presented to the jury. In addition, the testimony of the jailhouse informants was diluted. One of them, a convicted murderer who had met Kimbell in state prison, recanted the testimony he gave at the first trial, saying he had been pressured into giving it. Called to testify at the second trial, he cited his Fifth Amendment protection and elected to remain silent. A second informant had died.

Kimbell was cleared of all charges and released in 2002.

Larry Osborne
Kentucky

When Larry Osborne was freed from custody in the summer of 2002, he became the 102nd prisoner to be exonerated from death row since 1973, the fourth in 2002, and the first in Kentucky since that state restored the death penalty in 1976. He was also one of the youngest, having been only seventeen years old when the crime was committed. Osborne's conviction and death sentence were a classic case of police "flipping" a suspect—offering favors to one suspect for help in convicting the man who was their true target.

Osborne was charged with the 1997 slayings of Sam Davenport, eight-two, and his wife, Lillian, seventy-six, after a break-in at their home in Whitley County, Kentucky, where they had lived for forty-six years. They were hit over the head and their house was set on fire. The cause of death was smoke inhalation. Osborne and his friend, Joe Reid, who was fifteen, said they heard glass shattering when they passed the Davenport house on a motorbike the night of the murders. Larry phoned his mother, Pat Osborne, who in turn called the police. When they arrived at the scene, the house was in flames.

The police decided that Larry and his mother were suspects. They had suspected for some time that Mrs. Osborne was the mastermind of a local crime syndicate, although she had an IQ of 54, generally considered retarded, and had difficulty performing even simple tasks. The police also were eager for an arrest since there had been a series of murders in Whitley County and pressure was growing for the authorities to bring the spree to an end.

As Larry was considered their prime suspect, the police elected to take Joe Reid, alone, to the police station for questioning. Reid was questioned on December 14, the day after the murders, again on December 16, and once more on New Year's Eve. He told the same story repeatedly, insisting that he and Osborne had nothing to do with the crime. But the New Year's Eve session was a long one, continuing for at least four hours. During that interrogation, which was taped, the police told Reid all the details about how the crime was committed. They drew a map of the scene and showed him photographs that were taken there. Then he was given a lie-detector test. He stuck to the same story he had been telling and was told that he had failed the test. There followed a forty-minute break in the tape, after which Reid came back on, saying that Osborne had committed the murders while he watched from the outside. Police assured him they would tell the prosecutors that he had cooperated with them. "Is that going to get me out of all this stuff?" Reid asked. Osborne was arrested that same night.

Not long afterward, before he could testify at his friend's trial in 1999, Reid drowned while swimming in Jellico, Tennessee. His death was ruled accidental. He had never been cross-examined or spoken with a lawyer in his own behalf. Nonetheless, the prosecution read Reid's statement at trial. The defense objected, arguing that evidence taken from a dead man was inadmissible because there was no possibility of cross-examination. The trial judge overruled the objection. Osborne was convicted and sentenced to death.

The Kentucky Supreme Court reversed the conviction, finding that the trial court had allowed hearsay evidence to be presented. Osborne was retried without Reid's statement being presented to the jury. He testified in his own behalf at the five-day trial, saying what he had said from the start: "I didn't have anything to do with this." He was acquitted and walked free after spending three years on death row.

Richard Neal Jones
Oklahoma

Richard Neal Jones was convicted and sentenced to death in Oklahoma for the gangland-style murder of Charles Keene in 1983. Jones's defense was that he had passed out in a car and was unconscious while three codefendants beat up the victim, shot him, and threw his weighted body in the river.

The Court of Criminal Appeals of Oklahoma remanded the case for retrial. In a two-to-one decision, the court held that the jury was prejudiced by the improper admission of hearsay testimony and the introduction of inflammatory photographs. The trial court, according to the decision, had allowed into evidence incriminating postoffense statements by Jones's three codefendants, none of whom testified in court and therefore could not be cross-examined. The court also agreed that the case should have been remanded on the basis of prosecutorial misconduct. It noted further that the case against Jones was not "overwhelming" and that his involvement was disputed by some of the evidence. The dissenting judge stated that the only hearsay statement that actually implicated Jones should still have been allowed in as a prior consistent statement and that, at the very least, Jones was present at the crime scene and a party to the conspiracy leading to the murder.

Jones was released from death row in 1987, retried, and acquitted in 1988.

Gary Nelson
Georgia

Gary Nelson spent eleven years on Georgia's death row, the result of a textbook case of inadequate representation by counsel. In a capital trial that lasted only two days, Nelson was defended by a sole practitioner who had never tried a death-penalty case, who was experiencing financial difficulties, and was being paid between $15 and $20 an hour. Nelson's request for cocounsel was denied and no funds were provided for an investigator or for an expert witness. In his closing, Nelson's attorney spent about two minutes delivering a 250-word summation.

Nelson's appeal was taken by a respected Atlanta law firm, and he eventually was cleared of all charges and released in 1991. The prosecution admitted that "there is no material element of the state's case in the original trial which has not subsequently been determined to be impeached or contradicted." Nelson's original defense attorney was later disbarred for other reasons. During the eleven years Nelson spent on death row, fifteen people were executed in Georgia's electric chair.

Roberto Miranda
Nevada

Roberto Miranda fared no better than Nelson with the attorney appointed to defend him for capital murder. Miranda had come to the United States from Cuba during the Mariel boatlift. He was not in the United States very long before he found himself accused of fatally stabbing Manuel Rodriguez Torres in Nevada in 1981. The state offered Miranda a plea bargain, which would have allowed him to serve as little as ten years in prison and saved him from the specter of the death penalty. He turned down the offer, insisting he was innocent and claiming that a man he knew had framed him. At trial, he was represented by a lawyer with less than one year's experience who had inherited the case when his colleague died. Miranda was convicted and sentenced to death.

Fourteen years later, Clark County Senior District Judge Norman Robison overturned the conviction because of incompetent representation. Judge Robison wrote, "The lack of pretrial preparation by trial counsel . . . cannot be justified." The day after he was released from death row, with only the clothes on his back and a few personal belongings, Miranda was picked up and incarcerated by the Immigration Service. He was subsequently released pending a deportation hearing.

• • •

Benjamin Harris
Washington

After thirteen years of life on death row, Benjamin Harris had his murder conviction overturned and his death sentence vacated when U.S. District Judge Robert Bryan found that his trial lawyer had been incompetent. The charge against Harris was that he had hired a hit man named Bonds to murder Jimmy Turner in 1984.

Harris, who suffered from mental illness, offered several inconsistent stories concerning his whereabouts and involvement in the murder. At one point he said he and Bonds had taken turns in shooting Turner. In another version he admitted driving Bonds to the scene and providing him with the murder weapon. But at no time did he say he had hired a hit man, an admission that would have mandated the imposition of the death penalty under Washington state law.

Harris's attorney interviewed only three of thirty-two witnesses listed in police reports and spent less than two hours consulting with Harris before trial. Judge Bryan ordered Harris released from custody if not given a speedy retrial; his codefendant had been acquitted. The state appealed Bryan's ruling, but it was upheld by the Ninth Circuit Court of Appeals on September 12, 1995.

The prosecution chose not to retry Harris. Bonds refused to testify, and the federal court had ruled his confession, which his attorney claimed he had fantasized, to be inadmissible. Having decided not to retry him, the prosecution sought to have Harris committed to a mental institution as insane, based on a petition from hospital psychiatrists, although the state originally had argued that he was mentally competent to stand trial. Harris was confined at Western State Hospital until July 16, 1997, when a jury determined that he should be kept in a less restrictive environment. He continued to insist he was innocent, maintaining that he had been framed.

Clarence Richard Dexter
Missouri

When Clarence Richard Dexter's wife of twenty-two years was found murdered in 1990, police quickly fingered Dexter as their cheif suspect and apparently did not dig much deeper. They overlooked significant evidence that the murder was committed during the course of a botched robbery, and Dexter was tried, convicted, and sentenced to death. The defendant's trial lawyer, who was in poor health and under federal investigation for tax fraud, failed to challenge blood evidence presented at the trial. The Missouri appeals court overturned the conviction in 1997 because of prosecutorial misconduct. Then, careful examination of the blood evidence showed that the conclusions presented at trial were incorrect. The state's blood expert admitted his previous findings overstated the case against Dexter. A retrial was scheduled, but the day before it was to begin, the prosecution dismissed the charges and Dexter was freed.

• • •

Alfred Rivera

North Carolina

Alfred Rivera spent twenty-two months on North Carolina's death row before his conviction was reversed. Rivera had been charged with the murder of two drug dealers. At his trial in 1997, the jury was not allowed to hear testimony that he may have been framed by others who later pleaded guilty to the murders. The North Carolina Supreme Court overturned the conviction and ordered a new trial. Rivera was retried and found not guilty.

When he was released, Rivera publicly denounced the system that nearly killed him after putting him away for nearly two years. He said he believed that many of the men he had lived with on death row were innocent, specifically mentioning David Junior Brown, who had become a rallying point for opposition to capital punishment because there seemed to be serious doubts about his guilt. Pleas to Governor Jim Hunt to commute Brown's sentence were ignored, however, and he was executed. David Junior Brown was "a man executed innocent," Rivera told Patrick O'Neill, a writer for the *Independent Weekly* in North Carolina.

Chris Fitzsimon, of the Common Sense Foundation, an organization that opposes capital punishment, noted that the official cause of death listed on an executed prisoner's death certificate in North Carolina is homicide. "It's time to stop calling what our state does 'executions,' " Fitzsimon said. "It's time to stop calling it capital punishment. Folks, what we're doing is murder."

• • •

Kerry Cook

Texas

The name Kerry Cook does not appear on any of the lists of innocent people released from death row, although he clearly belongs near the top of the register. Cook served almost twenty years on death row, wrongfully convicted of murder, but he was not officially exonerated until two years after he pleaded no contest in a deal that restored his freedom.

In 1978, Cook, who was twenty-two years old and living in Tyler, Texas, was arrested for the murder of Linda Jo Edwards, an acquaintance who lived in the same apartment complex. Edwards was a college student and was having an affair with her married professor. Cook had been invited into her apartment once and had left a fingerprint on a sliding glass door.

Three months after Cook had met with her, police raided the club in which he worked as a bartender and arrested him, despite the weight of evidence that implicated the victim's much older, married boyfriend. Investigators were aware that the club was known chiefly as a gay bar. They conjectured therefore that Cook was a "degenerate homosexual" who hated women and had brutalized the body of the victim. At his trial, a fingerprint expert testified that he could date Cook's fingerprint to be twelve hours old when the body was discovered, placing him in the apartment at the time of the murder. The testimony went unchallenged although it is scientifically impossible to date a fingerprint. The only other evidence offered by the prosecution was the testimony of an eyewitness who said she had seen Cook in Edwards's apartment and that of a jail inmate, Eddie "Shyster" Jackson, who said he heard Cook confess. Cook was found guilty and sentenced to death.

In 1988, the U.S. Supreme Court ordered the Texas court to review its decision just eleven days short of Cook's execution date. His conviction was overturned in 1991, and his retrial a year later ended in a hung jury. In 1993, a state district judge ruled that prosecutors had engaged in systematic misconduct, suppressing key evidence, and in 1994 Cook was tried a third time. This time he was convicted and again sentenced to death. But the system continued to grind away.

On November 6, 1996, the Texas Court of Criminal Appeals reversed the conviction, saying that "prosecutorial and police misconduct has tainted this entire matter from the outset." The court also ruled that key testimony from the 1994 trial could not be used in any further prosecution. A fourth trial was scheduled for February 1999. However, concerned about the possibility of yet another wrongful conviction, Cook accepted a deal. He pleaded no contest to a reduced murder charge, was sentenced to time served, and was released.

It was later learned that the eyewitness had originally identified Edwards's professor as the man she saw in the apartment but then changed her testimony and named Cook. Jackson, the jailhouse informant, recanted his testimony entirely. The fingerprint expert admitted it was impossible to date a fingerprint and said he had been coerced into testifying as he did by the District Attorney's Office. Most important, DNA tests conducted two years after Cook's release showed that the semen found on the victim matched the professor's, not Cook's.

Since his release, Cook has married and become the father of a son. The boy is named Kerry Justice. "After twenty-three years," Cook says, "Justice has finally arrived."

Part IV

THE SNITCH SYSTEM

In the argot of the criminal justice system, they are called jailhouse snitches; in more formal terms, they are known as incentivised witnesses. But there is nothing ambiguous about their function: They offer courtroom testimony for the prosecution in exchange for an incentive, usually the dropping of a criminal charge or its reduction to a lesser charge. If the witness is already incarcerated, he is likely to have his sentence reduced or his parole accelerated. The hazards of such a system hardly need explaining. How much trust can be invested in the testimony of a convict promised early release if he is ready to say what the authorities tell him to say? Yet dozens of innocent people have been sent to prison, many of them to death row, on the weight of bartered testimony that, in effect, has been bought by police or prosecutors. Law-enforcement agents insist that well-placed informants are an integral part of the process, that the surest way to justice is to squeeze one suspect or prison inmate to provide the incriminating evidence needed to convict another. It is by no means a technique of recent invention. Its roots are set deep in the practice of Anglo-American law.

In eighteenth-century England, the use of crown witnesses was accepted as a central tool in the criminal justice system. It was a straightforward arrangement known both to prosecution and defense and therefore entirely without subterfuge. Informants for the state escaped prosecution and received for their services a stipend referred to as "blood money." It was an arrangement that not only countenanced perjury but encouraged it, proving along the way that there was little honor among thieves. Of course a crown witness of renown might well have suspected that a day would come when he would fall victim to a witness no more credible than he was. That is what happened to Charles Cane.

Cane had offered the testimony that delivered two men to the hangman in 1755. The following year, he found himself in the prisoner's dock confronted by another witness for the crown and suffered the same inglorious end. The perceptive clergyman that ministered to him noted that it was no surprise to Cane. He had, the clergyman said, expected "nothing less than hanging to be his fate at last, but not of the evil day's coming so soon."

More than two centuries later, the United States proved that it conceded nothing to the Mother Land when it came to producing "professional" informants. Leslie Vernon White had established a reputation as the best in the business and in 1989 was featured on a segment of the television program *60 Minutes*. White's story was first chronicled by *Los Angeles Times* reporter Ted Rohrlich. A career criminal, White fabricated confessions in at least a dozen cases. He would pick up details about crimes from news sources and get information via the prison telephone. He noted that his was a competitive business, with many informants seeking an edge in collecting information that would make their stories credible. They even celebrated their calling with slogans such as "Don't go to the pen, send a friend" and "If you can't do the time, just drop a dime."

Two reporters for the *Chicago Tribune*—Ken Armstrong and Steve Mills—studied the role that snitches and other incentivised witnesses played in the cases of ninety-seven people who were released from death rows throughout the United States between 1976 and 1999. Their findings were analyzed in a research report by Rob Warden for the Center on Wrongful Convictions.

The study found that prosecutors used incentivised witnesses in 39 percent of the ninety-seven cases. The thirty-eight people wrongfully convicted on the basis of that testimony served a total of 291 years in prison before they were released, an average of nearly eight years each. Sixteen of the thirty-eight defendants were convicted on the testimony of jailhouse snitches, almost all of whom said they had heard the defendants confess. Other informants, some of them suspects in the same case, testified against the remaining twenty-two. In eighteen cases, informants with incentives were the sole basis for conviction, and police or prosecutorial misconduct contributed to more than one-third of those cases. Of the thirty-eight states that practice capital punishment, seventeen had wrongful convictions based at least in part on incentivised testimony. Recantation by the informants was the reason for exoneration in almost half the cases.

It is not possible to estimate how many innocent people might have been sent to death row or, worse, executed, as a result of such fabricated testimony. It is nearly certain, however, that at least one innocent man was put to death solely on the basis of the incentivised testimony of two witnesses.

• • •

Sonia Jacobs and Jesse Tafero
Florida

Justice came too late for Jesse Tafero. He and Sonia "Sunny" Jacobs, his common-law wife, were sentenced to death in Florida for the murder of two highway patrolmen in 1976. They were convicted largely on the testimony of a third accomplice who to all appearances was the actual killer. Jacobs's conviction was overturned in 1992 on a writ of habeas corpus when it was discovered that the prosecution witnesses had lied. Tafero, who was convicted on the same evidence, would likely have been released as well. But by then he had been dead two years, executed in brutal fashion in the electric chair.

Early on the morning of February 20, 1976, state highway patrol trooper Philip Black and a visiting Canadian constable named Donald Irwin approached a green Camaro parked at a rest stop on Interstate 95 in Broward County. Asleep in the car were Jacobs, Tafero, and Walter Rhodes, an ex-con whom Tafero had met while both were serving prison terms. The patrolmen thought they saw a gun on the floor of the car. They woke the occupants and asked Tafero and Rhodes to get out. At some point after that, both police officers were shot dead. Jacobs, Tafero, and Rhodes fled the scene in the police car, but soon ditched it and resumed their flight in a stolen car. Shortly afterward, they were caught at a police roadblock and arrested.

Ballistics tests indicated that both policemen were shot with the same gun. Tests also showed that Rhodes definitely had fired a gun, since he was the only one who tested positive for gunpowder residue. Tafero, it was determined, might have fired a gun or simply handled a gun after it was fired. Tafero had told police that Rhodes had shot the policemen and then handed him the gun so that Rhodes could drive the getaway car. Rhodes was in fact behind the wheel when the car was stopped at the roadblock. However, Rhodes named Tafero as the shooter and agreed to take a polygraph test. Police said he passed the test but withheld the results from the state. Yet it was on the basis of the lie-detector test that the prosecutor justified a plea bargain for Rhodes, who agreed to testify against Tafero and Jacobs and plead guilty to second-degree murder in return for a life sentence.

Tafero and Jacobs were tried separately but were convicted on the same basic evidence. In addition to Rhodes's testimony, jailhouse informants said that Tafero and Jacobs had confessed to them. There also was testimony from two eyewitnesses. One said he saw a man in brown, which was what Tafero was wearing, spread-eagled and leaning over the hood of the police car when the shots were fired. Another said he saw a man wearing blue, Rhodes, move from the front of the car to the rear just before the shooting. However, neither witness was able to identify the shooter on sight. Both Jacobs and Tafero were found guilty. The jury recommended a term of life imprisonment for Jacobs and a death sentence for Tafero. The judge overruled the jury and sentenced Jacobs to die as well.

In 1981, the Florida Supreme Court commuted Jacobs's sentence to life in prison after her lawyers learned that the polygraph test was inconclusive and indicated that Rhodes might have been lying. The following year, Rhodes recanted, saying it was he who had fired the gun. He later recanted on his recantation, then recanted again and altered his story repeatedly over the years.

Tafero's conviction was affirmed in 1981. Various motions and appeals in state courts were denied in 1983, 1984, 1987, 1988, and 1990. The Eleventh Circuit Court of Appeals, a federal court, reviewed the case in 1986 and 1989 and confirmed the conviction each time. The appeal process finally ran out for Tafero; so did time. In May 1990, he was executed in horrifying fashion. During the execution, Tafero's head seemed to catch fire, with flames and smoke shooting through the top. The electric current was interrupted and resumed three times. Witnesses said that Tafero continued to breathe and move after the first interruption. His brutally slow, painful death prompted many to consider whether continued use of the electric chair might violate the Eighth Amendment's injunction against cruel and unusual punishment.

As for Jacobs, who grievously mourned Tafero's death, her prospects were growing somewhat brighter. A childhood friend of hers, filmmaker Micki Dickoff, had taken an interest in her case. Scanning court transcripts, affidavits, and old newspaper clippings, Dickoff found errors in the state's case. It was learned that Rhodes had failed the polygraph test, and withholding the results from the defense was a violation of the defendants' constitutional rights. A federal appeals court determined that only Rhodes could have fired the gun. The testimony of the state's witnesses was found to be false. The prosecution had suppressed the statement of a prison guard that corroborated Rhodes's recantation of his initial testimony. Dickoff assembled a color-coded brief and presented it to the Eleventh U.S. Circuit Court of Appeals. The court overturned Jacobs's conviction on a writ of habeas corpus.

Rather than risk the likelihood of an acquittal on retrial, the Broward State Attorney's Office offered Jacobs a deal. If she would enter a plea in which she did not admit guilt but agreed not to bring a civil suit, she would be released immediately. Jacobs, twenty-nine years old when she was sent to prison, now forty-five and the mother of two grown children, accepted the offer. She walked free on October 9, 1992. Since the tainted evidence that resulted in Jacobs's release was virtually identical to that which sent Tafero to his death, it is a near certainty that he too would have been freed and that an innocent man had been executed.

When Jacobs was released, her first priority was to reunite with her two children. Eric, a son by her first marriage, was now twenty-five years old and had a four-year-old daughter of his own. Tina, her daughter by Tafero, had been ten months old and still nursing when her mother went to prison; she was now sixteen.

In an interview with Sydney P. Freedberg of the *St. Petersburg Times* seven years after her release, Jacobs recalled, "Getting back family is the hardest part. They live with embarrassment for so long: You say you didn't [commit the murder], but everyone says you did."

Immediately upon leaving prison, Jacobs, who now lives in Los Angeles and teaches yoga, phoned her son, then headed to North Carolina where he lived with his wife and daughter.

When she met her granddaughter for the first time, the child asked, "Grandma, were you lost?"

"Yes," Jacobs answered, "I was."

Peter Limone
Massachusetts

The case of Peter Limone is like no other. His thirty-three years in prison—four and a half on death row—make him the grand-daddy of all those wrongfully convicted who were later exoner-ated. But that is just the beginning of his story. Limone, convicted of a gangland hit, was framed by an unlikely cadre of racketeers and rogues. Some were members of the Mafia; others were FBI agents. One was the longtime, once-revered director of the bureau, J. Edgar Hoover.

On March 12, 1965, a small-time hood by the name of Edward "Teddy" Deegan was shot to death in an alley in Chelsea, Mass-achusetts, a suburb of Boston. The murder remained unsolved for more than two years. Then, a high-up Mafia hit man, Joseph "The Animal" Barboza, who moonlighted as an FBI informant, put the finger on Limone and three others—Joseph Salvati, Henry Tamelo, and Louis Greco. Barboza was a well-known figure in the Boston area, and his appearance on the witness stand attracted its share of attention. U.S. marshals surrounded the courthouse every day he testified, and of course all of his tes-timony was given under a grant of immunity.

It served Barboza's interest to have the case cleared, because he himself was involved in the killing. He knew the four men he named were innocent and so did the FBI. The FBI's interest was served as well. Barboza was one of their top Mafia informants, and agents of the Bureau were as protective of their snitches as they were of the reputation of their director. Solely on the strength of Barboza's testimony, which had been orchestrated and rehearsed in cooperation with FBI agents, Limone and the three others were convicted of capital murder and sentenced to die in the electric chair. They escaped death when Massachusetts abolished the death penalty in 1974, and their sentences were commuted to life. Both Tamelo and Greco died in prison. Salvati was released in 1997 when the governor commuted his sentence. Only Limone, whose criminal record included a youthful offense for an attempted break-in and a few gambling-related charges for running a dice game, continued to serve time. He had been denied parole in 1987, some twenty years into his sentence, and there appeared to be little hope that he would ever set foot outside the prison gates. Thirteen years later, his outlook would change.

In 2000, the U.S. Justice Department opened an investigation into corruption in the Boston office of the FBI. The investigation was to reach back to the 1960s, and what it began to uncover was not pretty. It turned up documents that showed that officials at FBI headquarters, including Hoover, were aware that Boston agents were employing killers and gang leaders as informers and were protecting them from prosecution. Among the copious files relating to the Deegan case was a report showing that two days before Deegan was killed, an FBI informant told special agent H. Paul Rico that Vincent "Jimmy the Bear" Flemmi, the brother of another informant, planned to kill Deegan and that then-New England Mafia boss Raymond L. S. Patriarca had approved the hit. The report, written by Rico and agent Dennis Condon, both since retired, named four other men, including Barboza, who were involved in the plot. None of the men later convicted of the crime was named in the list.

Further documentation included a memorandum from the Boston field office to Hoover, dated a week after the murder, stating, "Informants report that . . . Vincent James Flemmi and Joseph Barboza, prominent local hoodlums, were responsible for the killing." The memo goes on to describe in detail how the murder was carried out. Hoover and his agents knew before the trial that four innocent men were being railroaded and perhaps sent to their deaths for a crime committed by one of their informants. But Barboza was considered too valuable a snitch to be sacrificed in the interest of justice. After the trial, he became the first person ever to be placed in the federal witness protection program.

Based on the emerging revelations, Limone's attorney, John Cavicchi, requested that his client's conviction be overturned and that he be granted a new trial. At a hearing near the end of December 2000, Middlesex Superior Court Judge Margaret Hinkle, clearly sympathetic to Limone's plight, took the unusual step of lifting attorney-client privilege so that Joseph J. Balliro Sr., a well-known Boston defense attorney, could divulge information he was told decades earlier about Deegan's murder. Balliro then told the court that Vincent Flemmi had confessed to the crime in the 1960s before his death. The attorney had written an affidavit stating that Vincent, the brother of Stephen "the Rifleman" Flemmi, another gangster who worked in the service of the FBI, had told him that Limone and the three other convicted men had nothing to do with the crime.

Early in January 2001, Judge Hinkle vacated Limone's conviction and ordered his release from prison. Two weeks later, she threw out the conviction of Salvati, who had been paroled in 1997, saying, "The conduct of certain agents of the Bureau stains the legacy of the FBI." Salvati's attorney, Victor Garo, said his client had been the victim of a conspiracy. "J. Edgar Hoover and senior members of the FBI conspired to murder my client," Garo told UPI reporter P. Mitchell Prothero. "This was not the work of rogue agents."

The congressional investigation, led by Representative Dan Burton, Republican of Indiana, chairman of the House Government Reform Committee, turned up evidence that the Boston FBI field office had allowed several informants to seize control of the city's organized crime operations and manage them under the protection of federal law-enforcement officials. Mobsters James "Whitey" Bulger and Stephen Flemmi were indicted for about twenty murders that were allegedly covered up by FBI agents protecting their key informants. It was charged that Bulger and Flemmi were permitted to carry out crimes, including murder, in exchange for providing the FBI with information about rival mob families.

The committee hearings continued at least through 2002. At one point, the noted lawyer F. Lee Bailey testified that he believed the FBI had coached Barboza on how to lie on the witness stand. Bailey, who had represented Barboza briefly in 1970, said, "He told me he had quite a bit of help. I believe the testimony was furnished."

A key witness for the congressional committee was Jeremiah T. O'Sullivan, who was in charge of the New England Organized Crime Strike Force and later a U.S. attorney in Boston in the 1970s and 1980s. O'Sullivan testified that he was aware that informers were committing murders and receiving protection from the FBI, but he took no action because he feared reprisals. "With the FBI," he said, "if you go against them, they will try to get you."

One of the first casualties of the investigation was John J. Connolly Jr., a retired FBI agent who was sentenced to ten years in prison in September 2002 for racketeering and obstruction of justice. Connolly, it was charged, had in effect become a member of Whitey Bulger's gang.

Bulger has been indicted for racketeering and involvement in twenty-two murders. He disappeared in 1995 after Connolly told him about the secret indictment. He remains a fugitive and is second on the FBI's Most Wanted List behind Osama bin Laden. Ironically, Bulger's brother, William M. Bulger, is president of the University of Massachusetts and former president of the state senate.

Stephen Flemmi was convicted of extortion and money laundering and sentenced to ten years in prison. He still faces ten federal murder charges and state murder charges in Oklahoma and Florida.

Peter Limone, sixty-seven years old when he was released, resides in Medford, Massachusetts, with his wife of forty-five years, Olympia. They have four children and eight grandchildren.

James Richardson

Florida

Had it all started just a few years later, events might have played out differently for James Richardson. But it was 1968, the whole country seemed to be on fire, the South was seething with a century's worth of racial hostility, and small backwater towns like Arcadia, Florida, were still dishing out their own version of Southern justice. A black, poverty-ridden fruit picker like James Richardson was easy prey when a quick arrest was needed for a horrendous crime. And the crime of which Richardson was accused was as horrendous as one could imagine. He was charged, convicted, and sentenced to death for murdering all of his seven children.

Arcadia, the seat of DeSoto County, is located in a remote pocket of Southwest Florida between Sarasota and Fort Myers, about thirty-five miles inland from the Gulf of Mexico. The lush citrus groves fueled a large part of the local economy, and James and his wife, Annie Mae, worked in those fields, picking oranges and earning 25 cents for each box they filled. Both were illiterate; James had an IQ of about 75—not quite retarded but low enough to be classified a "slow learner." All the same, he was well liked in the community and reputed to be a devoted father. It was all the more shocking therefore when he was arrested on October 31, 1967, and charged with murdering his children.

The Richardson children, aged one to seven, had been poisoned five days earlier, their food laced with parathion, a highly toxic agricultural pesticide. Arcadia's police chief, Richard Barnard, and DeSoto County Sheriff Frank Cline shared responsibility for the investigation. They searched the house and a small shed in the backyard and found nothing suspicious. Cline noticed a metallic scent, which he knew to be parathion, but none was found on the premises. However, the following day police received an anonymous phone call saying that a sack of parathion had been found in the shed behind the house. Cline knew his search had been thorough. "It wasn't there yesterday," he told the press. But it was there now, casting the first shadow of suspicion on Richardson. At the same time, word began drifting through town that Richardson had recently purchased a $14,000 life insurance policy for the children. The police now had what they believed to be motive, means, and opportunity. Richardson was promptly charged with murder. Annie Mae also was arrested and charged with child neglect.

The prosecution should have sensed that something was wrong with its case at the coroner's inquest. One of those testifying was Bessie Reese, the Richardsons' next-door neighbor who had been watching the children the day they were poisoned. It was Reese who served the children lunch that day and, according to another neighbor, Charlie Smith, it was Reese who suggested they search the shed for the poison. Another witness, Gerald Purvis, an insurance salesman, testified that he tried to sell Richardson life insurance for his children, but Richardson said he couldn't afford it and no sale was made. The assistant prosecutor, John "Red" Treadwell, nonetheless persuaded the coroner's jury that Richardson might have believed that a policy had been purchased. The jury returned with an indictment: the Richardson children had been murdered with premeditation.

John Spencer Robinson, a thirty-year-old civil rights activist from Daytona Beach, became interested in the case as he watched it unfold on local television. Richardson said he liked the similarity in the sound of their names and chose Robinson to represent him from a list of lawyers offered to him by the head of the Arcadia NAACP. It was, in some respects, an unfortunate decision, for while Robinson was convinced of Richardson's innocence and totally committed to his cause, he was principally a family-law attorney and had never tried a murder case. He and his partner, Richard Whitson, took the case at no charge.

At the outset, circumstances looked promising to Robinson. Bail was set at $7,500, incredibly low for a case involving seven murders. A few days later, an anonymous benefactor posted the bail, and Richardson was released. In addition, the child-neglect charges against Annie Mae were dropped. It appeared to the defense that the prosecution knew it had no case. They expected all charges would be vacated at a hearing to be held on March 25, 1968. However, they soon discovered that the prosecutors had a new card to play; in fact they had two cards. Their names were Ernell Washington and James Weaver, and they were ready to tell a jury that Richardson had confessed to them when they were together in the Arcadia jail. It was the first hard evidence the state had, and the judge thought it to be convincing. Bail was revoked and Richardson was returned to jail. The trial was set for the end of May.

The entire legal proceeding moved quickly. The jury, all white, was selected on the first day. The following day, Weaver took the stand and told his "confession" story. Washington was not able to appear in court. After testifying at the March hearing, he was released from prison and a few weeks later was shot to death in a local bar. But the state had sent in a replacement from its bench. James Cunningham, a former inmate, testified that he too had heard Richardson confess. On the third day, the state rested. The defense tried to impeach Washington's testimony, showing that he had been given probation on his attempted-murder charge in exchange for his testimony. A few other character witnesses were called, but it meant little. It took the jury just ninety minutes to return a verdict of first-degree murder. Since there was no recommendation of mercy, the judge imposed the mandatory sentence—death in the electric chair.

Not long after Richardson was sent away, Mark Lane, a New York attorney who had achieved national renown in the sixties as the author of a book advancing a conspiracy theory for the assassination of President Kennedy, came to Arcadia. Lane was intrigued by the case and had begun doing research for a book entitled *Arcadia* that would be published two years later. As he interviewed some of the central characters, he became increasingly convinced of Richardson's innocence, and he began to have doubts about the role played by Bessie Reese. He learned, for example, that Reese had trouble holding on to her husbands. She had been convicted of killing her second husband in 1955 and had served four years of a twenty-year sentence before being paroled. Lane also discovered that her first husband had died under curious circumstances and that some suspected the cause of death was food poisoning. Charlie Smith told Lane that it was Reese who had found the bag of parathion in the shed, as he had testified at Richardson's trial. Finally, Lane learned that Reese had a grudge against Richardson. Her third husband had left her for Richardson's cousin, and she blamed Richardson and threatened to "get" him.

On April 21, 1971, a year after Lane's book was published, the appeals court unanimously affirmed Richardson's conviction and sentence. But the specter of execution would soon be lifted. On June 30, 1972, the U.S. Supreme Court handed down its decision in *Furman v. Georgia,* nullifying more than six hundred death sentences throughout the country. As the seventies passed, Robinson withdrew as Richardson's attorney and was replaced by Lane and Florida cocounsel Ellis Rubin. In 1988, Lane returned to Arcadia for a public rally in support of Richardson and got possession of the state's nearly thousand-page file of the Richardson case, which apparently had been pilfered years earlier from the office of Assistant DA Treadwell. The file contained numerous bits of information that Lane thought was suppressed evidence. Encouraged by his findings, Lane visited Bessie Reese at a nursing home where she was spending her last years, suffering from Alzheimer's disease. Two aides at the home told Lane that Reese had confessed many times that she had poisoned the children.

The case was beginning to break open now. Lane turned the mildewed Richardson file over to Governor Bob Martinez and petitioned the governor for his immediate release. He also petitioned the state supreme court for a new trial. Unexpected help came from a young woman, Virginia Dennis, who was an eight-year-old friend of the Richardson children at the time of the crime. Virginia said she had eaten breakfast with them on the day they died, but neither she nor they had gotten ill. That meant that the poison had to be added to their food at lunch, after both James and Annie Mae had left for work.

Martinez ordered a new investigation and turned the case over to one of the state's top prosecutors, Dade County District Attorney Janet Reno, who later served as U.S. attorney general in the Clinton administration. Two months later, on April 11, 1989, Reno filed her report. It contained a litany of prosecutorial misconduct and perjured testimony—information withheld from the defense; witnesses, including Sheriff Frank Cline, who had lied under oath; a jailhouse snitch who had recanted. At a hearing on April 25, retired Circuit Court Judge Clifton Kelly, who had been recalled to service to hear the case, said he did not believe Richardson had been given a fair trial. "The enormity of the crime," he said, "is matched only by the enormity of the injustice [done] to this man." The judge set aside the conviction and ordered Richardson released.

Richardson, who learned to read and write in prison, filed suit against DeSoto County for wrongful conviction. He was awarded a settlement of $150,000, most of which went to his lawyers. Having spent nearly twenty-two years of his life in prison, he was ineligible for Social Security benefits. He and his wife, who stuck with him during his years of imprisonment, were later divorced. Richardson, who had suffered two severe heart attacks, remarried and now lives with his wife, Theresa, on the ranch of his cardiologist in Wichita, Kansas. He does light work to pay for his room and board. Bessie Reese died of Alzheimer's disease at the nursing home in 1992.

James Creamer
Georgia

James Creamer and six codefendants were convicted of murdering two physicians in Marietta, Georgia, in a 1973 trial that a

U.S. district court judge said "bordered on the Kafkaesque." He was not exaggerating. The judicial proceeding was tainted from the start and included perjured testimony from an accomplice, prosecutorial misconduct, and junk science that involved the introduction of evidence secured during sessions of hypnosis.

Drs. Warren and Rosina Matthews were found shot to death in their home in May 1971 in what looked like an attempted robbery gone awry. Creamer and six other suspects were taken into custody and prosecuted almost entirely on the word of Deborah Ann Kidd, who said she had accompanied the men to the Matthews home. Testifying under a grant of immunity, Kidd named Creamer as the shooter. The seven suspects were found guilty by a Cobb County jury. Six were given life sentences. Creamer, the presumed shooter, was sentenced to death. In 1974, the Georgia Supreme Court unanimously upheld all the convictions and sentences.

The case began to unravel a year later, following an investigation by the *Atlanta Constitution*. The newspaper's probe revealed that Kidd initially had claimed that she had been high on drugs the day of the crime and was unable to recall any of the events that took place. Later, in a hypnotic state induced by a police-appointed hypnotist, she said she remembered that Creamer had committed the murders, with the other six defendants serving as accomplices. The prosecution had intentionally withheld from the defense the transcripts of the statements Kidd had made prior to testifying. The transcripts revealed that she had offered a number of conflicting descriptions of what had transpired at the crime scene. The identity of the shooter changed from one version to another and so did her identification of those who were present. At one point, she confessed to having shot the victims herself. The *Constitution* also discovered that Kidd was romantically involved with one of the detectives assigned to the case.

Charging the prosecution with willful destruction of the taped testimony, District Court Judge Charles A. Moye ordered all the convictions to be reversed. The state appealed, but its case was dissolving rapidly. Kidd admitted she had lied in her trial testimony. To clinch matters, Billy Birt, a prisoner already on death row for another crime, confessed that he and two other men—one who was in federal prison and another who was then a fugitive—had murdered the two doctors. Charges against Creamer and the other six were dropped and they were released in 1975. The district attorney, however, said he was not convinced of their innocence and he declined to prosecute Deborah Kidd for perjury.

Anthony Brown
Florida

The testimony of a codefendant also was the basis on which Anthony Brown was convicted of murdering a deliveryman and sentenced to death in Florida in 1983. The only evidence against Brown was offered by a codefendant who escaped a death sentence and was given a term of life imprisonment for his testimony. The jury had recommended a life sentence for Brown as well, but the judge saw fit to impose the death penalty. Brown's conviction was reversed on appeal when it was learned that he had not been notified of a critical deposition taken by the state and thus had been deprived of his constitutional right to confront and cross-examine a hostile witness. At the retrial, in 1986, the codefendant admitted that his original testimony incriminating Brown had been perjured, and Brown was acquitted.

Neil Ferber
Pennsylvania

A jailhouse snitch was instrumental in getting Neil Ferber, a thirty-nine-year-old furniture salesman, convicted of carrying out what appeared to be a professional hit on a Philadelphia mobster in 1981, but not without some help. There was the mistaken testimony of two eyewitnesses and a police conspiracy that a judge called a "Kafkaesque nightmare" and a "malevolent charade."

On the evening of May 27, 1981, Chelsais "Steve" Bouras, a well-known underworld figure, was gunned down by two men while dining in the Meletis Restaurant in South Philadelphia. His dinner companion, Jeanette Curro, also was slain. A month later, Ferber was arrested after being identified by two eyewitnesses—a man and his wife—who said they saw the killer run out of the restaurant, remove a ski mask, and flee down the street. The woman identified Ferber in a police photo spread only to change her mind after seeing him in person in a police lineup. Her husband, however, maintained that Ferber was the man he saw that night.

At the trial, the most incriminating testimony was provided by Gerald Jordan, a former cellmate of Ferber's at the Philadelphia

Detention Center. Jordan, who had spent much of his adult life serving time for petty crimes, told the jury that Ferber had admitted being one of two gunmen who had shot Bouras and Curro. No further evidence was presented and none was needed. Ferber was convicted and sentenced to death.

The District Attorney's Office as well as some Philadelphia homicide detectives appeared to have lingering doubts regarding the case that was presented. About two years after Ferber was convicted—years he spent on death row—the DA's Office told the court that Jordan had failed a lie-detector test concerning Ferber's guilt, a fact that had not been shared with the defense. At around the same time, Jordan recanted his testimony and said he never believed Ferber had had anything to do with the murder. On January 3, 1986, his last day in office, District Attorney Edward G. Rendell asked Common Pleas Judge Robert A. Latrone to grant Ferber a new trial. Latrone immediately threw out Ferber's conviction, and Rendell's successor, Ronald D. Castille, declined to retry him. He was freed the following day.

Ferber did not lose much time in filing suit against the city, contending he had suffered bleeding ulcers and a nervous breakdown as a result of his unjust imprisonment. In 1993, a Common Pleas Court jury awarded him $4.5 million. As reported in the *Philadelphia Inquirer,* the jury found that Ferber had been framed by homicide detective Daniel Rosenstein and a police sketch artist, Dominic Frontino. The award was overturned by Common Pleas Judge John Herron because of technical changes in the liability laws. But the judge made it clear that he believed Ferber had been railroaded by corrupt officials and noted that

DENNIS STOCKTON was almost certainly innocent when he was executed for murder in Virginia in 1995. Stockton, who spent twelve years on
death row, insisted on his innocence right to the end. His story is told by Joe
Jackson and William F. Burke Jr. in their 1999 book, *Dead Run. Photo by John
H. Sheally II.*

JOSEPH BURROWS was convicted and sentenced to death in Illinois, largely
on the testimony of the actual killer. Burrows was exonerated following an investigation by a reporter for the *Champaign-Urbana News Gazette.* He had spent five
years on death row. *Photo by Loren Santow.*

DELBERT TIBBS, a young theology student at the time, attracted a great deal of public attention when he was sentenced to death for murder and rape in Florida in 1974. The case against Tibbs was so weak that the prosecutor said he would testify for the defense if Tibbs were retried. *Photo © 2003 Andrew Gordon.*

The case of **GARY GAUGER** was a clear example of a false confession being extracted by police from an unwitting suspect. Gauger, convicted of killing his parents in 1993, was exonerated three years later with the help of Northwestern Law School Professor Lawrence Marshall. *Photo © 2003 Andrew Gordon.*

PERRY COBB (above) and **DARBY TILLIS** (below) were convicted and sentenced to death following two mistrials because of hung juries in 1979. It took two more trials to free them after they had spent eight years on death row. They were among the first to have their death sentences reversed in Illinois. *Photos by Loren Santow.*

VERNEAL JIMERSON (top) and **DENNIS WILLIAMS**
(**above**)   were two of the Ford Heights 4, a textbook example of corrupt
practices involving prosecutorial and police misconduct in Illinois. Much of the
investigative work that led to their release was done by three students at the
Medill School of Journalism at Northwestern. By that time, 1996, Williams had
been imprisoned for eighteen years and Jimerson for eleven, much of it on death
row. Williams died of undisclosed causes in March 2003 at the age of forty-six.
Photos by Loren Santow.

After ten years on death row, **RONALD JONES** became one of the first to benefit from DNA testing when he was proven innocent of the 1989 rape and murder of a Chicago woman. The judge who sentenced Jones to death, John E. Morrissey, originally denied the request for a DNA test, but the Illinois Supreme Court reversed the judge and ordered the testing. *Photo by Loren Santow.*

CARL LAWSON was the victim of an unusual case of conflict of interest when he was sentenced to death for murdering an eight-year-old boy in Illinois. The public defender assigned to Lawson's case had been the assistant state's attorney at the defendant's arraignment. After serving six years on death row, Lawson was found not guilty in 1996. In 2002, Governor George Ryan pardoned Lawson on the basis of actual innocence. *Photo by Loren Santow.*

Funeral arrangements had already been made for **ANTHONY PORTER** (top), who was scheduled to die in Illinois's death house in 1998 for a double murder in 1982, but he was released when another man confessed to the crime. Porter's case was one of those that prompted Illinois Governor George Ryan to impose a moratorium on the death penalty in January 2002. *Photo by Loren Santow.*

STEVEN SMITH (above) was the eleventh death-row inmate set free in Illinois between 1987 and 1999. During that time, the state freed as many inmates from death row as it had executed after the death penalty's reinstatement in 1977. Smith had been convicted in the 1985 shooting death of a prison official. *Photo by Loren Santow.*

SONIA "SUNNY" JACOBS is one of only two women who were exonerated after serving time on death row. Jacobs and her common law husband, Jesse Tafero, were convicted of murdering two Florida highway patrolmen in 1976. Her conviction was overturned on a writ of habeas corpus, and she was set free in 1992. It was too late for Tafero; he had been executed two years earlier. *Photo © 2003 Andrew Gordon.*

DAVID KEATON, an eighteen-year-old star football player in Quincy, Florida, who planned to enter the ministry, was sentenced to death for killing an off-duty deputy sheriff during the holdup of a grocery store in 1971. Charges against him were dropped when the actual killer was identified and convicted. *Photo © 2003 Andrew Gordon.*

KERRY COOK served almost twenty years on Texas's death row for the 1978 murder of a female acquaintance who lived in his apartment complex. Cook was freed in 1996 after pleading no contest to a reduced murder charge in return for a sentence of time served. Two years later, he was exonerated when a DNA test established his innocence. *Photo © 2003 Andrew Gordon.*

Largely on the basis of a sloppy DNA test, **ROBERT EARL HAYES** was convicted of murder and rape and sentenced to death in Florida in 1991. Better DNA testing established his innocence, and he was acquitted after a retrial in 1997. *Photo © 2003 Andrew Gordon.*

From left to right, **BRAD SCOTT, ROBERT HAYES, SONIA JACOBS, RANDALL PADGETT, AND DELBERT TIBBS** are among the six wrongly convicted people whose stories are told in *The Exonerated,* a play written by Jessica Blank and Eric Jensen, and directed by Bob Balaban, which has been playing in New York since 2002. Among the actors in the rotating cast have been: Jill Clayburgh, Richard Dreyfuss, Brooke Shields, Robert Vaughn, Jeff Goldblum, and Montel Williams. *Photo © 2003 Andrew Gordon.*

the wronged man could seek further recourse in federal court. Herron described Ferber's trip through the criminal justice system as a "Kafkaesque nightmare of the sort which we normally characterize as being representative of the so-called justice system of a totalitarian state." He found that police had manipulated witnesses, "withheld important information, tampered with identification evidence, and misled judicial officers."

Ferber declared his intention to press his case for damages, but in 1996 the city agreed to a settlement. Ferber was granted $1.9 million, a sum Rendell called "fair and appropriate, and a fraction of what a jury would have awarded." In settling the civil suit, the city did not acknowledge any impropriety in its handling of the case.

Joseph Green Brown
Florida

Joseph Green Brown is fifty-two years old now. He is known as Shabaka—Swahili for "uncompromising"—and has spent most of the past fifteen years working at a drop-in center in Washington, D.C., feeding homeless drug addicts, counseling alcoholics, and helping people with mental problems. He has supplemented his income by working at a drive-in convenience store. He also lectures against capital punishment, a subject with which he is intimately familiar, having spent thirteen years on Florida's death row for a crime he didn't commit.

In 1974, a Hillsborough County jury convicted Brown of raping and murdering Earlene Treva Barksdale, the owner of a

Tampa clothing store and wife of a prominent Florida lawyer. The case turned on the testimony of a companion of his, Ronald Floyd, who turned state's evidence in exchange for lenient treatment on a robbery charge. Floyd had an added incentive for fingering Brown, since Brown had implicated him in a robbery in which both men had participated.

Floyd told the authorities that he was riding in a car with Brown and another man when they pulled up in front of the clothing store. Floyd said he stayed in the car while the other two entered the store. A few minutes later, he said, he heard a gunshot and rushed inside where the victim was lying on the floor, apparently dead. The man who was alleged to have accompanied Brown was never found or identified.

Also introduced as evidence was a .38-caliber handgun that the prosecutor, Robert Bonanno, claimed was the murder weapon. An FBI ballistics expert had determined that the presumed smoking gun could not possibly have fired the fatal bullet, but that was a piece of expert testimony that surfaced after Brown was convicted; it never reached the jury. Other revelations were soon forthcoming.

Eight months after the trial, Floyd admitted that his story implicating Brown was a fabrication. Under cross-examination at the trial, Floyd said he had been offered nothing in return for his testimony against Brown. It later came to light, however, that the state had cut a deal with Floyd, promising to go easy on the robbery charge if he cooperated. Despite the new facts that were emerging, Florida courts offered no relief. Brown was destined to spend another twelve years on death row. In the fall of 1983, Governor Bob Graham signed a death warrant.

Brown was fifteen hours away from execution when a federal judge in Tampa issued a stay. Two and a half years later, the U.S. Court of Appeals for the Eleventh Circuit ordered a new trial because "the prosecution knowingly allowed material false testimony to be introduced at trial." Without Floyd's testimony and the smoking gun, the state had no case. The charges against Brown were dropped and he was released.

In 1999, twelve years after he was freed, Brown described life on death row for Amnesty International.

> It was a six-by-eight-foot cell, where you could take five feet forward and five feet backward. You have a little iron bunk and a sink and commode combination. You did everything in that cell. You were allowed out of that cell for two hours once a week, for recreation, weather permitting. If you violated any rules of the institution, whatever privileges you had, such as visitation and mail, were taken for thirty days.

> Once a prisoner's death warrant is signed, he is removed from death row and placed in what was called death watch.

> Death watch is a cell located exactly thirty feet from the electric chair. You spent an average of twenty-one to twenty-three days in that cell and there were only two ways out—in a pine box or by a stay of execution. But while you were in that cell, you were treated to what we jokingly called the "presidential treatment." This consisted of listening to that chair being tested twice a day,

and knowing it was being done in your honor. . . . I can't tell you how it is to stand outside of that cell and have a gentleman come and put a tape measure around your chest, around your waist, the inseam of your legs, and measure you for your burial suit.

After the prison tailor took his measurements, Brown told Sydney Freedberg of the *St. Petersburg Times,* he was put back in his cell kicking and screaming. He declined to order the traditional last meal. "You got to realize," Brown said, "you put a man in a cage and treat him like a dog, talk to him like a dog, feed him like a dog . . . there's gonna come a time he wants to bite like a dog."

Sixteen men were executed while Brown was in Florida State Prison, and the memory of what it was like remained sharp even twelve years later. "There is a stink that hangs around for a couple of weeks," he recalled. "You can't get rid of it." Brown's anger, too, was unabated. "Yes, I'm bitter," he said. "I'm frustrated. The state of Florida didn't give me nothing. They didn't give me an apology. When they released me, they didn't even give me bus fare home."

James Robison

Arizona

James Robison was little more than a bit player in a Mafia-style slaying that had about it all the melodrama of a Hollywood film noir from the forties, except for the happy ending, for this story had no real ending at all. The case centered on the 1976 murder of Don Bolles, an investigative reporter who covered organized crime for the *Arizona Republic*. Bolles died from injuries suffered when a bomb exploded in his car, which was parked outside a hotel in downtown Phoenix. As Bolles lay in a pool of blood outside the car, he whispered, "They finally got me, the Mafia, Emprise. Find John Adamson." Emprise was a corporation with ties to the dog-track industry and was suspected of being closely connected to the mob. John [Harvey] Adamson was a well-known crime figure who had called Bolles and asked to meet him at the hotel.

As requested, the police found Adamson and arrested him. Adamson admitted placing the bomb but said it was detonated by Jimmy "The Plumber" Robison. He also said that he and Robison had been hired to kill Bolles by a local contractor and land developer named Max Dunlap. There was considerable speculation that Dunlap arranged the hit to return a favor he owed to Kemper Marley, a powerful Phoenix businessman who some called the Arizona Godfather, but who never had been directly implicated in any illegal activity.

Charged with first-degree murder, Adamson was quick to cut a deal. He pleaded guilty to second-degree murder for which he would receive a sentence of twenty years plus two months. The agreement included a provision that the original first-degree murder charge could be reinstated if he breached the terms of the plea bargain. In exchange, Adamson agreed to testify against Robison and Dunlap. Both were convicted, almost entirely on Adamson's testimony, and Robison, the presumed detonator of the bomb, was sentenced to death. Dunlap received a long prison term.

Both convictions were overturned by the Arizona Supreme Court in 1980 because the defendants' lawyers had not been permitted to fully cross-examine Adamson, and a new trial was ordered. Aware that his testimony was critical to the state's case, Adamson tried to bargain his way out of prison. He refused to testify at the retrial unless he was released. But the maneuver backfired. Prosecutors concluded that he had violated his plea agreement and reinstated the first-degree murder charge. The Arizona Supreme Court agreed that he could be retried. A jury convicted him, the judge sentenced him to death, and the state supreme court upheld the sentence. But Adamson's rocky trip through the criminal justice system was not nearly over.

In 1986, the Ninth Circuit Court of Appeals reversed the sentence on the grounds that Adamson had been subjected to double jeopardy. In 1987, the U.S. Supreme Court reversed the circuit court's double-jeopardy ruling. The guilty verdict remained intact, but the lower court struck down the sentence because the judge, not the jury, had imposed the death penalty. On successive days in 1990, the high court, by a five-to-four vote, upheld the constitutionality of Arizona's sentencing law, but then barred Adamson's execution by a four-to-three vote, with Justices Sandra Day O'Connor and Anthony M. Kennedy, who had voted with the majority the day before, not taking part in the decision.

Adamson was later released into a witness protection program. Robison and Dunlap were retried in separate trials in 1993. Robison was acquitted, but he was not free for long. He subsequently was convicted of conspiring to kill Adamson and later joined him in witness protection. Dunlap was convicted and remains in prison.

As the *Arizona Republic* noted on the twenty-fifth anniversary of Bolles's murder, it still remains "something of a mystery. . . . The truth is buried in police files, media morgues and, on the 25th anniversary of Bolles's death, the graves of some who were involved. A few of Bolles's graying colleagues still sift through his notes and stories on organized crime, seeking clues to the past and present, seeking closure."

Muneer Deeb

Texas

On the night of July 13, 1982, three teenage girls were brutally murdered in what Associated Press reporter Michael Graczyk described as "a frenzy of rape, torture, and knife butchery" in Lake Waco's Koehne Park in Texas. Their throats were slashed and their bodies pierced with up to thirty stab wounds before being dumped in a nearby park. The ferocity of the assault horrified the citizens of Waco, and the crime became known as the Lake Waco murders.

The police focused their attention on a forty-year-old local man, Wayne David Spence, who had a history of violent attacks that included beating, biting, and knifing and who conveniently was already in custody. Spence was serving a ninety-year term for aggravated sexual abuse using a knife. Arrested as his accomplices were two brothers, Anthony and Gilbert Melendez. But it was the arrest of Muneer Mohammad Deeb that tied the case together by providing authorities with a motive. They theorized that Deeb, a Jordanian immigrant who ran a local convenience store and was studying to become a computer programmer, had hired the three men to kill an ex-girlfriend on whom he had a $20,000 life insurance policy. There was no hard evidence linking Deeb to the killings, and as the prosecution's story unwound, its credibility seemed to evaporate further. In fact, the woman who was alleged to be the target of the plot was not even one of the victims.

The premise advanced by the prosecution was that Deeb, looking to cash in on the insurance policy, agreed to pay Spence and the Melendez brothers a total of $5,000 to murder his former girlfriend, Kelly. Unfortunately, eighteen-year-old Jill Montgomery, one of the victims, bore a close resemblance to Kelly. In a case of mistaken identity, Spence and the brothers botched the job by killing Jill and then murdered the two others who witnessed the attack. Armed with that story, the prosecution went to trial.

The case broke when the state called as a witness a man who had shared a jail cell with Spence. Spence, the man claimed, had told him on several occasions how Deeb had described the murder-for-hire scheme in great detail and how he would benefit from Kelly's death. In addition, he said Deeb had asked Spence if he knew someone who could carry out the plan. One of the Melendez brothers also testified that he was present when Spence and Deeb conspired to murder the young woman. The trial judge permitted the testimony, holding that it fell within a conspiracy exception to the rule barring hearsay evidence— evidence that cannot be attributed directly to its source. The

Texas Court of Criminal Appeals disagreed. In 1991, it over-turned Deeb's conviction on the grounds that the hearsay evidence should not have been allowed in. Melendez declined to testify at the retrial, and Deeb was acquitted and set free in 1993.

The Melendez brothers pleaded guilty. Gilbert was given a life term, and Anthony was sentenced to ninety-nine years. Spence was executed by lethal injection on April 3, 1997. He insisted all the way to the death chamber that he was innocent. It was the second execution in Texas in as many days.

Steven Manning
Illinois

In 2000, Steven Manning became the thirteenth prisoner released from Illinois's death row because of wrongful conviction, but he was not exactly set free. He was shipped immediately to Missouri where he previously had been sentenced to one hundred years in prison on an unrelated kidnapping charge. Manning was a former Chicago policeman gone bad. His felony record, in addition to the kidnapping charge, included burglary, theft, official misconduct as a police officer, and the felony murder charge that landed him on death row in Illinois.

The murder victim was James Pellegrino, Manning's former partner in the trucking business. He had been missing for almost three weeks when, on June 3, 1990, his body was found floating in the Des Plaines River near Chicago. His wrists and ankles were bound with duct tape and his head was in a plastic bag and covered with a towel. An autopsy report said he had died of a single gunshot wound to the back of the head. Manning was the prime suspect right from the start. Pellegrino's wife, Joyce, told police that when her husband left the house on May 14, he told her that Manning had "ripped him off for a lot of money" and that he was going to get it back. If he turned up dead, he told her, she should call the FBI and say that Manning had killed him.

When Pellegrino did turn up dead, Manning was promptly arrested and sent to the Cook County jail. He was placed in a cell with a career criminal named Thomas Dye, a con man and jailhouse snitch whose own prior record included ten felony convictions. He had most recently been sentenced to fourteen years for burglary. Three other felony charges were pending. Dye wasted no time in seeking an edge by helping to convict Manning. He contacted the prosecutors and told them that Manning had confessed to killing Pellegrino. Given Dye's reputation as a liar and a snitch, his word carried little weight with the State Attorney's Office. But Assistant State Attorneys Patrick J. Quinn and William G. Gamboney offered Pellegrino a chance to prove his claim. They wired him and told him to record conversations with Manning and get his confession on tape. Speaking freely, Manning told Dye much about his past criminal activities but said nothing that implicated him in Pellegrino's murder. All the same, the state decided to try Manning for the crime and use Dye as its star witness.

The prosecution's case rested principally on Dye's testimony and, in a critical judicial error, the tapes of the conversations between Dye and Manning. Circuit Court Judge Edward M. Fiala Jr. had allowed the tapes to be entered as evidence even though they contained no mention of Pellegrino. The tapes established for the jury that Manning was a man with a sordid past, but there was no reference to the case that was being tried. Nonetheless, the jury found Manning guilty and, after he waived his right to a jury sentencing hearing, the judge imposed the death penalty. Shortly after testifying, Dye's fourteen-year burglary sentence was reduced to six years. But before he served much of that term he was paroled and placed in the federal witness protection program.

On April 16, 1998, the Illinois Supreme Court ruled that the admission of the tapes into evidence constituted judicial error because they contained irrelevant and prejudicial references to other crimes Manning was involved in while making no mention of the crime for which he was being tried. The court also held that Joyce Pellegrino's statements about her conversations with her husband should have been excluded as hearsay evidence. Manning remained on death row for another twenty-one months before the state dismissed the charges and sent him to prison in Missouri.

Jeremy Sheets
Nebraska

A taped confession that did not pass legal muster also was instrumental in getting Jeremy Sheets released after four years on Nebraska's death row. The tape was made by an alleged accomplice, Adam Barnett, who conveniently had committed suicide before the case against Sheets could be heard; the tape could not be entered as evidence since Barnett was not available for cross-examination. Sheets's good fortune did not resonate well within the Omaha community in which the crime took place nor among those in the criminal justice system, for Sheets was not the type to elicit sympathy, and there were many who continued to believe that he was in fact guilty.

The case began in 1992 when the body of a seventeen-year-old high-school honor student, her throat slashed, was found dumped in a wooded area north of Omaha. The girl, Kenyatta Bush, had been kidnapped outside Omaha North High School on her way to class on September 23. The case went unsolved for four years, but in 1996 police arrested Barnett, who admitted participating in the murder and named Sheets as an accomplice. In a taped confession, Barnett told police that, after a night of getting high on drugs, he and Sheets decided to rape a black woman as a way of getting even for the black men who date white women. Barnett said Sheets stabbed the girl after they took turns raping her. In exchange for the taped confession, Barnett was granted a plea bargain in which he was not charged with first-degree murder, did not have an additional weapons charge filed, and received a commitment that his safety would be assured while he was incarcerated. The last was no small issue when a white man who raped a young African-American girl was to be placed in a largely black population of convicted felons. Barnett apparently did not fare well in any event; within a matter of months he hanged himself in his cell.

Testimony presented at Sheets's trial in 1997 indicated that he was something of a racist. According to witnesses, he previously had threatened an African-American neighbor and was intrigued by Nazism, drawing swastikas and at one point shaving his head to look like a skinhead. But the only evidence that tied him directly to the crime were the taped words of his now-deceased accomplice. It was enough for the jury. Sheets was found guilty of first-degree murder and sentenced to death.

In September 2000, the Nebraska Supreme Court overturned the conviction, saying the tape recording was the kind of statement deemed "highly suspect," "inherently unreliable," and hence inadmissible without the defendant having the opportunity to cross-examine the witness. A year later, the U.S. Supreme Court declined to hear the state's appeal of the ruling, and Sheets was set free. Douglas County Attorney Jim Jansen saw no point in retrying the case. "The tape was the sole focus as identifying Sheets as the murderer," he said, but he remained convinced of Sheets's guilt, adding, "We hear so much about innocent people being convicted; this is the reverse of that."

Upon his release, Sheets won no favor with the public when he requested a refund of the monies deposited in his behalf in the state's victims' compensation fund. The Nebraska attorney general denied the request, pointing out that the reversal of Sheets's conviction was not on the basis of actual innocence. He said it was not even considered a "disposition of charges favorable" to the defendant unless the case is subsequently dismissed because the prosecution is convinced that the accused was innocent. It was not.

● ● ●

Henry Drake
Georgia

After being tried three times, convicted twice, and spending eight years on Georgia's death row, Henry Drake was set free on the grounds of actual innocence. Drake and a codefendant, William Campbell, were found guilty in separate trials of stabbing to death a seventy-four-year-old barber in his shop during the course of a robbery in 1977. The barber apparently put up a struggle because there were pools of blood on the floor and blood smears on the wall of the shop. Two blood-soaked pocket knives were found on the floor.

When Campbell was arrested for the murder, he said he was not present at the scene and named Drake as the killer . He later told his attorney that he committed the crime by himself and that Drake had nothing to do with it. He offered many conflicting versions of the story before settling on one that did not implicate Drake. It was this story that his lawyer expected to hear when Campbell testified at his own trial. However, Campbell flipped again and surprised his attorney by testifying that he was entirely innocent and that Drake attacked the barber while Campbell was getting his hair cut. The jury didn't buy the story, and Campbell was convicted and sentenced to death.

Drake was tried later, and Campbell testified against him, supporting the prosecution's claim that Campbell, an older man suffering from emphysema, was not strong enough to have committed the murder by himself. The only forensic evidence introduced at trial was testimony that the bloodstains found at the scene suggested there had been two assailants. The blood types, however, were never matched with Drake's and there was no physical evidence connecting him to the crime. Drake also had an alibi that was confirmed by several witnesses. Nonetheless, he was found guilty and condemned to die.

Campbell, for his part, continued to change his story. Shortly before he died of natural causes in 1983, he recanted his trial testimony in a signed affidavit and declared that Drake was not involved in the murder. In 1984, the circuit court of appeals vacated Drake's death sentence and a year later ordered a new trial. This time the jury was hung, splitting ten-to-two for acquittal. In 1987, at a third trial, Drake was again convicted, but this time he was sentenced to life in prison.

Six months later, partly on the testimony from the medical examiner that the bloodstains at the crime scene did not necessarily support the two-assailant theory, the Georgia Board of Pardons and Paroles declared Drake factually innocent and voted unanimously to release him.

Willie Brown and Larry Troy
Florida

Willie Brown and Larry Troy were already in prison when they were convicted in 1981 of stabbing to death Earl Owens, a fellow inmate, at Florida's Union Correctional Institution. The two men were held as suspects in solitary confinement for seventeen months before they were formally charged with the crime. Then three inmates came forth and identified Brown and Troy as the murderers. Since two of the inmates were known to have mental problems, the word of the third man, Frank Wise, became the pivot of the state's case. Wise was not a prosecutor's ideal witness. He was doing time for murdering Troy's cousin and was quoted before the trial as saying that he hated Brown and Troy so much that he would like to see them executed whether they were guilty or not. He now had the opportunity to fulfill his wish. Wise testified at the trial that he saw both men leaving the victim's cell shortly before the body was discovered. His testimony resulted in Brown and Troy being convicted and moved from the prison's general population to death row.

Salvation, at least for the time, came to the pair in the form of a German anti-death-penalty activist, Esther Lichtenfels. In the course of her work, Lichtenfels visited Florida's death row on several occasions, and she and Brown fell in love. She was determined to help free him, and over the next several years invested $70,000 in her own investigation of the case. Her efforts were given impetus in 1987 when the state supreme court reversed the convictions because the prosecutors did not share with the defense statements they received during prison interviews.

While awaiting a new trial, Lichtenfels managed to set up a sting operation that freed both men from death row. Wearing a legally authorized tape recorder and fitted with a hidden microphone, she recorded Wise saying that he had lied in his testimony and offering to recant and tell the truth in exchange for $2,000. On the basis of the recorded admission, all charges against Brown and Troy were dropped, and Wise was charged with committing perjury.

Brown, who was also serving twenty years on a robbery charge, left prison in 1988 and had hardly tasted freedom when he and Lichtenfels were married. Neither they nor Troy lived happily ever after. Troy, who had been serving a twenty-five-year sentence for another murder, was released in 1990, but he was not free for long. Seven months after leaving prison, he was arrested for selling cocaine and was sent to the Charlotte Correctional Institution in North Carolina. Brown's life continued to be driven by drug use and robberies. He was returned to prison for robbing a bank in Springfield, Massachusetts, and later arrested for holding up a bank in Dunedin, Florida, brandishing the handle of a broomstick, and then leading police on a high-speed chase in a stolen car.

Brown insisted that the authorities had unfairly made him a target. "In their eyes, I was never exonerated," he said from jail. "There's enough pain in this stuff to last a lifetime."

Walter McMillian
Alabama

Walter "Johnny D" McMillian came close to becoming a victim of Southern justice in 1988 when he was sentenced to death for killing a white eighteen-year-old store clerk in Monroe County, Alabama. McMillian, a black logger, was railroaded in a trial that took less than two days and convicted on the testimony of three criminal suspects. The death sentence was imposed by the judge, who overrode the jury's recommendation that McMillian be given a life term in prison. Fittingly enough, the judge was named Robert E. Lee Key Jr. It took the efforts of a zealously committed defense attorney, Bryan Stevenson, under the bright light of publicity provided by the television show *60 Minutes,* to save McMillian's life.

McMillian was convicted of killing Ronda Morrison while robbing the shop in which she worked. Arrested with him was Ralph Myers, who agreed to testify against McMillian in return for consideration from the state. The prospect of just treatment looked dim for McMillian from the outset. The fact that he had a white girlfriend and his son had married a white woman did not sit well in that part of the country. Shortly after his arrest, the Monroe County sheriff told him, "I ought to take you off and hang you like we done that nigger in Mobile, but we can't." Nonetheless, what followed was in every sense the equivalent of a judicial lynching.

Two weeks after his arrest McMillian was placed on death row, although he had no prior criminal record. Amnesty International believed that no other defendant in the United States had ever been placed in a death-row cell while still awaiting trial. On a change of venue the trial was moved from Monroe County to Baldwin County, the locale of *To Kill a Mockingbird,* Harper Lee's well-known novel about racism in the South.

The trial, a caricature of criminal justice, was, in Thomas Hobbes's phrase, nasty, brutish, and short. The core of the state's case was the perjured testimony of three witnesses, including a convicted murderer, who placed McMillian at the scene of the crime. The defense, by contrast, produced twelve black witnesses who testified that McMillian was at a church fund-raising fish fry when the murder occurred. The jury returned a verdict of guilty and voted seven-to-five against the death penalty. However, Judge Robert E. Lee Key Jr. thought the jury to be too forgiving. He imposed the death penalty, and McMillian officially took his place as a denizen of death row.

The case attracted the attention of Bryan Stevenson, a Montgomery, Alabama, attorney and director of the Equal Justice Initiative of Alabama. Stevenson had been representing condemned inmates in the South for thirteen years, and as he began to look into McMillian's case he discovered that much was amiss. The prosecution, he learned, had withheld exculpatory evidence, most critically concealing the existence of a witness who had seen the victim alive after the time she was presumed to have been murdered by McMillian. There also was an unedited police tape that differed markedly from the one that had been given to the defense and appeals teams. It contained a statement by a prosecution witness complaining that the police wanted him to frame an innocent Johnny D. For added measure, all three prosecution witnesses recanted their testimony and admitted they had lied.

Despite the mounting evidence of official misconduct, state courts denied appeals on four occasions. At that point, Stevenson decided to go public. He took McMillian's story to CBS-TV and was interviewed by Ed Bradley on *60 Minutes*. With the story now in the open, the Alabama Court of Criminal Appeals reversed the conviction. The county district attorney acknowledged that the case had been bungled and joined the defense in getting the charges dropped. McMillian finally was freed in 1993 after serving nearly six years on death row. "Often times," Stevenson said, "obtaining evidence suppressed by prosecutors or police can take many years of litigation."

In 1997, Stevenson argued before the U.S. Supreme Court that McMillian should be permitted to sue the county sheriff who suppressed evidence that would have benefited his defense. The court ruled against him, but McMillian settled with other parties involved in the case for an undisclosed sum. In 2001, Alabama passed a statute granting compensation to prisoners who have been exonerated.

"No man who has had to withstand the psychic trauma of sitting on death row should have to go through such rigmarole to get reimbursed," Stevenson said. "The presumption should be, if you were exonerated, the state should compensate you for the time you were in prison and to help make your transition easier into the real world. I think that's something society owes someone who has been deprived of the liberties we take for granted."

Curtis Kyles
Louisiana

Curtis Kyles became something of a career defendant, having been tried five times for the same crime and imprisoned for fourteen years before being freed on a federal writ of habeas corpus. At one point he had come within thirty hours of execution.

Kyles was arrested in 1984 for the murder of Dolores Dye during a car theft in a store parking lot in Gretna Parish, Louisiana. The case against him hinged on the testimony of four eyewitnesses and what seemed to be compelling physical evidence: the murder weapon, a spent cartridge, and the victim's purse were found in his apartment. Nevertheless, his first trial, in November 1984, ended in a hung jury. A month later, he was retried, convicted, and sentenced to death. His appeals to state courts won him a remand for an evidentiary hearing, which would determine whether the existing evidence was sufficient to sustain the verdict, but the state trial court denied relief. He fared no better in the the state supreme court; his application for discretionary review was denied.

During the appeals process, one of the eyewitnesses recanted, stating in an affidavit that she had not seen the killer's face but was pressured by police and prosecutors to identify him. One prosecutor, she said, told her that "all the other evidence pointed to [Kyles] as the killer." To make certain that she would be able to pick out the defendant in the courtroom, she was told that "the murderer would be the guy seated at the table with the attorney and that [he] was the one I should identify," the affidavit said. It was also discovered that the state had withheld critical information about another witness—a paid informant who might have been the actual killer. While the informant had given detailed testimony implicating Kyles, there was undisclosed evidence indicating that the snitch himself had had possession of the victim's belongings and might well have planted the incriminating items in Kyles's apartment. In addition to deflecting suspicion from himself, the informant, who fit another eyewitness's description of the murderer, might also have been motivated by a reward that had been offered in the case.

Having lost all his appeals in the state courts as well as the U.S. Court of Appeals for the Fifth Circuit, Kyles found relief from the U.S. Supreme Court on a habeas corpus petition in April 1995. In a decision rendered just a few days before he was to be executed, the high court remanded the case based on failure of police and prosecutors to turn over exculpatory evidence to the defense before the trial and denounced the "uncritical readiness" of the prosecution to accept the informant's questionable story. The court ruled that Kyles was entitled to a new trial because there was "reasonable probability" that the disclosure of the concealed evidence would have produced a different result.

But Kyles's long journey into the night of the criminal justice system was far from over. His third trial, in October 1996, ended in a deadlocked jury, and subsequent trials in the next two years had the same result. After the fifth trial and fourth mistrial, prosecutors decided to drop the charges and Kyles was released.

Though Kyles suffered the oppressive indignities of wrongful conviction, he might count himself fortunate that his petition for habeas corpus came as early as it did. Just a few years later, the bar for habeas petitions was raised in deference to the jurisdiction of state courts. Had the strict time lines and standards of the Anti-Terrorism and Effective Death Penalty Act—passed in 2001 in response to the 9/11 attack—been in effect in 1995, Kyles might well have been returned to Louisiana's death row to await execution.

Federico Macias
Texas

Like Kyles, Federico Macias was freed on a writ of habeas corpus within two days of execution. In his case, however, it was not the misconduct of the prosecution that led to his wrongful conviction, but the mishandling of the defense by his own attorney.

Macias was sentenced to death in 1984 for hacking a couple to death with a machete during a burglary at their home in El Paso,

Texas. The critical testimony against him was offered under a grant of immunity by a coworker and an alleged accomplice who said he drove Macias to the crime scene on the night of the murders. His testimony was corroborated by the ubiquitous jailhouse informant who said he heard Macias confess and by a nine-year-old playmate of Macias's daughter who said she had seen the defendant with blood on his hands and shirt the day of the crime.

After his conviction was affirmed by the Texas Court of Criminal Appeals, a volunteer legal team from the New York firm of Skadden Arps Slate Meagher & Flom came to his aid shortly before his scheduled execution. It soon became apparent that Macias had been afforded virtually no defense. His court-appointed attorney had failed to call two alibi witnesses who could have placed him elsewhere at the time of the murders and had failed to cross-examine either a purported eyewitness who had not been at the scene of the crime or the nine-year-old girl, whose testimony turned out to be false. The attorney acknowledged having performed no investigation at all for the sentencing phase, his only preparation being a talk with Macias and his wife during the lunch break at the sentencing proceeding. In addition, he had based his trial decisions on a fundamental misunderstanding of Texas law.

On a habeas corpus petition, a federal district court reversed the conviction in 1992 on the basis of ineffective counsel and ordered a new hearing. The court found that "[t]he errors that occurred in this case are inherent in a system which pays attorneys such a meager amount." A grand jury refused to reindict because of lack of evidence, the prosecution dropped the case, and Macias eventually was cleared of all charges.

Charles Smith
Indiana

The ineffective assistance of counsel also led ultimately to the acquittal of Charles Smith, who had been sentenced to death for murdering a young woman during a robbery in Allen County, Indiana, in 1983. An accomplice, who claimed to be the getaway driver, testified against Smith in exchange for the dismissal of all charges against him. Smith had a solid alibi but was prohibited from introducing it by the trial judge because his attorney had failed to file a pretrial alibi notice.

After initially affirming the conviction and death sentence, the Indiana Supreme Court granted a retrial in 1987 because Brown had not received an adequate defense. At the retrial, the alibi was presented to the jury along with evidence that the eyewitness had falsely accused Smith of committing the crime. Brown was acquitted and released in 1991.

Jesse Keith Brown
South Carolina

Jesse Keith Brown was the victim of another type of ineffective counsel; he made the mistake of representing himself. Brown was convicted in 1983 of the murder of John Horace McMillen during the course of an armed robbery at McMillen's home in Spartanburg, South Carolina. The main evidence for the prosecution was the testimony provided by Brown's half brother, who turned out to be the real killer and who was permitted to plead to lesser charges in exchange for testifying against Brown.

The South Carolina Supreme Court overturned the conviction in 1986 and ordered a new trial because the prosecution had given an improper closing argument. Brown was retried, before a different judge, and again was convicted and sentenced to death. In 1988, the state supreme court ordered another new trial because the judge had given improper instructions to the jury. At a third trial a year later Brown was acquitted when new evidence was presented that indicated that his half brother had committed the murder. Brown was later convicted on robbery charges arising from the same crime.

Part V

FALSE CONFESSIONS

No evidence is more compelling than a suspect's confession. Rarely is anything else needed to convict, for why would anyone confess to a crime he did not commit? Yet false confessions have become legion in the criminal justice system. Of the convictions that have been reversed on the basis of DNA evidence—those in which there is no doubt of error—20 percent involved a false or coerced confession. Studies indicate that about 75 percent of juries will vote to convict when the defendant has confessed, even if convincing physical evidence and the testimony of other witnesses suggest that the defendant is innocent. Such confessions have become a growing national problem, particularly in cases involving minors or the mentally ill; they result not only in the wrong person being imprisoned or possibly executed, but in the guilty party remaining at large.

People confess to crimes they did not commit for reasons that run the spectrum from plea bargains or police coercion to psychological compulsions whose complexity is not easily gauged. The old rubber-hose, third-degree treatment made famous in

B-grade movies of the forties and fifties was outlawed nationally by the U.S. Supreme Court in 1933. It has been replaced by more subtle psychological techniques that often enlist attrition as an ally. Detectives take turns interrogating a suspect until, twenty or thirty hours later, a confession might seem a small price to pay for a ticket home or a night's rest. Those more open to suggestion, like the young or mentally retarded, might in fact come to believe that they committed the crime after all. "The difference between the third degree and psychological interrogation," Peter Carlson wrote in the *Washington Post,* "is akin to the difference between getting mugged and getting scammed."

When a crime has been highly publicized and the suspect is likely to be familiar with the details of the case, a technique of hypothetical questioning can sometimes pry loose a confession that includes some telling details. For example: "Let's just say you were going to commit this crime, what type of weapon would you use? You wouldn't use a gun, would you, because that would have attracted too much attention, right? Yes, you would use a knife, and if you used a knife, what would you have done with it after you killed her? Of course you would have disposed of it, but first you would wipe the blood off, wouldn't you?" Each time the suspect agrees, the noose is drawn tighter, and if he begins to agree to details that would be known only to police and the person who committed the crime, he is that much closer to confessing.

Sometimes suspects can be tricked into offering a confession. Alleged accomplices are often questioned separately, with each being told that the others have implicated them in the crime. On other occasions they are told they failed a "voice stress" test that showed they were lying. Under such circumstances, wrote crime reporter Jim Dwyer in the *New York Times,* social scientists say "a false confession may seem like an exit ramp from an impossible predicament, just as a bear might chew off its own foot to escape from a trap."

The issue of false confession came into sharp focus in 1963 with the well-publicized "career-girl murders" on New York's Upper East Side. Police questioned hundreds of suspects but had gotten nowhere until, six months later, James Whitmore Jr. was arrested and interrogated in another case. Whitmore, who was mentally slow, voluntarily went into detail about how he had stabbed to death Janice Wylie and Emily Hoffert while burglarizing their apartment. It was soon discovered that Whitmore was elsewhere at the time of the murders, and the actual killer, Richard Robles, was later convicted and sentenced to twenty years to life.

But at the time of his confession, the double charge of capital murder made Whitmore a likely candidate for Sing Sing's electric chair and produced some lasting changes in the justice system. The prospect of an innocent man being executed was instrumental in the New York state legislature's decision to abolish capital punishment in 1965. On the national level, the Supreme Court also took note. The tactics used by police to elicit Whitmore's confession were cited extensively in the court's 1966 Miranda ruling, which required police to advise suspects of their right to remain silent or have an attorney present when they are questioned.

Four decades later, false confessions again were at the center of debate when five teenagers who had confessed to raping a young woman who later became known as the Central Park Jogger, were found to be innocent of the crime. The confessions of the youths were videotaped and played on television regularly, and they appeared to be as authentic as one could wish. But another man confessed thirteen years after the crime was committed, and DNA tests proved that he had raped the victim and the Central Park Five had not.

Between 1963 and 2002 there were doubtless scores, perhaps hundreds, of instances of false confession. It is impossible to estimate the true number because the cases are hidden from view until brought to light, usually by a chance occurrence. But we know for certain that a number of innocent people have been dispatched to death row on the basis of confessions that turned out to be false. Wilbert Lee and Freddie Pitts were two of them.

Wilbert Lee and Freddie Pitts
Florida

Early on the morning of August 1, 1963, the Gulf County Sheriff's Office received a report that the MoJo service station in Port St. Joe, located in the Florida Panhandle, was open and the two attendants were missing. Also missing were a .38-caliber Smith & Wesson revolver and a paycheck that Freddie L. Pitts had cashed at the station. The following morning, at around eight-thirty, two women on their way to go fishing found the bodies of the two attendants lying in a secluded spot in a wooden area.

Pitts, Wilbert Lee, and his wife, Ella Mae, and three companions had made two trips to the station on the night of the murder.

First, at around midnight, while Lee had used the pay phone, others in the group had gotten into a dispute with the attendants, who refused to let them use the rest rooms. Two hours later, after filling up on beer and moonshine, Pitts, Lee, and a woman named Willie Mae Lee returned to the station to buy some vodka. What happened next would be the subject of legal proceedings that lasted twelve years. When questioned by police several days later, along with others who had visited the station that night, Lee, Pitts, and Willie Mae were said to have told the following story:

At around two A.M., Pitts and Wilbert Lee held up the gas station with the gun they had stolen on their first visit about two hours earlier. They abducted the two attendants and drove approximately twelve miles to an isolated area in the woods. The attendants were forced to climb through an iron gate and marched deeper into the woods near a canal. The victims were beaten with a tire iron and then shot in the head. Willie Mae Lee testified that she heard two shots before the defendants returned to the car. The three of them then drove away. She said she had taken no part in the crime and that when the defendants drove her home, they warned her that if she told anyone about the events she would never see her daughter again.

Prior to finding the bodies, the Sheriff's Department acted as though they were dealing with a missing persons case. They surmised that the attendants had gotten drunk and wandered off with the money. A polygraph officer arrived at Port St. Joe at around noon on August 2 to perform exploratory tests on those who had visited the service station on the night of July 31. Because of factual differences in their statements, some of those questioned were advised of their rights and asked to take lie-detector tests. Wilbert Lee was tested first, and the results indicated he was not telling the truth. When Pitts was tested, he said that he and Lee returned to the station and robbed it, but did not abduct the attendants, who were alive when they left. This was the first the authorities had heard of the station being robbed. The critical test was the one performed on Lamberson Smith, one of the drinking buddies who had been partying with Pitts and Lee between visits to the service station. He said Pitts, Lee, and Willie Mae had left Lee's house at around two A.M. and returned two to three hours later. His test reflected no deception; Smith was presumed to be telling the truth.

Pitts and Lee were taken to the county jail. They were arraigned on August 7. The judge appointed attorney Fred Turner to represent them. Both men confessed and told Turner that they had not been mistreated by the police. Turner inquired about the murder weapon and Pitts told him he had run out on the sand dunes and thrown the gun as far as he could. Turner tried to negotiate a plea to a lesser charge but failed. The judge promised Turner a "mercy trial" if the defendants pled guilty. They agreed, and new indictments were handed up by the grand jury. The "mercy trial" was held on August 28, but a majority of the all-white jury did not recommend mercy, and Lee and Pitts received none. Based largely on their confessions and the testimony of an alleged eyewitness, both were convicted and sentenced to death.

Several months later, Pitts and Lee told FBI agents who interviewed them that their confessions were beaten out of them. Pitts said he had been taken for a ride after his polygraph test and that he was knocked unconscious on several occasions. Lee said he too was beaten and that law-enforcement officers had threatened to shave his wife's head if he didn't confess.

Pitts and Lee filed a direct appeal with the Florida Supreme Court, challenging the manner in which the judge determined the defendants' sentences. Specifically, they alleged that they had pled guilty to an indictment that did not stipulate the degree of the offense with which they were charged and that the judge took the unorthodox step of impaneling a jury to decide whether they should be granted mercy. The court ruled that the judge's actions did not constitute reversible error and affirmed the sentence. A petition for a writ of certiorari with the U.S. Supreme Court, which would have required the lower court to submit the record of the case for review, also was denied, as were petitions on other grounds filed with the circuit court and the district court of appeals.

The first break for Lee and Pitts came in 1966 when a career criminal by the name of Curtis Adams Jr. admitted killing the two attendants at the MoJo station. Adams already was serving time for committing a similar crime. On August 16, 1963, he had robbed a service station, taken the attendant into the woods, and shot him. Pitts and Lee filed a new motion on the basis of Adams's confession, but at the petition hearing Adams changed his story. He admitted robbing the station on the night in question but denied killing the attendants. In fact, he further incriminated Lee and Pitts. He said that when he used the rest room he heard someone inside the store shout, "Don't anybody move or I'll shoot." He said he looked out the door and saw Pitts and another man taking the two attendants away. Adams testified that he had confessed because sixteen black men had beaten him while he was in Broward County jail and threatened to do further damage if he did not confess to the crime.

Although their petition was denied, Lee and Pitts found a new ally. *Miami Herald* reporter Gene Miller took up the case when he learned of Adams's confession. It appeared that two black men were being pushed toward their death for a crime committed by a white man. He wrote a series of articles, and through his persistent efforts events began to shift in Lee's and Pitts's favor. Miller's most critical discovery was that the eyewitness in the case had recanted her testimony in 1968, but the prosecution had failed to share that bit of news with the defense. On May 13, 1969, finding that the state had withheld evidence, the circuit court vacated the convictions and ordered a new trial. However, the District Court of Appeals of Florida reinstated the verdicts and sentences the following year, ruling that the evidence withheld was immaterial because the defendants had pleaded guilty and were tried only on the issue of punishment.

The attorney general soon weighed in on the side of the petitioners. He conceded that the state had unlawfully suppressed evidence and filed a "motion in confession of error." The state supreme court ordered a new trial. On March 15, 1972, Lee and Pitts again were found guilty and sentenced to death by an all-white jury that knew nothing of Adams's confession, which the trial judge refused to allow into evidence. Their appellate attorney said that the defendants, "although totally innocent, were convicted because they were black." Nevertheless, the convictions and sentences were both affirmed on appeal. Twelve years after the first convictions, the case finally wound to a conclusion favorable to the defendants. Governor Reubin Askew granted Lee and Pitts a full pardon, saying, "I am sufficiently convinced that they are innocent."

After being set free in 1975, Lee and Pitts moved to Miami. Lee, whose family left him while he was on death row, worked for the state counseling troubled juveniles, then was hired to counsel inmates in Miami-Dade's jails. Pitts, who had not seen his two daughters since being sent to prison, worked for a while in security and then took a job as a truck driver. He remarried and lives in Miami Shores. Both lecture frequently against capital punishment.

Some years after they were released from prison, the Florida legislature awarded each man $500,000. It was the first time that state had ordered restitution for persons wrongly sentenced to death. "It's like giving the monkey some peanuts," Lee said.

Gary Gauger

Illinois

The case of Gary Gauger was a classic example of a confession extracted by hypothetical prompting. Gauger, an organic vegetable farmer who lived and worked on his parents' farm in McHenry County, Illinois, near the Wisconsin border, was charged with killing his parents at their home on April 8, 1993. His induced confession was offered up after he was interrogated for sixteen hours without a lawyer being present. He was convicted and sentenced to death by lethal injection.

The Gaugers, Morris and Ruth, both in their seventies, were

found dead, their throats slashed, and Gary was taken into custody for questioning. He was interrogated through the night, and the authorities came away with what they claimed was a confession. Gary insisted on his innocence and denied having confessed. He said he had offered, at the urging of the police, a hypothetical account of how he might have committed the double murder. He had been told that he failed a polygraph test and that clothes soaked in his parents' blood had been found in his room. Neither statement was true, but Gary had no way of knowing that. If indeed the bloody clothes were found in his room and he flunked the lie-detector test, how might he account for that? His interrogators asked him to consider the possibilities, just hypothetically of course. Gary responded that if he had in fact killed his parents, it must have been during a blackout because he remembered nothing about it. That was enough of a confession for the sheriff's deputies. Gauger was charged with the crime, and on May 5 a grand jury returned an indictment on two counts of murder. At a pretrial hearing, Gary described his interrogation and explained how he had been maneuvered into speculating about his guilt, but a motion to suppress the confession was denied.

The confession formed the backbone of the prosecution's case, and the deputies filled in the details at the trial. They testified that Gary told them he had come upon his parents from behind, pulled their heads back by the hair, and cut their throats. Additional state's evidence was offered by a pathologist who performed autopsies on the bodies and a forensic scientist who examined loose hairs found near Ruth's body. The pathologist, Dr. Lawrence Blum, testified that the wounds were consistent with the prosecution's account of how the victims' throats were cut. Under cross-examination, however, he acknowledged that it was equally likely that the Gaugers had been bludgeoned first. The forensic scientist, Lurie Lee, said that the hairs found near Ruth's body and presumed to be hers had been stretched and broken in a manner that was consistent with the prosecution's version of the murder. But as with Blum, Lee conceded under cross-examination that the hairs also could have been broken during combing or brushing. The state then dusted off and presented to the jury a jailhouse snitch named Raymond Wagner who was a fellow inmate of Gary's at the McHenry County Jail when he was awaiting trial. A twice-convicted felon, Wagner testified that Gary often described how he had gone about killing his parents.

The state's jerry-built case was deemed sufficient by the jury. Gauger was found guilty on both charges. He waived his right to be sentenced by the jury that convicted him and heard his death sentence pronounced by Judge Henry L. Cowlin on January 11, 1994.

Gauger was fortunate enough to have his case taken on appeal by Northwestern Law School professor Lawrence Marshall, and nine months later Judge Cowlin reduced his sentence to life in prison. Two years later, his prospects grew even brighter. On March 8, 1996, the Appellate Court for the Second District in Illinois unanimously reversed his conviction and remanded the case for retrial because Cowlin had failed to grant the motion to suppress Gauger's confession. The court declared the entire interrogation unconstitutional and ruled that since the arrest itself was made without probable cause, any statements made by Gauger should not have been admitted at trial.

Without the confession, the state had no case. All charges were dropped, and Gary was set free.

The issue of his actual innocence, however, was not completely resolved until June 1997 when officers of the U.S. Bureau of Alcohol, Tobacco and Firearms came across a wiretap recording that cleared Gauger of any involvement in the crime. Investigating a conspiracy among members of a Wisconsin motorcycle gang called the Outlaws, federal officials heard a tape recording in which one of the gang members, Randall E. Miller, said that the authorities had nothing to link him to the Gauger murders because he had been careful to leave no physical evidence. A federal grand jury in Milwaukee indicted Miller and another gang member, James Schneider, for thirty-four acts of racketeering, including the murder of the Gaugers. Schneider pleaded guilty to the crime in 1998; Miller was convicted in U.S. District Court in 2000.

Gary, now married, works the family farm with his wife, Sue. He recently was one of thirty-one exonerated death-row inmates who took to the stage of Northwestern's Thorne Auditorium to demonstrate their opposition to capital punishment. "Until this happened," Gauger said, "I really believed in the criminal justice system."

Robert Lee Miller Jr.
Oklahoma

The "confession" that led to the conviction of Robert Miller for the rape and murder of two elderly women in Oklahoma City was based on the contents of a dream that he shared with detectives who were questioning him about the crime in 1988. For Miller, the dream soon turned into a nightmare that ended with his spending seven years on death row. For most of that time the state had withheld DNA evidence that would have established his innocence.

Zelma Cutler, a ninety-two-year-old widow who lived alone in a corner house in the Military Park section of Oklahoma City, was found dead in her bed four months after another widow, Anna Laura Fowler, eighty-three years old, had suffered a similar fate. Both women had been raped. No property was taken from their homes. There was no murder weapon. Both women appeared to have been suffocated by the weight of the man who attacked them. The murders were part of a crime spree that had begun in 1987 and spread panic through the neighborhood. A task force of twelve detectives was assigned to the case. The only hard evidence they had to go on were the identification of A-positive blood types in the semen of the rapist and what was described as three "Negroid" hairs found on the sheets covering Mrs. Cutler's body.

Police questioned more than one hundred black men in the area. Blood samples were taken from twenty-three of them. One of those with A-positive blood was Robert Miller, a twenty-seven-year-old unemployed heating and air-conditioning repairman. When questioned, Miller told police he was eager to help in any way he could. He was taken in for questioning, and his nightmare was about to begin. Miller was a drug user given to an occasional hallucinatory dream, and he made the mistake of describing one for Detectives Jerry Flowers and David Shupe.

His revelations were recorded on nearly twelve hours of video-tape. During those hours, Miller told the detectives that he dreamt about the murders and proceeded to regale his inter-rogators with an array of dreams and visions that regularly invaded his sleep, offering premonitions, paranoid warnings, and insights into events that had already occurred. They were clearly the detached fragments of a mind not fully in control, but the detectives believed they were on to something. They worked Miller hard, coaxing, cajoling, suggesting various scenarios of the murders until one would ignite Miller's imagination. Finally, they thought they had gotten enough. Miller, they said, had given them details of the crimes that only the killer would know. He was charged with the murders of the two women.

The prosecution went to trial with an A-positive blood sample, three hairs that an expert witness said were Negroid and could have come from Miller, and a twelve-hour videotape played for the jury that sounded nothing like a confession. The district attorney was Robert Macy, the same "Cowboy Bob" whose tactics during the prosecution of Clifford Henry Bowen were condemned several years earlier (see p. 102). This time Macy pulled from his bag of tricks a pair of Fruit of the Loom underpants that had been left at the murder scene. It was the same brand that Miller wore, and the prosecution contended that when Miller was questioned he knew that such an item of clothing had been left behind.

There was little of consequence the defense could present by way of rebuttal, as the prosecution's case was void of substance. The blood was one of the most common types, and the hair samples were not specifically matched to Miller's. The secret details of the crimes that Miller was presumed to have knowledge of were actually known to many people in the neighborhood, according to at least one defense witness, a neighbor of Miller's who described him as a peaceful man who often performed helpful chores for others in the area. On the videotape, which was the core of the state's case, Miller was heard proclaiming his innocence. But in its way, the trial was over before it began. The all-white jury convicted Miller in 1988 of two murders, two rapes, and two burglaries. He was sentenced to two death penalties plus 725 years in prison.

Robert Miller's case, however, was a long way from decided, as shown in a detailed description and analysis in *Actual Innocence,* a book by Barry Scheck and Peter Neufeld, founders and directors of the Innocence Project, and Jim Dwyer, a reporter and columnist for the New York *Daily News.* Lee Ann Peters, a young appellate lawyer in the Oklahoma City Public Defender's Office, had been following the case with more than casual interest because her grandmother lived in the Military Park area. Now, assigned to handle Miller's appeal, she noticed that while twenty-three black men had undergone tests for their blood types, twenty-four had been checked for their hair. The man whose blood had not been sampled was named Ronald Lott, and, as it developed, his omission from the blood list was apt to be more than just an oversight.

Working with retired homicide detective Bob Thompson, Peters discovered that the Military Park crime spree had not ended with Miller's arrest. Two other elderly women were attacked later in precisely the same manner. Both in their seventies, they survived the attacks, and nothing was stolen except for a handgun that the intruder had taken away from one of his victims. A few days later, Lott was arrested for the two rapes.

The stolen gun was in his possession and his fingerprints were found in the homes of the other victims. Blood tests turned up A-positive. He should have been considered a prime suspect in the Cutler-Fowler murders for which Miller was then being prosecuted. Furthermore, Peters and Thompson learned that the same prosecutor, Barry Albert, was handling both cases. Lott pleaded guilty to the two more recent rapes at precisely the same time pretrial hearings were being conducted in Miller's case. Albert said later that he had informed the judge that the existence of a suspect such as Lott constituted exculpatory evidence in Miller's behalf. The judge was unmoved. Albert withdrew from the case and was replaced by Macy and Assistant District Attorney Ray Elliott. Lott's arrest and guilty plea in almost identical crimes were kept secret throughout Miller's trial.

Peters in the meantime pressed on. She had the physical evidence against Miller tested for DNA, and the results cleared him conclusively; they did not exclude Ronald Lott. Peters presented her findings to the district attorney, who was not particularly moved. The only thing the DNA tests proved, he maintained, was that Miller did not rape the victims. They did not prove he was absent from the scene. The explanation was elementary: Lott had raped the women, but Miller killed them. He had confessed, hadn't he?

An examination of the interrogation transcript was a revelation. There were more than one hundred inconsistencies regarding what Miller said about his dream vision and his accounts of events, and he was incorrect about dozens of details. Also, when the detectives referred to the killer in the third person while describing their hypothetical scenarios, Miller went along with them. When they switched to the second person, substituting "you" for "he," Miller invariably balked and corrected them, saying, "It's not me." The questioning technique was at its shabbiest when detectives tried to elicit an admission that Miller had left a pair of his underwear at the scene. When asked what the killer had left behind, Miller suggested a variety of items including a shoe, a knife, hair, a shirt, "probably a knife" in a second guess, his hat, a ski mask, and gloves, as well as the possibility of underwear. But the detectives kept coming back to the underwear, finally asking at which of the two houses it was left and what brand of underwear it was. Miller replied, "I don't know." That was admission enough for the police.

By 1994, Lee Ann Peters had left the Public Defender's Office, and the new PDs handling Miller's appeal suggested that he take a deal with the DA's Office and accept a sentence of life without parole. Miller, who had been on death row since 1988, declined, and in 1995 the district attorney agreed that a new trial was warranted. The state's case this time would be even less compelling than the first, for little of its evidence was still available. The DNA showed that Miller was not the source of the sperm; the jailhouse snitch had recanted his testimony and disappeared. All that remained was the videotape of Miller's interrogation.

At a hearing to determine whether there were grounds for holding Miller for retrial, Judge Larry Jones made short work of the state's last piece of evidence. "There is nothing in these statements by defendant which would in any way be considered a confession," he said. "I get the impression . . . that Mr. Miller was attempting to tell the detectives what he believed they wanted to hear. And it is evident from the video that the detectives are directing many of the responses."

The issue should have been decided right there, but the DA's Office was not ready to let go. The prosecution appealed to a higher judge who it felt was likely to be of a different mind. Judge Karl Gray, though conceding that the confession was at best weak, ruled that enough of Miller's statements were accurate to justify probable cause. He decided that Miller could be held for retrial.

At this point, a friend of Miller's brother called Barry Scheck at the Cardozo School of Law in New York City. Scheck recommended that they contact an attorney named Garvin Isaacs, who had built a reputation as an attorney for the damned, taking and often winning cases whose prospects had long been abandoned. Isaacs took the case for $1 and went to work immediately. He had Miller given a polygraph test, which he passed. He then filed a series of motions. Early in 1998, all charges against Miller were dropped.

Elliott, who seemed determined to get Miller one way or another, offered Ronald Lott a deal. Lott was already serving a forty-year sentence for the two other rapes, and, given the presence of his semen at the Cutler and Fowler murder scenes, his outlook was not bright. Elliott made Lott an offer he thought Lott could not refuse. If he agreed to implicate Miller, Elliott would take the death penalty off the table and present Lott with the gift of a straight life sentence, which could result in his walking free in thirty to forty years. Lott declined the offer. Elliott now had nowhere else to go. He decided not to retry Miller, and Miller was released on January 22, 1998. Later that year, Elliott was elected a judge in Oklahoma County.

• • •

David Keaton
Florida

David Keaton, an eighteen-year-old star football player with plans to enter the ministry, became famous in his hometown of Quincy, Florida, for events not of his making. He and four others became known as the "Quincy Five," all accused of a murder they did not commit; only Keaton did time on death row before he was exonerated.

The Quincy Five were charged with killing an off-duty deputy sheriff during the holdup of a grocery store in 1971. About four months after the crime, local authorities were ready to file charges against six local black men, although there was no physical evidence linking them to the murder. What kept the Quincy Five from becoming the Quincy Six, however, was the inconvenient discovery that one of the suspects was in jail when the killing took place. One of the remaining five was found incompetent to stand trial, charges against another were dropped, and a third was tried and acquitted. Keaton and a young man by the name of Johnny Frederick were found guilty. Frederick was sentenced to life in prison; Keaton, the alleged trigger man, was sentenced to death.

Although he had an alibi, Keaton was held in custody for more than a week. During that time, he later maintained, he had been threatened, lied to, and beaten until he confessed. He believed that despite the confession, no jury would convict him when they heard his alibi, which placed him elsewhere when the murder was committed; he was wrong. The coerced confession was buttressed by the false testimony of five eyewitnesses, whose identification was prompted by photos they were shown by police. The jury found Keaton guilty.

The case became something of a cause célèbre, with local activist groups proclaiming his innocence, but Keaton remained on death row for two years. On appeal, the state supreme court reversed the conviction when the judge learned that exculpatory evidence had been withheld by the prosecution. A new trial was ordered, but it turned out to be unnecessary. Through an improbable series of events, three other men, all from Jacksonville, were arrested for killing the deputy. The evidence that implicated them included their fingerprints being found at the crime scene. Two of the men confessed and all were convicted. Keaton and Frederick were released in 1973.

Johnny Ross

Louisiana

False confessions from juveniles are commonplace in the criminal justice system. Teenagers rarely are acquainted with their rights, they are generally open to suggestion, and they are easily intimidated. As tough and streetwise as they might be, juveniles also tend to be uncertain and easily led in situations where they are clearly overmatched.

Johnny Ross, a sixteen-year-old black youth from Louisiana, was roused from sleep by police early one morning in 1975 and told he was suspected of having raped a white woman. He was taken to the scene of the crime and then to the station house for questioning. Without an adult being present, he waived his right to an attorney and subjected himself to intense interrogation. When the questioning was concluded, police came away with what they said was a confession. Ross contended that he had signed a blank piece of paper only after being beaten by the police. He was nonetheless charged with rape, which, at the time, was a capital crime in Louisiana.

Ross's trial lasted all of three hours. The prosecution's case consisted of a signed four-page confession and the tentative identification by the victim. No alibi evidence was presented in the defendant's behalf. Ross was convicted and sentenced to death under Louisiana's aggravated rape statute, which precluded consideration of mitigating evidence and made the death penalty mandatory. The conviction was upheld on appeal, but the death sentence was vacated when the U.S. Supreme Court ruled that the mandatory sentencing statute was unconstitutional. The case was remanded with instructions to impose a twenty-year sentence.

The Southern Poverty Law Center intervened in an effort to obtain a new trial. In 1980, tests revealed that the blood type of the sperm found in the victim did not match Ross's. Confronted with the new evidence and a writ of habeas corpus, the New Orleans district attorney agreed to drop the charges and Ross was released a year later.

• • •

Jerry Bigelow

California

Jerry Bigelow and Michael Ramadanovic had escaped from a Canadian jail in 1981 and were on the lam, hitchhiking their way south through California when an unsuspecting driver picked them up in Sacramento. The details of what ensued are muddled, but the driver ended up dead and Bigelow and his companion were arrested for murdering him.

In exchange for immunity from the death penalty, Ramadanovic agreed to testify that Bigelow had shot the victim. To further seal his fate, Bigelow confessed to the crime after he was told that he would receive a lesser punishment in return for his confession; he did not. The two men were tried separately. Ramadanovic pleaded guilty and was given a term of life imprisonment; Bigelow, who acted as his own attorney, was sentenced to death. The California Supreme Court did not think that Bigelow was a competent advocate. In 1983, it overturned his conviction on the grounds of inadequate representation of counsel and ordered a new trial.

At the 1988 retrial, his new attorney maintained that Bigelow had been intoxicated and was asleep in the back of the car when Ramadanovic shot the victim. Testimony was introduced from several witnesses who testified that Ramadanovic had boasted about the killing and told them he had acted alone and that Bigelow knew nothing about it. Evidence also was presented that Bigelow had, in the past, confessed to crimes he had not committed. The jury returned a verdict of not guilty, but the judge found some irregularities in the verdict forms and declared a mistrial. However, the California Court of Appeals ordered the trial court to accept the jury's verdict and Bigelow was exonerated and released.

John Henry Knapp
Arizona

John Henry Knapp was sentenced to death for setting the fire that killed his two young daughters in their Phoenix, Arizona, home in 1973. His first trial ended in a hung jury, but he was convicted when retried. The chief evidence against him was a confession he gave to police eleven days after the fire. He recanted within hours, stating that he was trying to protect his wife, who had fled the state almost immediately after the incident. He said he feared that if his wife were charged with the crime she would take her own life. The primary physical evidence offered by the prosecution was expert testimony that the fire could not have been accidental; it was definitely arson. There also were fingerprints on the gas can that started the fire, but the prosecution said they were smudged and unidentifiable.

More than a decade after the fire, new scientific evidence indicated that it could have been set accidentally, perhaps even by the young girls while playing with matches. It was also learned that other exculpatory information had been kept from the defense, including a tape recording of a phone call Knapp made to his wife moments after his confession in which he told her he was innocent but had confessed in order to protect her. When Knapp asked her to return home, she said, "They'll have to come and get me." In fact, she had been granted immunity but was never called to testify. Also withheld from the jury was the fact that the prints on the can were actually usable and that they belonged to someone other than Knapp. Conceivably, they might have belonged to his wife.

Given the new evidence, a third trial was ordered in 1991; like the first, it resulted in a hung jury. A year later, Knapp pleaded no contest to second-degree murder, was sentenced to time served, which was thirteen years, and was released.

The author of a book about the Knapp case said years later that "the irony is that John Knapp [who at one point had come within three days of execution] was used for years by death penalty advocates as an example of why we should have the death penalty. Now he is a perfect example for people who say we shouldn't have a death penalty."

Part VI

JUNK SCIENCE

A s far back as history can take us, the engines of human striving have been driven by the quest for absolute certainty. Socrates searched for truth and justice in their immutable forms. Aristotle ventured farther afield, seeking the heart of the matter in pursuits as different as drama and biology, poetry, and politics. The scientific method picked up where the frontier of philosophy ended. The laboratory became the temple in which those of serious mind bent a knee to worship. Each new advance brought us closer to a truth that could not be questioned, and that after all was the goal. Certainty, as difficult to apprehend as the Holy Grail, would free us from error and doubt and make us secure in our belief that truth was the coin of our noblest endeavors.

It took a while before we discovered that science was a fickle accomplice. Today's truth was at best tomorrow's probability. Scientific certainty was as fragile as any other. It seemed that the more we learned, the less we could be sure of, for each new discovery put in question all that preceded it. Every Ptolemy would be succeeded by a Galileo; for every true believer, a Darwin was waiting in the wings. Truth depended, finally, on the prism through which it was viewed. When what once passed for scientific certainty is eclipsed by new findings, it is disparagingly referred to as junk science.

In the courtroom, the introduction of scientific evidence is replete with hazards. There is always the question of whether the jurors—and in some instances even the judge—are able to comprehend it, and the more formidable question of how seriously that theory's application is treated by the forensic community. In recent years, the testimony of handwriting analysts has been called into doubt, and even more critically, the infallibility of fingerprint identification, once considered the very soul of absolute certainty, has become suspect.

In a 1993 case dealing with handwriting analysis, *Daubert v. Merrell Dow Pharmaceuticals,* the Supreme Court ruled that judges may exercise their own discretion in deciding whether to admit expert testimony regardless of their personal knowledge in that field. Judges in two subsequent cases took opposite views on the matter of handwriting analysis. One decided that it was not sufficiently scientific to be admissible. The other, citing a recent study, noted that the relatively new use of computer programs invested the technique with 98 percent accuracy.

Until the advent of DNA technology, fingerprints had long been considered the surest route to forensic certainty. The Chinese were said to have used thumbprints as a means of identification more than two thousand years ago, but the father of modern fingerprint technology was Sir William J. Herschel, a British government official in Bengal, India. Herschel's system, devised principally as a means of preventing impersonation, was in popular use by 1858. Sir Francis Galton founded the present system about thirty years later, and Juan Vucetich, of Argentina, applied it to criminal investigations for the first time in 1891.

The core of fingerprint analysis is the belief that no two individuals have the same set of prints. Of course that is a premise based on scientific projection. Not every set of prints has been compared with every other, but the sheer volume of instances in which the principle has held true without contradiction has wrapped fingerprint identification in a cloak of infallibility. Recently, however, it has come under closer scrutiny. In criminal investigations, the critical question is not whether two sets of prints can be exactly alike, but whether they can be similar enough to fool an analyst. There have been numerous cases in which fingerprints have been misidentified. Prints taken at a crime scene, for example, are often smudged or too indistinct to be identified with absolute certainty. The FBI's computerized fingerprint identification system is said to be more than 99 percent accurate, but when it is unable to tell the difference between two sets of prints, human analysts make the determination, and their conclusions often differ.

All the same, fingerprint analysis is still far more reliable than other forms of "junk science" evidence. Suspects have been wrongly convicted on the basis of faulty ballistics technology, inaccurate medical diagnoses, and testimony induced under hypnosis. Even DNA technology, now considered as close to infallible as one might ever hope, is subject to human error. If the test is not made with proper controls, it can lead to the conviction of the wrong man.

• • •

Robert Hayes
Florida

Largely on the basis of a sloppy DNA test, Robert Hayes was convicted of rape and murder and sentenced to death in 1991 in Broward County, Florida. Hayes, a groom at the Pompano harness track, was charged with sexually assaulting and strangling a coworker, Pamela Albertson.

In addition to the DNA evidence, matching Hayes with semen found on the victim's shirt, the prosecution introduced testimony from a witness who claimed to have seen Hayes with Albertson and heard her reject his advances shortly before the murder took place. However, Albertson, a thirty-two-year-old white woman, was found dead clutching several strands of sixteen-inch-long reddish-blond hair, apparently pulled from her attacker's head during the course of a struggle. That should have cast doubt on Hayes's status as a suspect because Hayes was a black man. In addition, it was common knowledge at the racetrack that Albertson was being pursued by another worker at the track who was heard making racist comments about her dating black men. The man had long, reddish-blond hair. Nonetheless, the jury found Hayes guilty.

He had been on death row four years when Barbara Heyer, an attorney in Fort Lauderdale, read about the case in the newspaper and agreed to represent Hayes pro bono. She succeeded in persuading the Florida Supreme Court to reverse the conviction. The court ordered a new trial, ruling that the band-shifting technique used to identify the DNA had failed to reach the level of scientific acceptance. In remanding the case, the court noted that "the record contains evidence suggesting that Hayes committed the homicide," but it "also contains objective physical evidence suggesting that someone other than Hayes was responsible."

New DNA testing, performed with proper controls, established that there was no match with Hayes's. At the retrial in 1997, evidence also emerged indicating that another man, who had since been convicted of rape in an unrelated case, might have been responsible for Albertson's murder. Hayes was acquitted.

He left prison with a pair of socks and sneakers in a plastic bag but no money. His lawyer bought him a bus ticket to his hometown of Canton, Mississippi, where he moved in with his grandmother. The racing commission denied him a license to work at a racetrack due to his felony conviction. Eventually, the town hired him to drive dump trucks and clean sewers. He continues to indulge his love of horses by caring for them at an amusement park owned by his uncle. He recently married Georgia Brown, a nursing-home worker.

"I'm trying to build my life back up," Hayes said in a recent interview, but he continues to have nightmares. "I might get thirty minutes sleep every hour, every night," he said. "I don't know who's gonna come down the hallway."

Randall Padgett
Alabama

The case against Randall Padgett seemed to be as solid as they get. The DNA in the semen and blood samples taken from the victim matched his, proving beyond a doubt, the prosecution maintained, that Padgett had raped and stabbed to death his estranged wife in a brutal attack in Alabama in 1990.

As it developed, however, the state's case was plagued with uncertainties from the very beginning. The expert witness for the defense disagreed with the testimony of the prosecution's DNA expert, testifying that there was not a perfect match. Late in the trial, the prosecution acknowledged that there were serious questions about the integrity of the tests. It was not even certain that the blood sample used for comparison with blood found at the scene actually belonged to Padgett. Despite the more-than-reasonable doubt raised by the defense, the jury found Padgett guilty and recommended a life sentence. The judge, apparently more firmly convinced than the jury, overrode the recommendation and sentenced Padgett to death.

The Alabama Court of Criminal Appeals wasted little time in reversing the verdict when it learned that the FBI crime lab had determined that the blood samples were not Padgett's and that the prosecution had suppressed those findings. There also was evidence presented that the crime might have been committed by another woman. Padgett was released in October 1997 after facing death in Alabama's electric chair for more than five years.

Reflecting on his trial some time later, Padgett said, "I think the jurors saw it as the righteous state of Alabama against the evil Randall Padgett." He said he felt as if the whole world was amassed against him. He was gratified, however, that he had been with his children on the night of the murder so they "never had any questions that their daddy hurt their mama."

Padgett had to sell his house to pay his legal bills, and at age forty-eight he moved in with his mother while working as a chicken farmer in Arab, Alabama. Noting that he was the seventy-fifth prisoner to be freed from death row since 1973, Padgett said, "If there's seventy-five people on death row who have gotten exonerated, I've got to believe there's a lot more that haven't gotten that chance."

Gregory Wilhoit
Oklahoma

Gregory Wilhoit's ordeal began in 1985 when his estranged wife, Kathryn, was found dead in her bed by neighbors who responded to the cries of her two infant daughters. She had been beaten and strangled while she slept. Wilhoit, an ironworker who recently had separated from Kathryn, was the likely suspect. He had no alibi for that night, but the authorities had little evidence. What they did have was a bite mark on the victim's body and a sympathetic Oklahoma jury.

Two dentists—expert witnesses for the prosecution—testified that the bite marks matched the configuration of Wilhoit's teeth. They also said there was a rare type of bacteria around the bite mark that also could be traced to Wilhoit. Despite the flimsiness of the state's case, Wilhoit was poorly armed to mount a strong defense. He was represented by a defense attorney who had suffered brain damage in a serious accident a year earlier and at the time of the trial apparently addicted to alcohol and prescription drugs. He had taken the case just three weeks before the start of the trial and never interviewed dental experts who could have rebutted the testimony of the prosecution's witnesses. After a two-week trial in 1987, Wilhoit was found guilty, and the jury recommended the death penalty.

Wilhoit took residence on death row in the state penitentiary in McAlester, Oklahoma. "I thought my life was over, literally over," he said later. But it wasn't. His neighbor across the cellblock was Ron Williamson [Part I—DNA], and the two men, each convinced of the other's innocence, struck up a friendship that helped them both find freedom.

Wilhoit was represented on appeal by Mark Barrett, a public defender who believed his client had been the casualty of ineffective counsel. Barrett fought for years to have the bite marks retested. He found eleven forensic dental specialists who were ready to testify that the bite marks on the victim were not left by Wilhoit. The experts also agreed that the bacteria the prosecution had characterized as rare actually was quite common.

The Oklahoma Court of Criminal Appeals found that Wilhoit had been deprived of competent counsel at trial, vacated the conviction, and ordered a new trial. With no evidence worth noting, the state retried the case in 1993, again contending that Wilhoit had brutally murdered his wife. The judge stopped the trial halfway through, declaring that the prosecution had no case, and set Wilhoit free.

● ● ●

Anthony Ray Peek
Florida

Anthony Ray Peek was only twenty years old in 1977, and life was headed downhill, fast. A drifter from New York, he was serving probation on a burglary charge in a halfway house in Winter Haven, Florida, when he was convicted of rape, for which he would be sentenced to twenty years to life. Even before he could start serving that sentence, he was found guilty of first-degree murder for beating and strangling Erma Carlson, a sixty-five-year-old nurse, in her nearby Winter Haven home in 1977. For that crime, he was sentenced to die in Florida's electric chair.

The critical evidence against Peek was two of his fingerprints found inside the victim's car parked outside the house. There also was a "Negroid" hair recovered in a torn stocking inside the dead woman's home. Peek testified that he never left the halfway house on the night of the murder; several witnesses corroborated his statement. The defense noted that periodic night checks at the halfway house indicated no unauthorized absences. As for the car, Peek said he came upon it the day after the murder, saw that the door was unlocked, and opened it. He looked through the glove compartment, found nothing of value, and left.

The conviction was affirmed by the state supreme court, but in 1983 Polk Circuit Court Judge John Dewell overturned the verdict and ordered a new trial because it was discovered that the state's hair analyst had testified incorrectly that the hair found at the scene belonged to Peek. In 1984, Peek was retried and again convicted during a trial in which the judge referred to Peek's family as "niggers." Once more, he was sentenced to death. The second conviction was vacated in 1985 because the judge had allowed testimony to be introduced regarding Peek's earlier rape conviction. Peek was acquitted in a third trial in 1987, ending his ten-year stint on death row.

He remains at Everglades Correctional Institution, where he sweeps the prison grounds while serving out his sentence on the rape conviction. The parole board recently extended Peek's release date by five years, to 2010. He says that his time on death row has taught him that he can handle anything. Pointing to a garbage bin in the prison visiting area, he said, "If you put a human being in there, he's gonna find a way to survive."

Dale Johnston
Ohio

Hypnosis has been used in many criminal cases to refresh the memory of witnesses and perhaps lead investigators to a likely suspect. Its status as a scientific tool, however, has been called to question, and there are serious doubts about its validity as courtroom testimony. For every physician or psychiatrist who is professionally trained to hypnotize patients as part of their therapy, there are many amateur practitioners who perform hypnosis for purposes of entertainment. When employed by an untrained person, hypnosis provides a frail foundation on which to build a criminal prosecution.

Dale Johnston was convicted of a double murder in Logan, Ohio, in 1984, chiefly on the testimony of a witness who had made his identification after being hypnotized by a person who lacked professional credentials. Johnston was convicted and

JUNK SCIENCE

sentenced to death for killing his stepdaughter and her fiancé, allegedly to keep them from blackmailing him with accusations of engaging in incestuous relations with his stepdaughter. The victim had complained publicly of Johnston's making such advances in the past.

The prosecution contended that Johnston had shot the couple in his home and dumped their bodies in a cornfield eleven miles away, where they were subsequently discovered. The state's key witness said he saw a man angrily order a couple into his car on a street in the town of Logan around the time of the murders. Placed under hypnosis nineteen days after the victims' bodies were found, the witness identified Johnston from a photograph in a newspaper and made the same identification at trial. Another witness, an anthropologist from North Carolina, testified that a boot print found near the bodies belonged to Johnston. The prosecution offered some physical evidence as well. Feedbags consistent with those found on Johnston's farm were found at the burial site of the victims, and some bloodstained items were seized from a strip-mining pit on the defendant's property.

The Ohio Court of Appeals vacated Johnston's conviction because the "hypnotically induced testimony was admitted without even minimal demonstration of its reliability." While awaiting retrial, defense attorneys found four witnesses who had seen the mother and daughter walking along railroad tracks near the cornfield and then heard gunshots. If these witnesses were correct, the pair seen by the prosecution's witness being forced into a car in Logan could not have been the victims. The defense also could demonstrate that Johnston was at home when the gunshots were heard. For added measure, it was revealed that the prosecution was aware of the four witnesses prior to trial but had chosen to withhold that information from the defense. The state dropped all charges against Johnston, and he was released in 1990.

Adolph Munson
Oklahoma

When a convenience-store clerk was kidnapped and murdered in Custer County, Oklahoma, in 1984, Adolph Munson no doubt seemed a likely candidate for a quick arrest. He was on work release at the time, having just served a sentence for a 1964 murder.

The most important physical evidence pointing to Munson were a .22-caliber bullet that police said they found in his motel room, presumably consistent with the weapon used in the murder; one of the victim's earrings, also recovered from his room; and a single strand of hair found in the car he was driving. A witness placed a car similar to Munson's near the store at about the time the kidnapping took place. To further bolster its case, the prosecution secured the help of a jailhouse informant who was ready to testify that Munson told him he had gone to "some little town," kidnapped a woman from a convenience store, killed her, and dumped her body in a wooded area.

The physical evidence appeared at best to be questionable, and the defense requested funds for an investigation. The request was denied, the evidence was presented with little convincing rebuttal, and Munson was convicted and sentenced to death. Both the conviction and the sentence were affirmed by the Oklahoma courts, and the U.S. Supreme Court declined to review the case.

Nine years of appeals and an investigation report by the American Bar Association established clearly that the state's entire case had been fabricated. As it turned out, the victim had not been killed by a .22-caliber bullet, and the strand of hair could not be proven to be hers. The pathologist who provided much of the forensic testimony, Dr. Ralph Erdmann, was subsequently convicted of seven felony counts involving fabrication of evidence and misrepresentation of facts in other cases, and his license was revoked. A number of witnesses contradicted a police officer's testimony that the earring was found in Munson's motel room, and the jailhouse snitch was dismissed as having lied when he denied offering his testimony as part of a deal with the state; the prosecutor had written a letter in his behalf to the pardon and parole board.

Perhaps most significant, investigators uncovered hundreds of exculpatory documents and photographs that had been withheld by the prosecution. Several witnesses said they had seen two white men (Munson is black) at the store when the clerk was abducted; one said she actually had seen these men carry the victim away in a truck. Another positively identified a white man who was known to have previously abducted convenience store clerks. Also withheld were photographs of tire tracks at the murder scene that did not match the tires on the car Munson was driving.

The Oklahoma Court of Criminal Appeals upheld the trial

court's decision to hold a new trial, and Munson was acquitted in April 1995.

Sabrina Butler
Mississippi

A flawed autopsy performed on her infant son, Walter, was largely responsible for sending Sabrina Butler to death row in Mississippi in 1990 for murdering the nine-month-old child. Butler, only eighteen years old at the time and borderline mentally retarded, had discovered the child was not breathing and tried unsuccessfully to resuscitate him by employing CPR before rushing the boy to a hospital emergency room. He was pronounced dead on arrival.

Butler gave the police several conflicting accounts of the events leading up to the child's death, and she was arrested the following morning. The charge was capital murder because the alleged homicide took place during the commission of another felony, child abuse. Following an autopsy, the prosecution contended that the cause of death was a blow to the stomach. The defense countered that the child's injuries were incurred while Butler, unskilled in CPR, tried to restore his breathing. Butler's attorneys provided little evidence to support their position, and apparently no account was taken of the possibility that the mother's mental condition might have been responsible for the disjointed story she told the police. A local newspaper described one of her lawyers as an "incompetent drunk."

The prosecutor was not a model of competency either. In his

closing argument, he told the jury it could infer guilt because Butler had not testified in her own defense. On those grounds, the Mississippi Supreme Court vacated the conviction and sentence and remanded the case for retrial. Butler was tried again in 1995, represented by an attorney who specialized in death-penalty cases. At the new trial, a neighbor of Butler's who had helped her try to revive the boy verified the defendant's story. The physician who performed the autopsy admitted that his work had been inadequate, and it was now believed that death was caused by either cystic kidney disease or sudden infant death syndrome (SIDS). The jury deliberated briefly before finding Butler not guilty on all charges. She was freed shortly before Christmas 1995.

Michael Linder
South Carolina

There was never any doubt that Michael Linder shot a highway patrol officer to death during a skirmish in 1979. The question that the South Carolina jury had to answer was whether Linder had fired back in self-defense. The prosecution maintained he had killed the officer without provocation, and expert witnesses testified that the officer's gun had never been fired. Linder insisted that he had shot the officer only after six shots had been fired at him. The jury voted with the prosecution. Linder was convicted and sentenced to death.

The conviction was thrown out because of trial error, and Linder was granted a new trial in 1981. He was represented this time by an experienced lawyer who uncovered conclusive evidence that the officer had in fact fired at the defendant. The defense also demonstrated that other evidence presented by the state had been distorted to make it appear that Linder had been the aggressor. This time, the jury voted to acquit. At the conclusion of the trial, one of the defense lawyers said, "If anyone thinks that our court system is not capable of actually executing an innocent person, they should look at this case."

Part VII

REASONABLE DOUBT

The concept of reasonable doubt is the linchpin of America's criminal justice system. It is the federal standard, and the standard of almost every state, the degree of certainty jurors must feel before finding a defendant guilty. Yet it is an inexact measure, for the phrase is pliant enough to fit almost any definition. As a consequence, its application varies wildly from state to state, jurisdiction to jurisdiction, and even from jury to jury. What is reasonable to one person often has little merit for the next.

The concept becomes a bit clearer if it is contrasted with the standard used to determine civil, rather than criminal, cases. In a civil suit, in which one party—the plaintiff—files a claim against another—the defendant—the case is decided on the basis of preponderance of evidence: which side seems to have presented the more credible argument. Tightening the focus to reasonable doubt in criminal cases is significant because it invests the defendant with the presumption of innocence. The state is obliged to prove to the jury that the defendant is guilty to the extent that a reasonable person could have no doubt about the verdict. The state bears the burden of proof. The defense is required only to create a doubt, often by introducing a plausibly alternative scenario, that the defendant committed the crime.

It is the specter of doubt that often prompts the police or prosecution to fabricate additional evidence even when their case appears to be sound. An article of clothing is planted at the scene, an eyewitness is persuaded that he saw more than he did, a felon doing time is offered a reduced sentence if he remembers hearing the defendant admit to the crime. The authorities are not, in many instances, trying to convict an innocent man, but attempting to make certain that a guilty one does not walk free. There are other instances, however, in which the prosecution seems determined to press its case with virtually no evidence at all. It appears to be hoping that the jury will be ready to convict on the basis of reasonable suspicion rather than doubt. A number of such cases have resulted in innocent people being sentenced to death, only to have their convictions overturned years later for lack of credible evidence. They have, in effect, been forced to serve hard time in isolated death-row cells because reasonable doubt was not applied in a reasonable manner. Of course it is equally true that the application of reasonable doubt has resulted in some guilty people being freed because the evidence against them was insufficient to sustain a conviction.

●　●　●

Anibal Jaramillo

Florida

A number of states—Florida is one—apply a standard that is even more stringent than reasonable doubt. It is called "sufficiency of evidence," and it requires the prosecution to eliminate every hypothesis other than guilt if it is to get a conviction. The necessary degree of certainty is elevated, since the jury must construe from the evidence that there are no possibilities other than the guilt of the defendant. Anibal Jaramillo was, in all likelihood, a beneficiary of this standard.

Jaramillo was convicted of a double murder in 1981 that had all the earmarks of a gangland execution. Gilberto Caicedo and Candellario Castellanos were found dead in their town house in southwest Dade County. They were tied up with cord and each was shot several times in the head. Jaramillo, an illegal Columbian immigrant, came under immediate suspicion. The authorities had information suggesting he had been a hitman in Colombia, and his fingerprints were found all over the murder scene—on a knife casing, a nearby table, and a grocery bag. The murder weapon, a machine gun equipped with a silencer, was never found.

Jaramillo had a reasonable explanation for his fingerprints being where they were. He said he was helping the victims' nephew stack cardboard boxes in the garage the day before the murder. He asked for a knife to cut the boxes, and the nephew told him he could find one inside a grocery bag on the dining room table. Jaramillo said he went inside, fetched the knife from the bag, and returned to the garage. He later put the knife back on the table where it was found after the murder. The victims' nephew, who could have corroborated Jaramillo's account, could not be located for the trial.

Confronted with a plausible explanation for the fingerprints, the prosecution tried to buttress its case with witnesses who, under cross-examination, further subverted the state's evidence. One prosecution witness admitted he had seen one of the victims' roommates, looking anxious, less than a mile from the scene shortly after the crime. Another witness said that she and her husband had driven the same man to the victims' town house a short while later. The roommate appeared to be a viable suspect, but no charges were ever brought against him. Despite the fact that the state's case had unraveled completely, the jury found Jaramillo guilty but unanimously recommended life in prison. Judge Ellen Morphonios-Gable overruled the jury and sentenced him to death.

Jaramillo spent only a year on death row. On appeal, the Florida Supreme Court made short work of the conviction, finding that the circumstantial evidence presented was "not legally sufficient to establish a prima facie case" against the defendant. "The proof," the court said, "was not inconsistent with Jaramillo's reasonable explanation as to how his fingerprints came to be on the items at the victims' home."

It is entirely possible that Jaramillo might have been found guilty in federal court or in a state court where reasonable doubt was the prevailing standard of proof. Under Florida law, however, Jaramillo's account of events could not be eliminated, and he was therefore turned loose, but not for long. The day he walked out of prison he was arrested by the Bureau of Alcohol, Tobacco and Firearms for lying on a government form when he bought a .45-caliber pistol from a gun shop in 1980. In 1983, a federal judge sentenced him to four years in prison. Jaramillo subsequently was deported to Colombia, where he was murdered in Medellin, probably in a confrontation involving drugs.

Robert Cox
Florida

Robert Cox also found salvage in Florida's rigorous "sufficiency of evidence" requirement. A onetime army ranger, Cox became an immediate suspect in the beating death of Sharon Zellers, a nineteen-year-old clerk at Disney World in Orlando, Florida, in 1978. He and his family were staying at the same motel where the victim's body was found, and on the day after the murder Cox required surgical treatment for a wound on his tongue that appeared to have been bitten badly during a struggle. Police checked further and found that Cox's blood type, O-positive, was the same as the young woman's and that a boot print at the crime scene was consistent with a military boot that Cox might have been wearing.

But the connections were not sufficiently convincing. Cox maintained that his tongue had been injured in a bar fight on the night of the murder. O-positive blood is a type shared by almost half the population, and the boot print could not be directly matched to any that Cox owned. In addition, he and the victim had never been seen together, there was no reason to believe they had ever met, and so there was no apparent motive. The case was deemed too weak to make an arrest.

Eight years later, in 1986, Cox was arrested and convicted of kidnapping and assault in California. Some of the circumstances of that crime seemed similar enough for Florida authorities to charge him in the murder of Sharon Zellers. Although there was no evidence beyond that which had been obtained in 1978, Cox was found guilty and sentenced to death.

His stay on death row lasted just one year. On appeal, the Florida Supreme Court, in a per curiam decision (a decision on behalf of the whole court rather than a single judge), ruled that the evidence offered, at best, "only a suspicion" of guilt. The court vacated the conviction and ordered the trial court to acquit Cox on all charges and release him.

Cox's freedom, however, was short-lived. He was promptly taken into custody and returned to California to complete his sentence on the kidnapping charge. Things did not get any better when he completed his term. Soon after returning to his boyhood home in Springfield, Missouri, he came under suspicion in the disappearance of a mother and two teenage girls. In Texas, police in Plano wanted him for questioning in yet another kidnapping. Cox was not charged in either of those cases, but in 1995 he was arrested for holding a gun on a twelve-year-old girl during a robbery in Decatur, Texas. He was convicted in that case and sentenced to life for armed robbery. He is not eligible for parole until 2025.

Jimmy Lee Mathers
Arizona

Rarely has someone been sent to death row on as little evidence as the state produced against Jimmy Lee Mathers. Even the judge who eventually vacated Mathers's conviction seemed at a loss trying to understand why he had been tried at all. Mathers had gotten himself involved with two other men—Teddy Washington and Fred Robinson—and there was trouble on the horizon. Robinson was in a volatile relationship with his common-law wife, Susan Hill. She had left him more than once, and Mathers had sometimes accompanied him on trips to retrieve her. On several occasions, Robinson had threatened to kill her if she didn't return.

In 1986, while all the principals were living in Banning, a small town in Southern California, Susan took off and went to stay with her sister in Hollywood. Robinson brought her back after a violent episode in which her sister and niece were tied up and Susan's life was threatened. A few weeks later, she persuaded Robinson to let her visit her father and stepmother— Ralph and Sterleen Hill—in Yuma, Arizona. The Hills and Susan's teenage stepbrother, LeSean, were aware of the threats and abuse to which Susan had been subjected, and they obtained a peace bond—the equivalent of a court injunction—prohibiting Robinson from entering their home. Susan informed Robinson of the order. She also extended her stay from a week to a month and then went to see her grandmother in California without telling him.

On June 8, 1987, Robinson's son, Andre, heard his father, Mathers, and Washington—who was wearing a red bandana— discussing a trip to Arizona. Mathers said he was going to "take care of some business." Late that afternoon, the boy said he saw the elder Robinson and Mathers putting guns into Robinson's car and driving toward Washington's house in a tan Chevette. Just before midnight that same day, there was a knock at the door of the Hills' home in Yuma. When LeSean answered, he saw a man there. The man tried to grab the boy, but he fled through the house and out another door. Ralph and Sterleen came out of their bedroom and heard a man, in a deep voice, say, "We're narcotics agents. We want the dope and the money." The Hills were herded back into their room, forced to lie facedown on the floor, and tied up. Ralph later recalled that before blacking out he saw the intruders, one wearing a red bandana, ransack the bedroom cupboards and drawers.

LeSean, in the meantime, had gone to a neighbor's house and telephoned the police. He told them he saw a tan Chevette speeding away from the scene. The police overtook the car and found Robinson behind the wheel. They also found a shotgun shell box, a red bandana, and some of Mathers's clothing. When police went to the Hills' home, they discovered that Ralph and Sterleen had been shot with a twelve-gauge shotgun. Ralph was badly injured and would lose an eye, but he survived. Sterleen was dead.

A shotgun found near the scene was later identified by Andre Robinson as the one he had seen being put in the back of his father's car earlier that day. Robinson was arrested that evening. Mathers was picked up the following day in Coachella, California, and returned to Arizona. A day later, Washington was taken into custody at his Banning home.

The three men were tried together for first-degree murder in 1987. At the close of the prosecution's case, Mathers's attorney moved for a judgment of acquittal on the grounds that the state had not presented sufficient evidence to support a conviction. The motion was denied. All three were found guilty of murder, attempted murder, aggravated assault, burglary, and armed robbery. For reasons not easily construed, the state maintained that Mathers had fired the shots. All three were sentenced to death.

In 1990, the Arizona Supreme Court reviewed Mathers's case and, "viewing the evidence in the light most favorable to the prosecution," found a "complete absence of probative facts" to support a conviction. The court held that the evidence presented at trial had "nothing to do with Mathers" and noted that even the trial judge had expressed doubt as to whether he had anything at all to do with the crime. The court set aside Mathers's conviction and sentence and entered a judgment of acquittal. Washington and Robinson remained on death row.

John C. Skelton
Texas

The case of John C. Skelton is red meat for those who are more concerned that the guilty might walk free than that innocent men might be executed. When the Texas Court of Criminal Appeals reversed Skelton's capital murder conviction in a two-to-one split decision, the majority said: "Although the evidence against appellant leads to a strong suspicion or probability that appellant committed the capital offense, we cannot say that it excludes to a moral certainty every other reasonable hypothesis except appellant's guilt."

Skelton had been sentenced to death in 1982 for killing a

former employee, Joe Neal, by placing a bomb underneath his pickup truck. As there was no forensic evidence linking Skelton to the crime, the prosecution's case was purely circumstantial, built largely on motive. The state showed that there was bad blood between the men, that Skelton had reason to want Neal killed, had made various threats against him, and had access to the general type of materials that were used in making the bomb. The defense produced several witnesses who testified that Skelton was eight hundred miles from the scene when the bomb exploded. However, such testimony was not what might have passed for an airtight alibi, since the manner in which the victim was killed did not require the presence of the killer.

All the same, while expressing its regret, the appeals court, in its 1992 ruling, found that the prosecution had not offered sufficient evidence to establish guilt. "Although this court does not relish the thought of reversing the conviction in this heinous case and ordering an acquittal, because the evidence does not exclude every other reasonable hypothesis, we are compelled to do so."

That is as good an explanation of reasonable doubt as one is likely to come by. The question of whether Skelton was innocent is not the same as asking whether he committed the crime. The first is strictly a legal matter, as a presumption of innocence is accorded every suspect until the state can prove his guilt beyond reasonable doubt. Actual innocence, as opposed to legal innocence, is not the province of the criminal justice system; it is decided in a higher court.

• • •

Andrew Golden
Florida

The conviction of Andrew Golden also was based solely on motive and overturned because of insufficient evidence and reasonable doubt. Golden, a high-school teacher, was sentenced to death for drowning his wife, Ardelle, in a lake near their home in Winter Haven, Florida, in 1989. Her body was found floating near a boat dock just a few feet from a partially submerged Pontiac Grand Am that her husband had rented. The prosecution contended that Golden pushed his wife off the boat dock and then drove the car into the lake to make the drowning appear to be accidental. But the medical examiner, finding no signs of foul play, had no alternative other than to rule the death an accident.

The state went to trial in 1991 with the flimsiest of cases. It presented no physical evidence, no eyewitness testimony, no confession, and nothing to indicate that Ardelle was the victim of murder by her husband or anyone else. The prosecution showed only that Golden had debts of more than $200,000 and that he stood to profit from more than $350,000 in life insurance policies he had taken out on his wife a year earlier. Golden's attorney presented no defense, offering no alternative to the prosecution's scenario.

Two years later, after the police investigator acknowledged that there was no evidence of murder, the Florida Supreme Court ruled unanimously that the prosecution had "failed to show beyond a reasonable doubt that Mrs. Golden's death resulted from the criminal agency of another person rather than from an accident." The court added that "a reasonable juror could conclude that he [Golden] more likely than not caused his wife's death." But it was equally reasonable to presume that Mrs. Golden might have driven the car into the lake at night from the unmarked, unlit boat dock. Consequently, the court vacated the conviction and ordered Golden to be released from death row.

When he left prison on January 6, 1994, Golden was met by his two sons. He lived for a while with his elder son and then moved to Texas where his life began to come apart. In 1996, he was arrested for molesting two girls, ages eight and nine. He later pleaded guilty to a new charge of engaging in indecent behavior with a child and was sentenced to a fifteen-year prison term. His attorney, John Giofreddi, said that the death of his wife, coupled with the trauma of spending two years on death row, contributed to his transformation into a "regressed pedophile."

Gary Drinkard
Alabama

The exoneration of Gary Drinkard after he had spent five years on death row in Alabama is a graphic illustration of how the presumption of innocence can become twisted to the point where the defendant is presumed guilty until he can prove he is innocent beyond a reasonable doubt.

Drinkard was convicted and sentenced to death for the robbery-slaying of Dalton Pace, an auto junk dealer in Decatur, Alabama, on August 18, 1993. He was alleged to have come away with $2,200 for his effort. The problem for the state was that there was no evidence connecting Drinkard to the crime—nothing that could place him at the scene, no sign that he had experienced a financial wind-fall. In fact, even a cursory look at the facts of the case would seem to exclude Drinkard as a suspect.

Thirty-seven years old at the time of the murder, Drinkard earned his living as a carpenter and was suffering from a severe back injury that made it difficult for him to continue practicing his trade. He was taking courses at a community college in search of a new vocation. On the day of the crime he had visited an orthopedic surgeon to discuss an operation. He was taking medication for the pain in his back, and he had been at home, in the company of others, on the night of the murder.

The prosecution's case rested on the testimony of several wit-nesses whose credibility was at best suspect, principally Drinkard's adopted daughter, Kelly Drinkard Harvell, and his half sister, Beverly Segars. Harvell, who stated originally that her father was at home when police said Pace was killed, changed her testimony to say he was not at home for the entire evening. Segars helped police build a case against Drinkard. She allowed herself to be wired with a tape-recording device and got Drinkard to discuss the murder. The recording was garbled, and the authorities tried to enhance its clarity, but the statements remained fragmented and difficult to comprehend. On the wit-ness stand, Segars said the defendant told her he didn't realize how big Pace was until he grabbed hold of him. Her common-law husband, Rex Segars, testified that Drinkard told him he killed Pace and made off with about $2,200.

Drinkard was represented by two court-appointed lawyers, one who specialized in collections and commercial work, and the other a recent law-school graduate who represented creditors in foreclosures and bankruptcy cases. Among the witnesses they failed to call for the defense was either of two doctors who would have told the jury that Drinkard's back injury made it physically impossible for him to have committed the crime, since it involved a physical struggle with a man of some size. There was also an elderly man who had visited the Drinkard's home with a friend that night and saw that Drinkard's pain was so severe he was barely able to move.

On appeal, the Alabama Supreme Court overturned Drinkard's conviction in 2000, and a team of lawyers and investigators from Alabama and the Southern Center for Human Rights in Atlanta spent hundreds of hours preparing his case for retrial. They learned that Harvell might have had a motive to change her testimony to suit the prosecution. A couple who managed a motel in Panama City, Florida, testified that Harvell had stolen some money when she worked for them, and Harvell admitted there were charges of grand theft and possession of a controlled substance pending against her in Florida. Beverly Segars's son, Robert Lambert, testified that his mother was known to play fast and loose with the truth and that he would not believe what she had to say, even under oath. Finally, two new witnesses, Willodene Brock and Thomas Carter, testified that they were at Drinkard's home on the night in question. Brock said she had gone there to help Harvell deliver her dog's puppies, and they did not leave until around ten o'clock. The murder was believed to have occurred at eight. Drinkard, they both said, had been there the whole time.

Drinkard was acquitted and released. He had spent seven years in prison, five of them on death row.

Samuel Poole

North Carolina

Samuel Poole was the second prisoner (David Keaton was first by a year) to be freed from death row after the Supreme Court's 1972 *Furman v. Georgia* decision restricting the use of the death penalty. Poole was sentenced to die in North Carolina after being convicted of breaking and entering with the intent to commit rape. The prosecution's case hinged on a button found in the victim's home that generally matched a button missing on Poole's shirt. The only other shreds of evidence were the fact that Poole owned the type of gun the victim saw and that he had been seen in the vicinity of the crime on the same day.

The case was flawed in more than one respect. In addition to the lack of evidence presented against Poole, he was convicted under a defunct mandatory sentencing law that precluded consideration of mitigating evidence. The North Carolina Supreme Court overturned the conviction in 1974 on the grounds that the evidence was insufficient to sustain the verdict. Three years later, in *Coker v. Georgia,* the U.S. Supreme Court declared the mandatory death penalty for rape to violate the Constitution's Eighth Amendment prohibition against cruel and unusual punishment.

Jonathan Treadway

Arizona

In Jonathan Treadway's case, there was not even a button to connect him to the crime. Treadway was convicted in 1975 for sodomy and first-degree murder in the death of a six-year-old boy in Arizona. What the state had was a set of palm prints on the outside window of the victim's house that presumably matched the defendant's. Treadway admitted he had looked in some windows on the night of the boy's death but denied he had ever entered the house or touched the boy.

The Arizona Supreme Court granted Treadway a new trial based on the incompetence of his counsel and because evidence of a prior crime by the defendant had been improperly admitted in court. At the retrial, five pathologists testified that there was no evidence that the victim had been sodomized or that he had died of anything but natural causes, probably pneumonia. The jury acquitted Treadway of all charges, noting that the state had not presented sufficient evidence to believe that Treadway had ever seen the inside of the victim's house.

Vernon McManus
Texas

Vernon McManus was sentenced to death in Texas in 1977 for murdering his in-laws with the assistance of his estranged wife. The most critical testimony offered against him was provided by McManus's ex-wife who, not surprisingly, received a life sentence after testifying against him. Complicating matters further, McManus's attorney was romantically involved throughout the trial with the prosecution's star witness, the defendant's former wife.

After spending more than ten years on death row, McManus was granted habeas corpus relief, and his conviction was reversed because of improprieties involving the selection of the jury. A new trial was ordered in 1988, but what little evidence the prosecution had during the first trial had by then evaporated. The state chose not to retry the case, all charges against McManus were dropped, and he was released from prison in 1988.

Robert Wallace
Georgia

Robert Wallace was sentenced to death for fatally shooting a police officer in Georgia in 1980. The fact that Wallace had shot the policeman was not in dispute. The point of contention was whether the shooting was intentional or, as Wallace contended, accidental. The prosecution argued that Wallace was intoxicated and had gotten involved in a scuffle over a gun with a police officer. At some point, Wallace gained possession of the gun and used it to shoot another cop who was on the scene. Wallace offered a different version of events. He said he was being beaten by the policemen and that during the course of the scuffle the police officer was accidentally shot.

Although there appeared to be more than reasonable doubt regarding Wallace's guilt, the jury returned a verdict of guilty, and Wallace was dispatched to death row. On a writ of habeas corpus, the U.S. Court of Appeals determined that Wallace had not been competent to stand trial and ordered a retrial. This time the jury found the shooting to have been accidental and he was acquitted.

Warren Douglas Manning
South Carolina

Warren Douglas Manning also was convicted of killing a police officer and sentenced to death. The prosecution claimed that Manning attacked a state trooper after a traffic stop on a South Carolina highway in 1988. He was being taken into custody for driving with a suspended license when, the police maintained, he turned on the officer and pistol-whipped him before shooting him at close range with his own revolver. The defense, for its part, contended that Manning had fled from custody when the trooper stopped another car. If the trooper's story were true, the defense said, Manning would have been covered with blood, but people who saw him minutes after the incident said they saw no blood on him. The jury found Manning guilty and he was sentenced to death. But Manning's trip through the criminal justice system was just beginning. He would be tried five times in all over the course of a ten-year stay on death row.

The conviction was overturned in 1988, a second trial ended in a mistrial, and Manning was convicted again in 1995. That conviction was vacated in 1997 when the South Carolina Supreme Court ruled that the trial court had abused its discretion by granting the state's motion to change the venue for the selection of a jury. The fourth trial ended in a mistrial, and the prosecutors decided to try their luck again. This time, Manning was represented by David Bruck, a death-penalty specialist, who demonstrated that there was no evidence on which to build a conviction. In his statement to the jury, Bruck emphasized that "the law requires that the state prove him guilty beyond a reasonable doubt. Without that, the law says you cannot find him guilty." Manning was acquitted after less than three hours of deliberation.

Addendum

THE CENTRAL PARK JOGGER

Nameless, her identity no more than a shadow cast across the conscience of a troubled city, she nonetheless became a part of the language of her time. For fourteen years she was known simply as the Central Park Jogger. In April 2003, Trisha Meili shed her anonymity with the publication of a long-awaited memoir. She told her story under the title *I Am the Central Park Jogger: A Story of Hope and Possibility*. The book was published on the anniversary of the event that propelled her into the headlines on April 19, 1989. At the time a twenty-eight-year-old investment banker at the Wall Street firm of Salomon Brothers, Meili was the most seriously injured victim on a night when forty Harlem teenagers introduced the term *"wilding"* to the vernacular of oppression. They invaded Central Park, randomly molesting, robbing, and assaulting strangers who were jogging or bicycling through the Upper East Side of the park.

Most victims escaped with minor injuries. The jogger, as she was described, was not so fortunate. She was found in the early morning hours lying unconscious in a muddy ravine north of a drive that crosses the park at 102nd Street. She was barely alive. Her body temperature was eighty-four degrees; she had lost 75 percent of her blood. She had been raped and beaten and left for dead. Her skull had been caved in with a heavy object. She would remain in a coma for twelve days. When she revived, she remembered nothing of the attack. She was unable to identify her assailant or even recall whether she had been assaulted by one or many. Finally conscious, her nightmare was just beginning.

Among the dozens of youths questioned by police that night were five Harlem teenagers whose names would become etched in the tableau of New York City's criminal justice system— Anton McCray, Kevin Richardson, Raymond Santana, Kharey Wise, and Yusef Salaam. They were charged with the brutal assault and gang rape of the young woman. All between the ages of fifteen and seventeen, they were about to embark on a nightmare of their own.

The only physical evidence the police had were hairs on the clothing of one of the boys that were said to be consistent with the hair of the jogger. But all five youths would soon be offering detectives what passed for confessions of guilt. The videotaped statements were the backbone of the prosecution's case. Salaam was the only one to take the witness stand. He was tried together with McCray and Santana. All three, represented by the seasoned defense attorney Michael Warren, were acquitted of attempted murder but found guilty of rape. They were sentenced to five to ten years under juvenile laws. Richardson and Wise were tried three months later. The forensic evidence, hairs presumably from the victim found on his shirt and underwear, was strongest against Richardson. After twelve tough days of deliberation, the jury found him guilty of attempted murder and rape. Wise, the oldest of the boys, was convicted on the lesser charges of sexual abuse and assault. Richardson was sentenced as a juvenile to five to ten years. Wise, at age seventeen, received five to fifteen years as an adult.

To all appearances, the case was settled now. The city breathed easier. The jogger had made a stunning, some said miraculous, recovery. She was well enough to testify at both trials, offering details of her activities before the attack and after she emerged from the coma, though she had no memory of the attack itself. Still, it was clear that she was on the road to recovery. Her assailants were safely tucked away behind bars. Justice, it seemed, had been done, and the jogger's ordeal receded in the memory of a city that adapts quickly to crisis. It was not altogether surprising, therefore, that little attention was paid more than a year later when, on July 13, 1990, a DNA expert testified in a Manhattan court that analysis of the semen found in the victim did not come from any of the five youths convicted of the crime. "That means," he said, "there was another rapist who is still at large."

In January 2002, a convicted murderer and serial rapist by the name of Matias Reyes told a prison guard at the Clinton Correctional Facility in upstate New York that he wanted to talk to authorities about the Central Park Jogger case. At the time, Reyes was serving a term of thirty-three and a third years to life for the rape and murder of a pregnant woman in Manhattan. He was interviewed by an investigator from the New York State Department of Corrections. Reyes, who had been in prison since 1991, explained that he had found God and felt compelled to confess that he and he alone had raped and assaulted the jogger. (He did not mention that his religious enlightenment had occurred shortly after the statute of limitations in the jogger case had expired.) The information was turned over to the District Attorney's Office in Manhattan. Aware that the initial DNA tests did not implicate the five Harlem youths, the DA arranged a DNA test for Reyes. The results came back in May. Reyes's DNA matched the semen taken from the jogger's body. The test also showed that the hairs found on Richardson did not belong to the jogger.

Reyes's confession was compelling. He re-created the details of the crime for investigators with startling accuracy. He said he hit the young woman over the head with a fallen tree branch, dragged her into a secluded wooded ravine, pulled off her jogging tights, and raped her. He then smashed her in the face and head with a rock and other objects. When she was found, she was tied up in the same manner as Reyes's previous rape victims. Her shirt was looped around her neck, tied to her wrists, and then wrapped around her mouth to gag her. In addition, the victim had a cross-shaped wound on her cheek, and Reyes wore a ring that was topped with a cross.

Reyes's past also stamped him as a likely suspect. This type of crime was not new to him. He had, in fact, committed a similar crime two days earlier in the same area of the park. Reyes had been identified as a suspect in that case, but he was never contacted or questioned. Nor had the police explored the possibility that the two crimes were connected. The earlier rape had been handled by the sex crimes unit and the second by homicide detectives because the jogger was not expected to survive. The two units did not share their information.

One of the gravest consequences of wrongful conviction is that the guilty party remains free to commit other crimes, and Reyes took full advantage of the opportunity. In the months following the jogger rape, he went on a rampage, raping, assaulting, and tormenting young women on the Upper East Side. On June 14, two months after the Central Park attacks, Reyes murdered Lourdes Gonzalez Serrano, a twenty-four-year-old pregnant woman, stabbing her to death in her apartment, while her children listened to her screams from another room. Two weeks later, on July 2, the police closed the file that had been opened on Reyes in the April 17 rape case. According to the *New York Times*, the report described how Reyes had been identified by the victim because of fresh stitch marks on his chin. But, it concludes, "The case was marked closed after initial efforts to contact the victim were unsuccessful."

The spree came to an end for Reyes in early August when a rape victim fled her apartment and ran down into the lobby of the building on East Ninety-first Street, with Reyes in pursuit. The building superintendent saw him coming, clubbed him with a mop, and held him for the police. He pleaded guilty to murdering the pregnant woman, raping three others, and committing a robbery. When he appeared in court for sentencing, on November 1, 1991, he went berserk. He swore at the judge, punched his lawyer, and assaulted several court officials until he was finally subdued. More than ten years would pass before he was heard from again.

If Reyes was telling the truth, and there was no reason to

doubt him, the case against the Harlem 5 would have to be reconsidered. Reyes's confession was by any measure the most coherent and complete account of the attack that had been offered so far. The DNA proved beyond a doubt that he had raped the jogger. Whether or not he acted alone was the chief question, and there was every indication that he had. He said he did not know any of the Harlem 5, and none of them had been able to pick him out in a photograph. Yet more convincingly, Reyes had a history of similar crimes, and he always worked alone. Serial rapists or killers are not inclined to seek company. Reyes was a loner who stalked, robbed, raped, and murdered as the impulse struck him. There was little likelihood that he was one of a party of six in the jogger case. The question then was: If the five youths had not raped the young woman, did they have anything at all to do with the attack?

Two basic issues needed to be addressed: the sequence of events that would determine whether the five youths could have been at the point of occurrence when the attack took place; and the confessions that were the pivot of two separate trials. When the events of that night were reconstructed, it appeared that the five, who were together all night, could not have been in the area where the jogger was assaulted.

She was on her way to commence her run at 8:55 when she met a neighbor in the lobby of their apartment building, at Eighty-third Street and York Avenue. By her own account, she ran the same route every night at a pace of a mile every eight minutes. The run generally took about forty minutes, which would have given her time to return home by ten o'clock when she had arranged to meet a friend. All estimates, including the one she later offered in court, suggested that the assault had begun between 9:10 and 9:20. The five youths were seen by a number of witnesses at other places in the park at that time.

The confessions were another matter entirely. The Harlem 5 had been in custody for several hours before the jogger was found. They were among a group of close to forty teenagers who had been brought in from the park that night for one offense or another. When the report about the jogger was received, they were all questioned as suspects. The detectives, some reputed to be among New York's best, apparently assumed that the jogger's attacker had been picked up in their sweep of the park. It was a scenario to be dreamed of: the culprits were in custody even before the crime had been discovered.

All five of the Harlem youths began by denying having taken part in the attack on the jogger or even being aware of it. But it was a long night and an even longer day ahead, and gradually each of the suspects started to give way. Finally, they all confessed to having been involved to one degree or another. The prosecution made much of the fact that their confessions were videotaped, but the cameras were not turned on until April 21, after the suspects had been in custody and questioned for as much as twenty-eight hours.

The youths' confessions were inconsistent with one another and at variance with the facts as they were known. There were conflicts about when, where, and how the rape took place and differing descriptions of the clothing the jogger was wearing. Three of the boys—Santana, Wise, and Richardson—were nearly an hour off when estimating the time of the attack. Wise said the victim was stabbed repeatedly, but there were no marks to indicate she had been stabbed at all. McCray had the time approximately right but put the location about seven blocks from where the victim was found. Salaam did not make a videotaped statement or sign a written summation of events because his mother arrived at the station house and summoned a lawyer.

The parents of three of the boys were present during the interrogation, but attorney Michael Warren thought they provided little in the way of guidance. In an interview with Chris Smith of *New York* magazine, Warren said: "To the extent that the parents were present at that time, it's really insignificant in terms of trying to assert that the parents voluntarily knew what was going on and agreed to it. That's just not the case. And the videotaping is the last stage of the process. At that point, the children will say whatever they've been scripted to say."

Throughout their prison terms, the youths maintained that they were innocent. They said they were tricked into making false admissions and often were responding to promises of leniency or threats of harsher treatment if they failed to comply. Salaam was told, falsely, that his fingerprints were found on the jogger's pants. Their insistence that the state had gotten the case wrong cost at least three of them a chance for parole. Richardson, Santana, and Salaam all denied any involvement in the jogger attack before the parole board, and in turn were denied parole because they failed to accept responsibility for their acts and showed no remorse. As for the other two, Wise's remarks were themselves contradictory and his responses too muddled to determine whether he was affirming or denying guilt. McCray served his sentence as a juvenile, so records of his parole hearings were unavailable.

Reyes's confession and his statement exonerating the Harlem 5 had given the case new legs. The office of Manhattan district attorney Robert M. Morgenthau began reexamining the evidence, and in December 2002 a report of its findings was submitted to the state supreme court. The report was in the form of a motion by Nancy E. Ryan, Morgenthau's chief of trials, to join the defense in seeking a dismissal of all charges against the youths. It said that the confessions had "serious weaknesses," and went on to note that they "differed from one another on the specific details of virtually every major aspect of the crime—who initiated the attack, who knocked the victim down, who undressed her, who struck her, who raped her, what weapons were used in the course of the assault and when the sequence of events in the attack took place." The report concluded that "there is a probability that the new evidence, had it been available to the juries, would have resulted in verdicts more favorable to the defendants, not only on the charges arising from the attack on the female jogger but on the other charges as well."

Two weeks later, on December 19, in a ruling that took just five minutes, State Supreme Court Judge Charles J. Tejada vacated all convictions against the five men, now between the ages of twenty-eight and thirty. They had all completed their prison terms of between seven and thirteen years. Santana, however, was back in prison, having pleaded guilty to drug possession in 1999 when police found crack cocaine in his apartment. On Christmas Eve, Santana was released on time served because his conviction in the jogger case had resulted in his drawing a longer sentence on the drug charge.

The action of the District Attorney's Office and the decision of the court did not sit well with the New York City Police Department. It commissioned a three-man panel to look into the case and make its own report. The panel included the deputy police commissioner for legal affairs, a former Queens DA and federal prosecutor, and a prominent New York City attorney. It predictably concluded that there was no misconduct in the police investigation of the case. It also determined that the Harlem 5 "most likely" was involved in the attack on the jogger to one degree or another.

Speaking for the panel, Michael F. Armstrong, a former federal prosecutor who was chief counsel to the Knapp Commission, which investigated police corruption in the 1970s, acknowledged the legal necessity for vacating the convictions. He noted, however, that Reyes's account was uncorroborated and that "the word of a serial rapist killer is not something to be heavily relied upon." The report concluded that the "most likely scenario" was one in which the five youths attacked the jogger before Reyes came upon her. "Our examination of the facts," the report said, "leads us to suggest that there is an alternative theory of the attack upon the jogger, that both the defendants and Reyes assaulted her, perhaps successively."

Both defense and prosecuting attorneys took issue with the police report, calling it a biased, last-ditch attempt to salvage the reputation of the police department. Myron Bedlock, one of Salaam's lawyers, said of the police, "They've got so much egg on their face, they're never going to be able to wipe it off." Three days after the report was released, James F. Kindler, chief assistant district attorney in Manhattan, supported the court's decision at a hearing before the City Council. "The theory that Reyes may have come along later," he said, "is a theory; there is no evidence to support it."

Now fourteen years after the fact, the jogger case is likely to remain a benchmark of sorts in the criminal justice system. It has focused attention on the consequences that can result from false confessions and the frequency with which they occur. According to records kept by the Innocence Project at the Benjamin N. Cardozo School of Law at Yeshiva University, twenty-seven people convicted of crimes based on confession were cleared by DNA testing in the past decade. Many more who falsely confessed were cleared by DNA evidence before trial.

Paul Cassell, a legal scholar, has pointed out that most false confessions are elicited from segments of the population that tend to be vulnerable, such as young people and the mentally handicapped. At the jogger trials, the psychological profiles and IQ scores of the defendants were not allowed into evidence. Had such information been admitted, it would have shown, for example, that McCray had an IQ of 87 and was reading at a fourth-grade level while in the ninth grade. Wise, with an IQ of 73, was reading at a second-grade level at the age of sixteen.

In an op-ed-page piece in the *New York Times,* Saul Kassin, a professor of psychology and chairman of legal studies at Williams College in Williamstown, Massachusetts, cites three steps that can be taken to verify false confessions. "The first step," he says, "is to see whether there were factors present that would have increased the likelihood of coercion—like the age or competency of the suspect as well as the conditions of custody and interrogation." The second step "requires considering whether the confession contains details that are consistent with the statements of others, accurate in their match to the facts of the crime and lead to evidence unknown to police." Finally, "a confession proves guilt if the accurate facts it contains are knowable only to a perpetrator."

In his examination of the jogger case, Kassin found the defendants to be exceptionally vulnerable to suggestion because of their age and the length of the interrogation. He notes the inconsistencies in their accounts and suggests the possibility that even if explicit promises were not made, they might have been implied or inferred. "A simple assertion like 'you can't go home, you're not cooperating,'" he writes, "could lead the accused to imagine that cooperation would bring freedom." Kassin also cautions that some questions might communicate to the suspect information he could not otherwise provide. As an illustration he notes that at one point the prosecutor asked Richardson, "Don't you remember somebody using a brick or a stone?" Such a question contains the answer the interrogator is seeking.

Kassin recommends that interrogations be videotaped from start to end. "This simple procedural reform," he writes, "will deter police coercion, deter frivolous defense claims of coercion, and enable trial judges and juries to assess the veracity of taped confessions."

As for Meili, whose soft-spoken good nature shines through her memoir and was apparent in an NBC-TV interview with Katie Couric on April 6, she is not indifferent to the truth of what happened to her that night, but has moved well beyond it. Now forty-two years old, married, and living in a Connecticut suburb, she has undergone years of rehabilitation but still suffers from impaired vision and occasional loss of balance. She works for a not-for-profit organization and takes part in public forums, counseling others who are trying to overcome physical disabilities. In May 2003 she was a speaker at an event to promote Sexual Assault Awareness Month.

Although she describes not being able to recall the brutal attack on her as a blessing, she says it also makes her feel helpless, "not as a victim but as someone who wants to contribute to the truth." The truth, she acknowledges, might never be known. When she learned that evidence pointed to Reyes as the lone assailant, she says, it "left me too stunned to respond. . . . Reyes became real to me in a way the five had not. I didn't want to see him in the papers or hear him talk on television." And it is "horrible," she says, to think that innocent people might have been sent to prison for something he did.

Afterword

UNITED STATES V.
CAPITAL PUNISHMENT

L aw-enforcement officials, Attorney General John Ashcroft among them, often call it the ultimate sanction. Others refer to it more directly as the death penalty or capital punishment. What it is, is state-sponsored execution, and it is carried out routinely in repressive dictatorships like Iraq, Cuba, and Libya, in Third World countries like Bangladesh and Uganda, in effete kingdoms like Saudi Arabia, and in one Western democracy— the United States of America. Every country in Western Europe has abolished the death penalty. Russia, while not officially banning it, recently declared a moratorium and commuted to life the death sentences of all seven hundred of its condemned prisoners. The number of countries that have stopped implementing the death penalty has grown to 105, more than half the countries in the world. The United States, on the other hand, is not beyond juggling venues in order to try a case in a state that is more hospitable to executions. It has, in recent years, become the most flagrant violator of the international ban on executing juvenile offenders. Texas alone has executed seven juveniles since 1985.

Executing the mentally retarded was permitted in twenty-two of the thirty-eight states that have capital punishment until the Supreme Court ruled in 2002 that the practice was cruel and unusual punishment and violated the Eighth Amendment.

The death penalty has been part of the dialogue of crime and punishment for about as long as history has been recorded. The first established death-penalty laws were contained in the Code of Hammurabi of Babylon in the eighteenth century B.C.E.; they applied to twenty-five different crimes. Perhaps the first abolitionist was William the Conqueror, in tenth-century Britain, who refused to allow executions except in time of war. At the opposite end of the spectrum was Henry VIII. Six centuries later, he allowed some 72,000 executions during his fifty-six-year reign. The number of capital crimes continued to rise in Britain throughout the next two centuries. By the 1700s, 222 crimes were punishable by death, including stealing, cutting down a tree, and robbing a rabbit warren. As the state found that juries were reluctant to convict in many capital cases because they thought death was too severe a punishment, the number of crimes in which it could be applied was cut roughly by half.

Like most of its other institutions, capital punishment was exported by Britain to the colonies. The first recorded execution in the colonies was that of Captain George Kendall, convicted of spying for Spain, in the Jamestown Colony of Virginia in 1608. In the late 1700s, a spirited though small abolitionist movement took root, mostly in Pennsylvania. Dr. Benjamin Rush, a signer of the Declaration of Independence, took aim at the heart of the concept, challenging the notion that the death penalty served as a deterrent. On the contrary, he said, it had a "brutalization effect" that actually stimulated criminal activity. Rush won the support of Benjamin Franklin and William Bradford, who later became U.S. attorney general. In 1794, Pennsylvania repealed the death penalty for all crimes except first-degree murder. In 1834, it became the first state to do away with public executions, moving them to correctional facilities. Michigan also was a pioneer in the abolition movement. In 1846, it became the first state to abolish capital punishment for all crimes except treason. Some years later, Rhode Island and Wisconsin did away with it entirely.

The abolition movement picked up steam shortly after the turn of the century. Between 1907 and 1917, six states completely outlawed the death penalty and three limited it to treason and the first-degree murder of a law-enforcement official. But the trend quickly reversed itself. The Russian Revolution of 1917 unleashed a witch-hunting frenzy in the United States as the fear of "creeping socialism" fed a paranoia that entered the marrow of the country and would not leave for some time. Five of the six abolitionist states reinstated the death penalty by 1924, and in the 1930s there were more executions than in any decade in American history.

It was in the rip-it-up decade of the sixties that sentiment worldwide began to shift away from the death penalty. A good many countries allied to the United States either abolished it or limited its use. In the United States, the number of executions dropped sharply. Between 1960 and 1976 only 191 people were executed, compared, for example, with an average of 167 a year in the thirties. Several Supreme Court decisions began chipping away at the arbitrary manner in which the death penalty was administered.

The one that finally broke new ground was *Furman v. Georgia* in 1972. Setting a new standard, the Court held that a punishment was cruel and unusual if it violated any of four precepts— if it was too severe for the crime, if it was arbitrary, if it offended society's sense of justice, or if it was not more effective than a less severe penalty. The ruling came in a five-to-four decision in which all nine justices wrote separate opinions. The effect was that Georgia's death-penalty statute was judged unconstitutional because it gave the jury complete sentencing discretion and could therefore result in arbitrary sentences. The decision voided the death-penalty statutes in forty states and commuted the sentences of 629 death-row inmates across the country. Thirty-five of the states affected set about rewriting their statutes to relieve jurors of the sole decision-making responsibility.

The majority of states, particularly those in the South, were not yet ready to give up the death penalty. Florida, Georgia, and Texas were quick into the fold, and the Supreme Court approved their revised statutes in a 1976 decision. At the same time, the Court held that the death penalty itself was not cruel and unusual punishment; other criteria would have to be met. The national moratorium on executions ended with much fanfare on January 17, 1977, when Gary Gilmore was shot to death by a firing squad in Utah.

The death chambers were up and running again, and some states appeared eager to make up for lost time. Since capital punishment was reinstated through January 2002, there have been 823 executions in the United States, 291 of them, or about 35 percent, were carried out in Texas. In 2002, that percentage was even higher; the Texas killing machine was responsible for nearly half the executions in the country—thirty-three of a total of seventy-one. Virginia was a distant second in executions carried out since 1977, with eighty-seven, followed by Missouri, Oklahoma, Florida, Georgia, South Carolina, Louisiana, Alabama, Arkansas, North Carolina, and Arizona. All told, the South executes people at a rate of more than four times the rest of the country—673 compared to a combined total of 150 in the West, Midwest, and Northeast. Twelve states—Alaska, Maine, Minnesota, Vermont, Hawaii, Massachusetts, North Dakota, West Virginia, Iowa, Michigan, Rhode Island, and Wisconsin—and the District of Columbia have abolished the death penalty. Five other states—Connecticut, Kansas, New Jersey, New York, and South Dakota—keep the statute on the books but have had no executions since 1976.

It is never easy to know when and on what battlefield events will occur that give a new shape to history. But when, in some future time, a more enlightened Supreme Court sits on the bench and the United States joins the other civilized countries of the world in consigning capital punishment to the dustbin of the past, the state of Illinois will be noted as a great battlefield of that war, and its conservative Republican governor, George H. Ryan, will have his name high on the honor roll.

The offensive against Illinois's death penalty started with the DNA exoneration of Anthony Porter in 1999, followed by a dozen others who were freed from death row after an exhaustive investigation by undergraduate students at the Medill School of Journalism under the guidance of Northwestern professor David Protess. A year later, Governor Ryan, who in 1977 was among the state legislators who voted to revive the death penalty, called a moratorium on executions. He noted that since 1976 the state had executed twelve prisoners while thirteen were exonerated. The numbers did not justify a system that was supposed to deliver justice. Ryan said he would review the cases of the 167 prisoners on death row to try to determine how many others had been wrongly convicted. It was becoming clear that a close examination of the system had led to Ryan's conversion to an abolitionist. Moral issues aside, he had begun to recognize that the system is flawed beyond repair, and it was not possible to prevent innocent people from being put to death.

With his term winding down, there was much speculation about how far Ryan would go in his mission to right the wrongs of how capital punishment was administered in Illinois. The first indication came on December 19, 2002. In a speech about the death penalty at the University of Illinois, he announced that he was pardoning Gary Gauger and Rolando Cruz—two of the thirteen who had already been freed—and Steven Linscott, who spent ten years in prison for murdering a young woman in Oak Park before being cleared by DNA evidence. The pardons expunged the convictions from the men's records. Ryan also stirred new conjecture about the fate of those still on death row when he said he would abolish the death penalty immediately if he could. The only thing that deterred him, he said, were the pleas from those who survived the victims.

All the same, on January 10, two days before he was to leave office, he took another step toward the inevitable when he issued four more pardons of men he said had been tortured into making false admissions:

- Aaron Patterson had confessed to the April 1986 stabbing of an elderly couple in Chicago. Patterson never signed the confession and during the interrogation had scratched these words into a bench with a paper clip: "I lie about murders, police threaten me with violence."
- Madison Hobley was convicted of killing seven people in an arson fire in 1987. Private investigators later turned up evidence that a metal can found at the scene, which had been used to connect Hobley to the crime, had been planted.
- Leroy Orange was sentenced to die for taking part in the stabbing of his former girlfriend, her ten-year-old son, and two others. Orange, who said he had been tortured, maintained that his half brother, Leonard Kidd, had committed the murders.
- Stanley Howard was convicted in 1987 of murdering a forty-two-year-old man. He confessed, he said, after police officers had kicked and punched him and placed a plastic typewriter cover over his head. Howard produced medical evidence supporting his charges.

Ryan noted that the "four men did not know each other, all getting beaten and tortured and convicted on the same basis of the confessions that they allegedly provided. They are perfect examples of what is so terribly broken about our system."

The lightning bolt came a day later. Before a packed auditorium at Northwestern University, the governor commuted the death sentences of all 167 prisoners on death row. They had served a collective two thousand years in prison for the murder of 250 people. Three prisoners had their sentences reduced to forty years; the others all received terms of life without parole. Ryan said that in reviewing every case he had found that they all "raised questions not only about the innocence of people on death row, but about the fairness of the death-penalty system as a whole. Our capital system is haunted by the demons of error: error in determining guilt and error in determining who among the guilty deserves to die."

In his indictment of the capital system, Ryan documented his case with statistics in Illinois that would likely be just as appropriate in most other states in the union. Since the state's attorney decides which defendants will face the death penalty, there is a vast disparity in how it is applied in various parts of the state. Someone convicted of murder in a rural area of Illinois, he said, is five times more likely to get a death sentence for first-degree murder than an offender in Chicago. He noted, too, that half the capital cases in Illinois had been reversed for either a new trial or resentencing. Ryan continued:

Thirty-three of the death-row inmates were represented at trial by an attorney who had later been disbarred or at some point suspended from the practice of law. Of the more than 160 death-row inmates, thirty-five were African-American defendants who had been convicted or condemned to die not by a jury of their peers, but by all-white juries. More than two-thirds of the inmates on death row were African-American. And forty-six inmates were convicted on the basis of testimony from jailhouse informants. . . . I asked myself and my staff: How does that happen. How in God's name does that happen? In America, how does it happen? I've been asking this question for nearly three years and so far nobody's answered this question.

Ryan said he listened for many months to those lobbying both sides of the issue. Then he explained why, after close examination of the capital punishment system, he had reached his bold decision:

The Legislature couldn't reform it, lawmakers won't repeal it, and I won't stand for it—I must act. Because our three-year study has found only more questions about the fairness of the sentencing, because of the spectacular failure to reform the system, because we have seen justice delayed for countless death-row inmates with potentially meritorious claims, because the Illinois death-penalty system is arbitrary and capricious—and therefore immoral.

The governor's action set loose a backlash of protest from states' attorneys, politicians, and the survivors of victims. John Piland, the president of the Illinois State's Attorneys Association, called it a "cruel hoax." Ryan's successor as governor, Rod R. Blagojevich, a Democrat, supports the death penalty but said he plans to extend the moratorium on executions until proper reforms are put in place. Prosecutors said they would try to challenge about twenty of the cases in which inmates were being retried, arguing that since they were not under an active sentence of death while they were being retried, they were not eligible for commutation. The most poignant cries of objection came from the families of victims, many of whom said they felt deprived of closure. But opponents of capital punishment pointed out that while the impulse for revenge is understandable, it should not be permitted to drive the criminal justice system, nor should revenge be confused with justice.

To one degree or another, capital punishment has troubled the national conscience for the better part of a century. As early as 1924, Clarence Darrow put the concept itself on trial when he defended Loeb and Leopold in a bench trial that has become ingrained in American folklore. Over the years, it has captured public attention as a stage play, a movie, a novel, and in various incarnations on television. Richard Loeb and Nathan Leopold, teenage intellectual whiz-kids from prominent Chicago families, had killed young Bobby Franks for the thrill of it and each was being fitted for the hangman's noose when Darrow, the wondrous and eloquent freethinker, entered the case. He pleaded his clients guilty and asked that the trial to determine their sentences be conducted without a jury. Darrow, best known perhaps for his clash with William Jennings Bryan in the Scopes trial, could bring magic to bear upon a jury, but here, he said, he wished the fate of the defendants to be determined by the judge alone; the responsibility for hanging two teenagers would not be divided by twelve.

In a dazzling closing argument that lasted several days and covers nearly one hundred pages in transcription, Darrow took on the death penalty long before such sentiment had become the fashion. As in most such matters, Darrow was decades ahead of the flow. In 1924, capital punishment was practiced in virtually every country in the world for more crimes than could be easily counted, and Chicago was intrigued by the possibility of a double hanging. "I never saw so much enthusiasm for the death penalty as I have seen here," Darrow said. "It's been discussed as a holiday, like a day at the races."

In his plea to the judge, Darrow introduced elements of psychology and philosophy; he reviewed a bit of the history of capital punishment, contending that as its use diminished, so did the crimes for which it was applied; he noted that when a pickpocket was hanged in public, other pickpockets seized the opportunity to work the crowd of spectators; he quoted liberally from the Persian poet Omar Khayyam. Near the end, he summed up the case against the death penalty: "I am pleading for the future," he told the judge and the world. "I am pleading for a time when hatred and cruelty will not control the hearts of men; when we can learn by reason and judgment and understanding and faith that all life is worth saving, and that mercy is the highest attribute of man."

The lives of Loeb and Leopold were spared. They were sentenced to life plus ninety-nine years. For a brief time, capital punishment became a popular, though largely intellectual, subject of debate. There were few abolitionists who felt compelled to act upon their views. The death penalty was used increasingly during the following decade, and it was not until the seventies and beyond that countries around the world began to take it off the books. France tore down its guillotine in 1972; Sweden did away with capital punishment the same year and the United Kingdom a year later. Many more countries dropped it in the eighties, and two dozen nations set it aside in the nineties.

By the turn of the century, the United States was the only industrialized country of the West that persisted in state-sanctioned execution. A few states even picked up the pace. In Texas, executions seemed to be only a bit less popular than football. When George W. Bush was governor, he expressed pride in the efficiency with which the state handled such matters. There have been few death-row exonerations in Texas, chiefly because so little time is wasted in sending inmates to the death chamber. In 2002, its thirty-three executions were nearly four times that of any other state. In 2003, the Lone Star State had already jumped out to an early lead. Seven executions had been carried out by early February, three of them in two days, matching the total in the rest of the country.

Still, it was becoming increasingly clear that public sentiment had begun to shift in most areas of the country, and the courts and members of the bar seemed to be taking note of deficiencies in the system. A comprehensive death-penalty study by lawyers and criminologists at Columbia University called attention to the fact that dozens of death-row inmates do not have lawyers to conduct their appeals. The situation was deemed critical because two out of three appealed death sentences are set aside as a result of errors by defense lawyers or prosecutorial misconduct. Supreme Court Justice Sandra Day O'Connor called the problem one troubling feature of a capital punishment system that "may well be allowing some innocent defendants to be executed." Justice O'Connor also noted that defendants with more money get better legal defense. "Perhaps it is time," she said, "to look at minimum standards for appointed counsel in death cases and adequate compensation for appointed counsel when they are used."

The issue of inadequate compensation was raised again in February 2003 when a New York State Supreme Court justice ruled that the pay scale for lawyers assigned to represent the poor was unconstitutional. Justice Lucindo Suarez ordered the city and the state to more than double the hourly rate at which assigned counsel is paid. The judge said the low fees have "created a crisis impairing the judiciary's ability to function" and are the reason for the shortage of attorneys willing to represent the poor.

The constitutional right to counsel was defined by the Supreme Court in the landmark *Gideon v. Wainwright* decision in 1963, when the court wrote, "The right of one charged with crime to counsel may not be deemed fundamental and essential to fair trials in some countries, but it is in ours." That ruling, however, has never been fully realized. In most of the twenty-two states that fund legal services entirely at the state level, financing is so inadequate that lawyers cannot afford to investigate cases and prepare sound defenses. The quality of representation is even worse in the twenty-eight states where municipalities are charged with providing the funding. In some Texas counties, defendants are held in jail for months before they gain access to a lawyer.

As Justice O'Connor noted, these deficiencies are most critical in death cases, possibly leading to the execution of innocent defendants. Two federal court judges—one in New York, the other in Vermont—recently mounted a more direct attack on the constitutionality of the death penalty, each from his own perspective. In July 2002, Judge Jed S. Rakoff, of U.S. District Court in Manhattan, found that the increasing number of exonerations of death-row prisoners indicated there was an "undue risk of executing innocent people" in violation of the Fourteenth Amendment's guarantee of due process. The death penalty, Judge Rakoff said, was unconstitutional and "tantamount to foreseeable, state-sponsored murder of innocent human beings."

Two months later, Judge William K. Sessions III, of the Federal District Court in Burlington, Vermont, ruled the death penalty to be unconstitutional because the practice of allowing evidence and procedures that were inadmissible at trial to be used in the sentencing process denies the defendant his right to due process. Judge Sessions said the law was incompatible with three recent Supreme Court decisions, including one that held that juries, rather than judges, must make the determinations of fact to support a verdict of death.

The movement away from the death penalty is not a mere chimera; Justice Department statistics are revealing. For the first time since 1976, the death-row population dropped in 2001, the most recent year for which data was available. The number of people on death row fell to 3,581 from 3,601 in 2000. In addition, the 155 defendants sentenced to die in 2001 were the fewest since 1973, less than half the number just five years earlier. Prisoners executed in 2001 had spent an average of almost twelve years on death row. The length of time between sentence and execution has been increasing for decades. In 2001, more people left death row than entered it, the first time that has been true since 1973. A total of sixty-six people were executed, nineteen fewer than the previous year. Another ninety had their sentences overturned or commuted, and nineteen died of natural causes or suicide. In sum, many more people left death row by a means other than lethal injection, which was the only method of execution used in 2001.

According to Austin D. Sarat, a professor of political science and law at Amherst College and the author of *When the State Kills: Capital Punishment and the American Condition*, "We're in a period of national reconsideration. People are asking if the death penalty is compatible with values which in the American mainstream are taken seriously: equal protection, due process, protection of the innocent."

Even a quick glance reveals that the manner in which capital punishment is carried out in the United States violates all of those values. It is racist; it favors the wealthy; and in many jurisdictions, guilt rather than innocence seems to be presumed. A recent study in Maryland found that the race of the victim plays a significant role in determining whether the killer will be sentenced to death while the race of the defendant is largely irrelevant. Since Maryland reinstituted capital punishment in 1978, half of the 1,311 cases eligible for the death penalty involved black victims. But of the seventy-six death sentences handed down, 80 percent of their victims were white. Maryland, which has executed only three men during that time period, is not a state with a deep devotion to the death penalty, and those who study the field believe the report is reflective of figures in many other states. Nationally, 82 percent of the victims of death row inmates were white, as of 2002, while only 50 percent of all homicide victims were white.

The disparity, the study found, has little to do with what happens in the courtroom. Prosecutors, not judges or juries, determine in which cases they will seek the death penalty, and the decision to charge a defendant with a capital crime outweighs by far anything that takes place later, including the sentencing phase of the trial. The critical statistic, then, is that prosecutors are twice as likely to ask for the death penalty when a black kills a white as in any other scenario.

F. Michael McCann, Milwaukee district attorney for more than thirty years, agrees that minorities are treated unfairly as the death penalty is applied. "It is rare that a wealthy white man gets executed, if it happens at all," he said in an interview with the *New York Times*. McCann's opinion counts for more than most because he has prosecuted some of the nation's most grizzly murder cases, including that of the serial killer Jeffrey L. Dahmer, who murdered, dismembered, and on occasion cannibalized at least seventeen boys and men. The death penalty was not at issue, since Wisconsin is one of the eighteen states without it, but McCann did not believe that even Dahmer should have been executed. "To participate in the killing of another human being," he said, "diminishes the respect for life, period. Although I am a district attorney, I have a gut suspicion of the state wielding the power of death over anybody."

John O'Hair, the Detroit district attorney, agrees. "Government is a teacher, for good or for bad," he told the *Times,* "but government should set the example. I do not believe that government engaging in violence or retribution is the right example. You don't solve violence by committing violence. I do not think the death penalty is a deterrent of any consequence in preventing murders."

That capital punishment does not deter capital crimes has been well documented in dozens of studies over at least the past five decades. A comprehensive study by the *Times,* based on Justice Department statistics from the year 2000, showed that the states that have not exercised the death penalty since 1976 did not have higher homicide rates than states with the death penalty. In fact, ten of the twelve states without capital punishment at that time had rates below the national average, while half the states with the death penalty have homicide rates above the national average, according to FBI statistics. Over the last two decades, states with capital punishment had homicide rates from 48 to 101 percent higher than states without the death penalty. The study also indicated that homicide rates within the states themselves had risen and fallen in about the same rhythm in states with and without capital punishment.

A comparison of neighboring states, where the demographics are roughly comparable, also indicates that the death penalty is of little consequence in deterring crime. According to FBI figures, the homicide rate in North Dakota, which does not have the death penalty, is lower than in South Dakota, which does. Massachusetts and Rhode Island, both non–capital punishment states, have a lower rate than Connecticut, and the homicide rate in West Virginia is 30 percent lower than in Virginia, which has one of the highest execution rates in the country.

Other commonly made arguments for capital punishment also collapse if examined closely. It is, for example, more costly to execute an offender than to pay for life imprisonment. Capital cases generally cost the state several million dollars to prosecute from beginning to end. Both the defense and the state spend more time on a capital case than one involving imprisonment. It takes longer to pick a jury and longer to present the state's case as well as the defense. Expert witnesses are an added expense and so is DNA or other scientific testing. After the trial, the appeal process can take years, with the state paying for the upkeep of the prisoner as well as incurring the cost of contesting the appeal.

The increasingly popular alternative to the death penalty is life without the possibility of parole, often referred to as L-WOPP. Advocates of capital punishment have contended that a prisoner who knows he has no chance to be freed has nothing to lose and therefore presents a threat to other prisoners and custodians. But there again they have it wrong. Prisoners serving L-WOPP sentences for a capital crime are confined in small isolation cells where they are held under lock for twenty-three hours a day, seven days a week, and are fed through a hole in the cell door. A long period of good behavior will earn them entry to a more livable environment. They will be housed in a larger, brighter cell, will be introduced into the general population, permitted to eat with other inmates, and receive privileges such as the right to watch television. A lifetime is a long time to spend in isolation, and states like Michigan, which has more than two thousand prisoners serving L-WOPP time, find it has worked well for everyone involved. Matthew Davis, a spokesman for the Michigan Department of Corrections, says that L-WOPP prisoners are generally quieter, less insolent, more likely to obey the rules, and less apt to try to escape. They are, in short, looking to do what most people do on the outside—achieve a better life for themselves.

The case against deterrence is compelling and appears to hold up from every perspective. According to the FBI's Uniform Crime Report for 2001, the South again had the highest rate of executions of the four regions of the country, accounting for almost 80 percent of prisoners put to death. It also had the highest murder rate, 6.7 homicides for every 100,000 in population, more than 50 percent higher than the Northeast, which had the lowest murder rate and carried out no executions during the year. By contrast, Texas, whose total number of executions is more than three times higher than any other state in the nation, had a 7.6 percent increase in homicides; its crime rate rose 4 percent, nearly five times the national average. It might even be suggested that the abolition of capital punishment reduces the rate of homicide in a society. In Canada, for example, the homicide rate is down 23 percent since the death penalty was abolished in 1975.

The arguments against capital punishment are straightforward and difficult to refute: it is applied arbitrarily, it is discriminatory, it is more costly than imprisonment, it does not deter, and it results in innocent people being executed. Proponents of the death penalty are left with little meat to pick from the bones. They insist that capital punishment is sometimes the only penalty suitable for a heinous crime, that the biblical injunction of an eye for an eye must be taken seriously while the biblical prescription for stoning to death adulterers is somehow merely symbolic, that the survivors of victims can achieve closure only if the guilty person is executed. All of those notions can be distilled quite simply into the all-too-human taste for revenge. In a debate on capital punishment with Alfred J. Talley, a New York judge, Clarence Darrow reduced the differences between their positions to the fundamentals:

In the end, this question is simply one of the humane

feelings against the brutal feelings. One who likes to see suffering, out of what he thinks is a righteous indignation, or any other, will hold fast to capital punishment. One who has sympathy, imagination, kindness and understanding, will hate it and defeat it as he hates and detests death.

Yet the legions who cling to the belief in the curative powers of capital punishment still outnumber the abolitionists, although the margin is shrinking. Unfortunately, one of capital punishment's most devoted advocates is the attorney general of the United States. Such a fan of the death penalty is John Ashcroft that early in 2003 he issued a decree that prosecutors should seek death in more cases. He was clearly unhappy with New York and Connecticut, both of which have capital punishment but don't use it. In ten cases in New York and two in Connecticut, he rejected the confidential recommendations of federal prosecutors who did not ask for the death penalty and insisted they do. He had his reasons. They were explained by Barbara Comstock, a Justice Department spokeswoman who plays Charlie McCarthy to Ashcroft's Edgar Bergen. When Congress passed the federal death penalty law, she said, it intended it to be applied "in a consistent and fair manner across the country. What we are trying to avoid is one standard in Georgia and another in Vermont."

It presumably never occurred to Ashcroft (who incidentally is committed to states' rights on most other issues) that it was equally possible to achieve consistency by reducing the number of death penalty cases in Georgia instead of increasing them in Vermont. Having abolished capital punishment for state crimes,

Vermont is not likely, after all, to seek them in federal courts. Critics of his edict—prosecutors as well as defense lawyers— were quick to point out other flaws in Ashcroft's quest for fairness. For example, while there will be more capital trials, there will not necessarily be more death sentences. Since capital punishment was revived in New York, six defendants have faced the death penalty on federal charges but none has been sentenced to death. There is also the possibility that defendants who might otherwise be found guilty will be acquitted if jurors do not think the death penalty is appropriate in their case.

Just a month before he ordered prosecutors to seek the death penalty more frequently, Ashcroft drew criticism from attorneys on both sides of the judicial system when he rejected seven guilty pleas in which defendants would have spared themselves the possibility of execution in exchange for a long prison term, probably life. Limiting plea bargaining, many said, would be costly and time-consuming and deprive prosecutors of an instrument that can sometimes pry loose an easy conviction. Steven M. Cohen, a former federal prosecutor in Manhattan, noted that "part of the process of being a prosecutor is the leverage that's created by pleas. The problem is, if you can't bargain away death, you will never get a plea."

Ashcroft apparently sees things differently. While every pulse beat in the country seems to be away from capital punishment, he is seizing any opportunity to apply it on a wider scale. But history will likely show that, even at the peak of his powers, John Ashcroft was already irrelevant. For he belongs to a dark and distant past when death was dished out with a carefree precision and the devout conviction in the sanctity of the state.

The future is on the way, its signs already visible in clear but subtle forms. The day will come when the lethal injection needle will take its place with the electric chair, the gas chamber, the hangman's noose, and the guillotine as relics of a more primitive time. Future generations will view them with awe and wonder, still no doubt grappling with the nature of justice, but knowing that now they are that much closer.

Wrongful Death Row Convictions by State

Alabama:
Gary Drinkard
Walter McMillian
Randall Padgett

Arizona:
John Henry Knapp
Ray Krone
Jimmy Lee Mathers
James Robison
Jonathan Treadway

California:
Jerry Bigelow
Patrick Croy
Troy Lee Jones

Florida:
Anthony Brown
Joseph Green Brown
Willie Brown and Larry Troy
Joseph Nahume Green
Andrew Golden
Robert Hayes
Sonia Jacobs
William Jent and Earnest Miller

David Keaton
Wilbert Lee and Freddie Pitts
Anthony Ray Peek
Joaquin Martinez
Juan Roberto Melendez
James Richardson
Bradley Scott
Frank Lee Smith
Delbert Tibbs

Georgia:
Jerry Banks
Earl Charles
James Creamer
Henry Drake
Gary Nelson
Robert Wallace

Idaho:
Charles Fain

Illinois:
Joseph Burrows
Perry Cobb and Darby Tillis
Robert Cox
Rolando Cruz and Alejandro Hernandez
Gary Gauger
Anibal Jaramillo
Ronald Jones

Carl Lawson
Anthony Porter
Steven Manning
Steven Smith
The Ford Heights 4: Dennis Williams, Verneal Jimerson, Kenneth
Adams, Willie Rainge

Indiana:
Larry Hicks
Charles Smith

Kentucky:
Larry Osborne

Louisiana:
Shareef Cousin
Michael Graham and Albert Burrell
Curtis Kyles
Johnny Ross

Maryland:
Kirk Bloodsworth

Massachusetts:
Lawyer Johnson
Peter Limone

Michigan:
Eddie Joe Lloyd

Mississippi:
Sabrina Butler

Missouri:
Eric Clemmons
Clarence Richard Dexter

Nebraska:
Jeremy Sheets

Nevada:
Roberto Miranda

New Mexico:
Thomas Gladish, Richard Greer, Ronald Keine, and Clarence Smith

North Carolina:
Timothy Hennis
Samuel Poole
Alfred Rivera

Ohio:
Gary Beeman
Dale Johnston

Oklahoma:
Ronald Keith Williamson
Charles Ray Giddens
Clifford Henry Bowen
Richard Neal Jones

Robert Lee Miller Jr.
Adolph Munsen
Gregory Wilhoit

Pennsylvania:
Neil Ferber
Thomas H. Kimbell Jr.
William Nieves
Jay C. Smith

South Carolina:
Jesse Keith Brown
Michael Linder
Warren Douglas Manning

Texas:
Randall Dale Adams
Clarence Lee Brandley
Kerry Cook
Muneer Deeb
Ricardo Aldape Guerra
Federico Macias
Vernon McManus
John C. Skelton

Virginia:
Earl Washington

Washington:
Benjamin Harris

Author's Note

This book covers more than one hundred cases of wrongful conviction. The factual information for each case was culled from a wide variety of sources. I am indebted to all those who have come to the subject before me, and I have endeavored to credit all of them. I apologize for any inadvertant omissions.

Special gratitude is owed to Rob Warden, executive director of the Center on Wrongful Conviction at Northwestern University, whose diligent research and thoughtful accounts provided me with valuable material on numerous cases (cited below) as well as background information that allowed me to establish a framework for the book.

The Death Penalty Information Center in Washington, DC, was a bottomless source of up-to-date statistics of every sort, viewed from every perspective. DPIC's Paula Bernstein was eager to help at every turn, and her well crafted *History of the Death Penalty* was remarkably complete and enlightening.

In Spite of All Innocence, by Michael L. Radelet, Hugo Adam Bedau, and Constance E. Putnam (Northeastern University Press, 1992), offered detailed reports on a number of cases (cited below) that proved extremely useful.

The same is true of *Actual Innocence,* by Barry Scheck, Peter Neufeld, and Jim Dwyer (Signet, 2001), for their comprehensive treatment of the case of Robert Miller.

While the facts of the cases have been gleaned from many sources, the opinions and views expressed throughout are those of the author alone.

The inspiration for this book was a gift from my longtime

friend and long-ago classmate, Herman Graf, president of Carroll & Graf Publishers, and Philip Turner, executive editor. Keith Wallman, associate editor, treated the manuscript with total commitment and painstaking care every step of the way. I am grateful to them all.

Sources

Preface:
Dennis Stockton
Amnesty International USA Death Penalty Web Site. http://www.amnestyusa.org/abolish/. The Program to Abolish the Death Penalty, Washington, DC.
Death Penalty Information Center Web Site. http://www.deathpenalty-info.org/. Death Penalty Information Center, Washington, DC.
Jackson, Joe and William F. Burke Jr. *Dead Run: The Shocking Story of Dennis Stockton and Life on Death Row in America*. New York: Walker Publishing Company, 2000.
Russell Colvin
Warden, Rob. Northwestern University School of Law Center on Wrongful Convictions Web Site.
http://www.law.northwestern.edu/depts/wrongul/.

Part I: DNA: Scientific Certainty
Introduction to Part I
Death Penalty Information Center Web Site. http://www.deathpenalty-info.org/.
Gary Dotson
Warden, Rob. Northwestern University School of Law Center on Wrongful Convictions Web Site.
Kirk Bloodsworth
Campaign for Criminal Justice Reform Web Site.http://justice.policy.net/cjreform/wrong/. The Justice Project. Washington, DC.
Chebium, Raju. "DNA Provides New Hope for Wrongly-Convicted Death Row Inmates." CNN.com, 16 June 2000. http://www7.cnn.com/2000/LAW/06/16/death.penalty.dna.main/.

Chebium, Raju. "Innocence Project Credited With Expanding Awareness of DNA Testing in Law Enforcement." CNN.com, 22 December 2000. http://edition.cnn.com/2000/LAW/12/22/innocence.project.crim/.

Chebium, Raju. "Kirk Bloodsworth, Twice Convicted of Rape and Murder, Exonerated by DNA Evidence." CNN.com, 20 June 2000. http://www.cnn.com/2000/LAW/06/20/bloodsworth.profile/.

Connors, Edward, Thomas Lundregan, Neal Miller, and Tom McEwen. "Convicted by Juries, Exonerated by Science." *Issues In Child Abuse Accusations*, Vol. 10. Institute for Psychological Therapies, 1998. http://www.ipt-forensics.com/journal/volume10/j10_3.htm.

Green, Frank. "Freed Inmates Tell Their Stories." *Richmond Times Dispatch,* 15 November 1998.

Rolando Cruz & Alejandro Hernandez

Amnesty International USA Death Penalty Web Site.

Connors, Edward, Thomas Lundregan, Neal Miller, and Tom McEwen. "Convicted by Juries, Exonerated by Science."

Higgins, Dr. Edmund. "Wrongfully Convicted." 2 January 2002. http://dredmundhiggins.com/.

Warden, Rob. Northwestern University School of Law Center on Wrongful Convictions Web Site.

Frank Lee Smith

"DNA Clears Man in Murder, 11 Months After He Died on Death Row." Associated Press. Truth in Justice Web Site.
http://truthinjustice.org/frank-smith.htm.

"Frank Lee Smith - Florida Death Row." P.A.T.R.I.C.K. Crusade Web Site. 14 March 2002. http://www.patrickcrusade.org/FRANKLEE-SMITH.html.

Higgins, Dr. Edmund. "Wrongfully Convicted."

Warden, Rob. Northwestern University School of Law Center on Wrongful Convictions Web Site.

Ron Williamson

Death Penalty Information Center Web Site.

Death Penalty Institute of Oklahoma Web Site. http://www.dpio.org/.

Ronald Jones
Warden, Rob. Northwestern University School of Law Center on Wrongful Convictions Web Site.

Earl Washington
Campaign for Criminal Justice Reform Web Site. The Justice Project.
Green, Frank. "DNA Clears Washington." *Richmond Times Dispatch*, 3 October 2000.

Charles Fain
Bonner, Raymond. "Death Row Inmate Is Freed After DNA Test Clears Him." *New York Times*, 24 August 2001.
"Death Row Inmate Is Freed After DNA Test Clears Him." *New York Times*, 24 August 2001. P.A.T.R.I.C.K. Crusade Web Site.
"Freed Death Row Inmate Not Bitter." Associated Press, 25 August 2001. P.A.T.R.I.C.K. Crusade Web Site.
McKim, Paul. "Another Death Row Prisoner Released." *Socialist Action*. September 2001 edition. San Francisco, CA.
"Not Ethically Blind." *Washington Post*, 25 August 2001. P.A.T.R.I.C.K. Crusade Web Site.
"Statement of Attorney General Al Lance Regarding : Charles Fain Case." State of Idaho Office of Attorney General Alan G. Lance press release. 6 July 2001. Office of Attorney General: Boise, ID.

Ray Krone
Death Penalty Information Center Web Site.
"History and Timeline." *The Ray Krone Story. York Daily Record*, 2001. http://www.ydr.com/page/krone/background/.
Wagner, Dennis, Beth DeFalco, and Patricia Biggs. "DNA frees Arizona inmate after 10 years in prison: 10 years included time on death row." *The Arizona Republic*, 9 April 2002.

Eddie Joe Lloyd
Wilgoren, Jodi. "Confession Had His Signature; DNA Did Not." *New York Times*, 26 August 2002.

SOURCES

Part II: Eyewitness Error

Introduction to Part II and Anthony Porter

Warden, Rob. Northwestern University School of Law Center on Wrongful Convictions Web Site.

Randall Dale Adams

Campaign for Criminal Justice Reform Web Site. The Justice Project.

Radelet, Michael L., Hugo Adam Bedau, and Constance E. Putnam. *In Spite of Innocence*. Evanston, IL: Northeastern University Press, 1992.

Warden, Rob. Northwestern University School of Law Center on Wrongful Convictions Web Site.

Ricardo Aldape Guerra

Guerra v. Johnson (95-20443) - Amici Brief. United States Court of Appeals. For the Fifth Circuit Court. Project Diana Web Site. http://www.yale.edu/lawweb/avalon/diana/guerra/20443.htm.

Warden, Rob. Northwestern University School of Law Center on Wrongful Convictions Web Site.

Silva, Marcial. "March Against 'Legal Murder'." *People's Tribune* (Online Edition). Vol. 20, No. 12. 22 March 1993.

Delbert Tibbs

"Case Histories: A Review of 23 Individuals Released from Death Row ." Florida Commission on Capital Cases. Locke Burt, Chairman. 20 June 2002. http://www.oranous.com/innocence/floridareport.htm.

Freedberg, Sydney P. "Freed From Death Row." *St. Petersburg Times*, 4 July 1999. Truth in Justice Web Site. http://truthinjustice.org/13survivors.htm.

Warden, Rob. Northwestern University School of Law Center on Wrongful Convictions Web Site.

William Jent & Earnest Miller

"Case Histories: A Review of 23 Individuals Released from Death Row." Florida Commission on Capital Cases.

"Florida's Exonerated Death Row Prisoners." Floridians for Alternatives to the Death Penalty Web Site. http://www.fadp.org/fl_exonerated.html.

301

Freedberg, Sydney P. "Freed From Death Row."
Miller v. Florida. 459 U.S. 1158 (1983). http://laws.lp.findlaw.com/getcase/US/459/1158.html.
Warden, Rob. Northwestern University School of Law Center on Wrongful Convictions Web Site.
Bradley Scott
"Bradley Scott Talks About His Three-Year Ordeal on Death Row." Transcript from Interactive Online Interview. CourtTV.com. 6 November 2000.
http://www.courttv.com/talk/chat_transcripts/110600scott.html.
"Case Histories: A Review of 23 Individuals Released from Death Row ." Florida Commission on Capital Cases.
Warden, Rob. Northwestern University School of Law Center on Wrongful Convictions Web Site.
Joseph Nahume Green
"Case Histories: A Review of 23 Individuals Released from Death Row." Florida Commission on Capital Cases.
"USA: Acquittal of Former Death Row Inmate —One More Reason For Abolition." Amnesty International. 17 March 2000. http://web.amnesty.org/library/index/ENGAMR510452000.
Warden, Rob. Northwestern University School of Law Center on Wrongful Convictions Web Site.
Perry Cobb & Darby Tillis
Luft, Kerry. "Spared Death Penalty, Cleric Now Seeks to Abolish It." *Chicago Tribune*, 15 September 1990. Illinois Death Penalty Web Site.
Myers, Linnet. "2 Acquitted of Murder After 9 Years in Prison." *Chicago Tribune*, 21 January 1987. Illinois Death Penalty Web Site. http://sun.soci.niu.edu/~critcrim/wrong/tillis.txt3.
Myers, Linnet. "4 Years on Death Row Trial after Trial, It All Became a Painful Joke." *Chicago Tribune*, 4 September 1988. Illinois Death Penalty Web Site.
Warden, Rob. Northwestern University School of Law Center on Wrongful Convictions Web Site.

Sources

Joseph Burrows

Warden, Rob. Northwestern University School of Law Center on Wrongful Convictions Web Site.

Steven Smith

Armstrong, Ken, and Todd Lighty. "Death Row Conviction Thrown Out." *Chicago Tribune*, 20 February 1999.

Warden, Rob. Northwestern University School of Law Center on Wrongful Convictions Web Site.

Larry Hicks

"Indiana Death Row." Office of the Clark County Prosecuting Attorney WebSite. http://www.clarkprosecutor.org/html/death/row/hicksl.htm.

Stanton, Nile. "The Ordeal of Larry Hicks: How an Innocent Man Was Almost Executed." 9 December 2001. http://faculty.ed.umuc.edu/~nstanton/Larry.html.

Warden, Rob. Northwestern University School of Law Center on Wrongful Convictions Web Site.

Eric Clemmons

Friends on Both Sides Web Site. http://www.friendsonbothsides.com/Prison%20Inmates/inmate%20pages/Men/Eric%20Clemmons-bey-legal.htm.

Halperin, Rick. *Abolish Archives*, 21 July 1998. http://venus.soci.niu.edu/~archives/ABOLISH/july98/.

Lambe, Joe. "Inmate's Legal Fight Overturns Execution." *The Kansas City Star*, 28 February 2000.

Shareef Cousin

Martin, Marlene. "Prosecutors Give Up Case Against Shareef Cousin." *The New Abolitionist*. February 1999 Vol.III, Issue 1. Campaign to End the Death Penalty Web Site. http://www.nodeathpenalty.org/newab010/shareefCousin.html. Chicago, IL.

Gary Beeman

Campaign for Criminal Justice Reform Web Site. The Justice Project.

Charles Ray Giddens

Banks, Gabrielle. "One Hundred Innocent Men." AlterNet, 22 April 2002. http://www.alternet.org/story.html?StoryID=12923. Death Penalty Information Center Web Site.

Lawyer Johnson

Johnson, Samantha. "Guilty until Proven Innocent: Lawyer Johnson's Prison Nightmare." ACLU of Massachusetts Web Site. http://www. aclu-mass.org/youth/risingtimes/9lawyerjohnson.html.

Timothy Hennis

Halperin, Rick. "News: U.S.A., N.C." *Abolish Archives*, 29 September 2000. http://venus.soci.niu.edu/~archives/ABOLISH/jun00/0558.

Part III: Corrupt Practices and Misconduct

Introduction to Part III

Warden, Rob and Protess, David. *Gone in the Night*. New York: Delacorte Press, 1993.

Warden, Rob and Protess, David. *A Promise of Justice*. New York: Hyperion, 1998.

The Ford Heights 4:

Verneal Jimerson

Dennis Williams

Willie Rainge

Kenny Adams

Armstrong, Ken, and Robert Becker. "Record Ford Heights 4 Payout May Not Be End." *Chicago Tribune*, 4 March 1999. Illinois Death Penalty Web Site. http://sun.soci.niu.edu/~critcrim/wrong/ ford4-suit.html.

Armstrong, Ken, and Maurice Possley. "Reversal of Fortune." *Chicago Tribune*, 13 January 1999. Illinois Death Penalty Web Site. http://sun. soci.niu.edu/~critcrim/wrong/tribpros13.html.

"Former Death Row Inmate Not Angry." Associated Press. http://www .suburbanchicagonews.com/joliet/prisons/executed/williams.html.

Higgins, Dr. Edmund. "Wrongfully Convicted."

"Long Road From Death Row to Freedom." Associated Press. http://www. suburbanchicagonews.com/joliet/prisons/executed/willias.html.

Warden, Rob. Northwestern University School of Law Center on Wrongful Convictions Web Site.

Thomas Gladdish, Richard Greer, Ronald Keine, & Clarence Smith

Death Penalty Information Web Site.

Detroit News. 16 December 1975.

Fight the Death Penalty in the U.S.A. Web Site. http://www.fdp. dk/uk/released.html.

"Infamous Crimes in N.M. History." *Albuquerque Journal*, September 19, 1999. http://www.abqjournal.com/2000/nm/future/10fut09-19-99.htm.

Radelet, Michael L., Hugo Adam Bedau, and Constance E. Putnam. *In Spite of Innocence.*

Warden, Rob. Northwestern University School of Law Center on Wrongful Convictions Web Site.

Earl Charles

Death Penalty Information Web Site.

Radelet, Michael L., Hugo Adam Bedau, and Constance E. Putnam. *In Spite of Innocence.*

Jerry Banks

Campaign for Criminal Justice Reform Web Site. http://justice.policy.net/. The Justice Project.

Radelet, Michael L., Hugo Adam Bedau, and Constance E. Putnam. *In Spite of Innocence.*

Clifford Henry Bowen

Armstrong, Ken. " 'True patriot' not quite a shining star." Outlaws Legal Service Web Site. 9 January 1999. http://www.outlawslegal.com/ vault/trib2.htm.

Clarence Lee Brandley

Radelet, Michael L., Hugo Adam Bedau, and Constance E. Putnam. *In Spite of Innocence.*

Warden, Rob. Northwestern University School of Law Center on Wrongful Convictions Web Site.

Patrick Croy
Campbell, Ward A. " 'Innocence' Critique." Pro-Death Penalty.com Web Site. http://www.prodeathpenalty.com/DPIC.htm.
"Erreurs Judiciaires Aux USA." AssociationRupture.org Web Site. http://assoc.wanadoo.fr/rupture/fr/court_errors.html. Paris, France.
"Exonerated from Death Row." Australian Coalition Against the Death Penalty. http://www.angelfire.com/stars/dorina/innocence1.html.
Jay C. Smith
Campbell, Ward A. " 'Innocence' Critique."
"Court Frees Jay Smith." *The Patriot-News*, 19 September 1992. Truth in Justice Web Site. http://truthinjustice.org/jay-smith.htm.
"Erreurs Judiciaires Aux USA." AssociationRupture.org Web Site.
"Exonerated from Death Row." Australian Coalition Against the Death Penalty.
Leask, Laird, and Pete Shellem. "Evidence Surfaces in Reinert Case." *The Patriot-News,* 29 March 1992. Truth in Justice Web Site. http://truthinjustice.org/jay-smith.htm.
Shellem, Pete, and Laird Leask. "Author Paid Trooper Probing Reinert Case." *The Patriot-News*, 5 April 1992. Truth in Justice Web Site. http://truthinjustice.org/jay-smith.htm.
Troy Lee Jones
Campbell, Ward A. " 'Innocence' Critique." Pro-Death Penalty.com Web Site. http://www.prodeathpenalty.com/DPIC.htm.
"Exonerated from Death Row." Australian Coalition Against the Death Penalty. http://www.angelfire.com/stars/dorina/innocence1.html.
Carl Lawson
Campbell, Ward A. " 'Innocence' Critique."
"Erreurs Judiciaires Aux USA." AssociationRupture.org Web Site.
"Exonerated from Death Row." Australian Coalition Against the Death Penalty.
Warden, Rob. Northwestern University School of Law Center on Wrongful Convictions Web Site.
William Nieves
Campbell, Ward A. " 'Innocence' Critique."

Carbin, Jenn. "A Matter of Life and Death." *Philadelphia City Paper*, 1-8 November 2001. http://www.citypaper.net/articles/110101/cs.cover1.shtml.

Dunham, Robert. "News: Analysis of William Nieves Case." *Abolish Archives*, 26 October 2000. http://venus.soci.niu.edu/~archives/ABOLISH/oct00/0487.

"Exonerated from Death Row." Australian Coalition Against the Death Penalty.

Galletti, Aria. "Innocent on Death Row." Voices Internet. March 2001. http://voicesweb.org/voices/cu/condemned0301.html.

Warden, Rob. Northwestern University School of Law Center on Wrongful Convictions Web Site.

"William Nieves." Canadian Coalition Against the Death Penalty Web Site. http://www.ccadp.org/williamnieves.htm.

Michael Graham & Albert Burrell

Campbell, Ward A. " 'Innocence' Critique."

Louisiana Coalition to Abolish the Death Penalty Web Site. http://lcadp.org/janfeb01.htm.

Reynolds, David. "DNA Testing Frees Death Row Inmate." *Inclusion Daily Express*, 3 January 2001.

Rimer, Sara. "Two Death-Row Inmates Exonerated in Louisiana." *New York Times*, 6 January 2001.

Thoming-Gale, Stormy. "Free Men Walking." *Justice Denied*. Vol. 2, Issue 3.

Joaquin Martinez

Campbell, Ward A. " 'Innocence' Critique."

Nguyen, Dong-Phuong. "Man Once on Death Row Acquitted of 2 Murders." *St. Petersburg Times*, 7 June 2001.

"Spaniard Returns Home After U.S. Death Sentence Quashed." Reuters, 10 June 2001. http://www.gospelcom.net/apologeticsindex/news1/an010611 06.html.

Juan Roberto Melendez

Berkowitz, Bill. "A Dead Man Walking Toward Freedom?" *WorkingFor Change*, 23 December 2001. Truth in Justice Web Site. http://www. truthinjustice.org/melendez.htm.

Campbell, Ward A. " 'Innocence' Critique."

"Exonerated from Death Row." Australian Coalition Against the Death Penalty.

Karp, David. "Judge Cites Prosecutor Trickery, Orders Retrial." *St. Petersburg Times*, 6 December 2001. http://www.oranous.com/JuanMelendez/cites.htm.

Thomas Kimbell

Campbell, Ward A. " 'Innocence' Critique."

Death Penalty Information Center Web Site.

"Ex-Death Row Inmate Acquitted." Associated Press, 4 May 2002. http://www.ccadp.org/thomaskimbell-news2002.htm.

Lash, Cindi. "From Death Row to Acquittal." *Pittsburgh Post-Gazette*, 4 May 2002. http://www.ccadp.org/thomaskimbell-news2002.htm.

"Thomas Kimbell." Canadian Coalition Against The Death Penalty Web Site. http://www.ccadp.org/thomaskimbell.htm.

Weinstein, Henry. "Pa. Death Row Inmate Acquitted at Retrial, Freed." *Los Angeles Times*, 7 May 2002. http://www.ccadp.org/thomaskimbell-news2002.htm.

Larry Osborne

Campbell, Ward A. " 'Innocence' Critique."

Canadian Coalition Against the Death Penalty Web Site. http://www.ccadp.org/larryosborne.htm.

"Exonerated from Death Row." Australian Coalition Against the Death Penalty. .

Floridians for Alternatives to the Death Penalty Web Site. http://www.fadp.org/fl_exonerated.html.

Yetter, Deborah. "Man Sent to Death is Acquited in Retrial." *The Courier-Journal* (Louisville, KY), 1 August 2002. http://www.truthinjustice.org/osborne.htm.

Richard Neal Jones

Campbell, Ward A. " 'Innocence' Critique."

Gary Nelson

Campaign for Criminal Justice Reform Web Site. The Justice Project.

Roberto Miranda

"Erreurs Judiciaires Aux USA." AssociationRupture.org Web Site.

"Exonerated from Death Row." Australian Coalition Against the Death Penalty.

Benjamin Harris

Campbell, Ward A. " 'Innocence' Critique."

Clarence Richard Dexter

"Innocence and the Death Penalty." Western Missouri Coalition to Abolish the Death Penalty. http://home.kc.rr.com/wmcadp/page9.htm.

Alfred Rivera

"Exonerated from Death Row." Australian Coalition Against the Death Penalty.

O'Neill, Patrick. "Call It Murder." *Independent Weekly*, 1 November 2000. http://indyweek.com/durham/2000-11-01/porch.html.

Kerry Cook

Death Penalty Information Center Web Site.

Goldwasser, Amy. "The Exonerated." Salon.com, 20 October 2000. http://dir.salon.com/news/feature/2000/10/20/exonerated/index.html.

Higgins, Dr. Edmund. "Wrongfully Convicted."

Part IV: The Snitch System
Introduction to Part IV

Warden, Rob. "The Snitch System." Research report presented April 25, 2002 at Arizona State University of Law, Tempe, AZ. http://www.law.northwestern.edu/depts/clinic/wrongful/documents/Snitch.htm.

Sonia Jacobs & Jesse Tafero

"Florida's Exonerated Death Row Prisoners." Floridians for Alternatives to the Death Penalty Web Site.

Freedberg, Sydney P. "Freed From Death Row."

Grassroots Investigation Project of Equal Justice, U.S.A. "Reasonable Doubts: Is the U.S. Executing Innocent People?" Equal Justice, U.S.A. 26 October 2000. http://www.quixote.org/ej/grip/reasonabledoubt/reasonabledoubt.pdf.

Warden, Rob. Northwestern University School of Law Center on Wrongful Convictions Web Site.

Peter Limone

Butterfield, Fox. "Ex-Prosecutor Tells of Ties Between F.B.I. and Mob." *New York Times*, 6 December 2002.

"FBI To Be Sued for $300 Million." TalkLeft.com, 25 August 2002. http://www.talkleft.com/archives/000759.html.

Finucane, Martin. "Man Freed After Serving 32 Years." Associated Press, 5 January 2001. Truth in Justice Web Site. http://www.truthin justice.org/limone.htm.

Lawrence, J.M. "Judge: Lawyer can reveal hit man's confession." *Boston Herald*, 23 December 2000. http://AmericanMafia.com/news/12-23-00_Hit_Mans_Confession.html.

Lawrence, J.M. "Lawyer urges judge to free man jailed in 1965 Mob killing." *Boston Herald*, 2 January 2001.

Limone, Olympia with Kathleen Powers. "My Story—I Knew My Husband Was Innocent." *Good Housekeeping*, October 2002.

Maguire, Ken. "Wrongly Jailed Man Gets Apology." Associated Press. Truth in Justice Web Site. http://www.truthinjustice.org/limone-apology.htm.

May, Allan. "Providence Mob." Court TV's Crime Library: Criminal Minds and Methods. http://www.crimelibrary.com/gangsters_outlaws/family_epics/providence_mob/1.html.

Prothero, P. Mitchell. "FBI 'knew innocent men were jailed'." UPI, 25 April 2001. http://www.gospelcom.net/apologeticsindex/news1/an010424 13.html.

Sherrer, Hans. "Four Men Exonerated of 1965 Murder After FBI Frame-up is Exposed." *Justice Denied*, Vol.2, issue 5. http://www.justicede-nied.org.fourmen.htm.

James Richardson

Against the Death Penalty Web Site. http://www.againstdp.org/natl-imp.html.

Armstrong, Ken and Possley, Maurice. "The Verdict: Dishonor." *Chicago*

Tribune. 10 January 1999. http://sun.soci.niu.edu/~critcrim/wrong/tribpros10.html.

Berlow, Alan. "Accumulating Aberrations." *The Atlantic Monthly,* November 1999. http://www.theatlantic.com/issues/99nov/9911wrongman2.htm.

"Florida's Exonerated Death Row Prisoners." Floridians for Alternatives to the Death Penalty Web Site.

Freedberg, Sydney P. "Freed from Death Row."

Radelet, Michael L., Hugo Adam Bedau, and Constance E. Putnam. *In Spite of Innocence.*

"Richardson 'Okay So Far' Following Heart Operation by Kansas Dr. Joseph Galichia." Galichia Medical Group Press Release, 18 September 1995. http://www.galichia.com.prrichardsonok.htm.

James Creamer

Georgia Moratorium Campaign Web Site. http://www.georgiamoratorium.org/.

Higgins, Dr. Edmund. "Official Misconduct." http://www.dredmundhiggins.com/officialmisconduct.htm. 2 January 2002.

Higgins, Dr. Edmund. "Wrongfully Convicted."

Radelet, Michael L., Hugo Adam Bedau, and Constance E. Putnam. *In Spite of Innocence.*

Warden, Rob. Northwestern University School of Law Center on Wrongful Convictions Web Site.

Anthony Brown

Brown, Anthony. "A Killing in Exile." *Eclectica Magazine,* Vol. 1, No. 11. http://www.eclectica.org/v1n11/inside.html.

Campaign for Criminal Justice Reform Web Site. The Justice Project.

"Exonerated from Death Row." Australian Coalition Against the Death Penalty.

"Florida's Exonerated Death Row Prisoners." Floridians for Alternatives to the Death Penalty Web Site.

Neil Ferber

Equal Justice, U.S.A. "Police Abuses in Philadelphia." http://www.quixote.org/ej/archives/mumia/corr2.html.

"Exonerated from Death Row." Australian Coalition Against the Death Penalty.

Fazlollah, Mark, Mark Bowden, and Richard Jones. "City Will Pay $1.9 Million to Man over Unjust Jailing." *Philadelphia Inquirer*. 15 August 1996.

Illinois Death Penalty Education Project. "Summaries of 46 Cases in Which Mistaken or Perjured Eyewitness Testimony Put Innocent Persons on Death Row." IllinoisDeathPenalty.com. Chicago, IL. http://www.illinoisdeathpenalty.com/eyewitness.html

Warden, Rob. Northwestern University School of Law Center on Wrongful Convictions Web Site.

Joseph Green Brown

Amnesty International. "Appendix: Statement of Joseph 'Shabaka' Green Brown." from "Fatal Flaws: Innocence and the Death Penalty." 1999. Amnesty International USA Web Site. http://www.amnestyusa.org/rightsforall/dp/innocence/innocent-8.html.

Campaign for Criminal Justice Reform Web Site. The Justice Project.

Campbell, Ward A. " 'Innocence' Critique."

"Florida's Exonerated Death Row Prisoners." Floridians for Alternatives to the Death Penalty Web Site.

Freedberg, Sydney P. " 'Yes I'm Angry—Yes I'm Bitter—I'm Frustrated.' " *St. Petersberg Times*, 4 July 1999. The Truth in Justice Web Site. http://www.truthinjustice.org/joegreenbrown.htm.

Illinois Death Penalty Education Project. "Summaries of 46 Cases in Which Mistaken or Perjured Eyewitness Testimony Put Innocent Persons on Death Row."

Warden, Rob. Northwestern University School of Law Center on Wrongful Convictions Web Site.

James Robison

Campbell, Ward A. " 'Innocence' Critique."

Lee, Robert W. "Cruel and Unusual Leniency." *The New American*, Vol. 6, No. 17. 30 August 1990. http://thenewamerican.com/focus/cap_punishment/vo06no17_cruel.htm.

Lovinger, Caitlin. "Life After Death Row." *New York Times*, 22 August 1999. www.texas-justice.com.

Texas Defender Service. "A State of Denial: Texas Justice and the Death Penalty." 2000. http://www.texasdefender.org/publications.htm.

Zehr, Edward. "John McCain, Warts and All." *Washington Weekly*, 14 February 2000.

Muneer Deeb

Campbell, Ward A. " 'Innocence' Critique."

Death Penalty Information Center Web Site.

"Erreurs Judiciaires Aux USA." AssociationRupture.org Web Site.

Graczyk, Michael. "Texas Executes Man Convicted of Lake Waco Murders." Associated Press, 4 April 1997. http://www.texnews.com/texas97/execute040497.html.

Hall, Michael. "Death Isn't Fair." *Texas Monthly*, December 2002. http://www.texasmonthly.com/mag/issues/2002-12-01/feature2.php.

"Statement on National Conference on Wrongful Convictions and the Death Penalty, November 13-15, 1998, Northwestern University Legal Clinic, Chicago, Illinois." TheElectricChair.com. http://www.patrickcrusade.org/national_conference_wrongful.htm.

Steven Manning

Campbell, Ward A. " 'Innocence' Critique."

"Exonerated from Death Row." Australian Coalition Against the Death Penalty.

Warden, Rob. Northwestern University School of Law Center on Wrongful Convictions Web Site.

Jeremy Sheets

Campbell, Ward A. " 'Innocence' Critique."

Creepin' Death Web Site. Source: *Lincoln Journal Star*. http://www.creepindeath.org/What_s_New/what_s_new.html.

"Exonerated from Death Row." Australian Coalition Against the Death Penalty.

Halperin, Rick. "Death Penalty News." *Abolish Archives*, 1 October 1997. http://venus.soci.niu.edu/~archives/ABOLISH/sep97/0248.html.

Halperin, Rick. "News: Jeremy Sheets to be Set Free." *Abolish Archives*, 15 May 2001. http://venus.soci.niu.edu/~archives/ABOLISH/sep97/0248.html.

Nebraskans Against the Death Penalty Web Site. http://www.nadp.in etnebr.com.

Ponnuru, Ramesh. "Bad List." *National Review*, 16 September 2002. Vol. 54, Issue 17.

Henry Drake

Campbell, Ward A. " 'Innocence' Critique."

"Statement on National Conference on Wrongful Convictions and the Death Penalty, November 13-15, 1998.

Northwestern University Legal Clinic, Chicago, Illinois." The Electric-Chair.com.

Warden, Rob. Northwestern University School of Law Center on Wrongful Convictions Web Site.

Willie Brown & Larry Troy

Campaign for Criminal Justice Reform Web Site. The Justice Project.

Campbell, Ward A. " 'Innocence' Critique."

Illinois Coalition Against the Death Penalty Web Site. http://www.ic adp.org/.

Warden, Rob. Northwestern University School of Law Center on Wrongful Convictions Web Site.

Walter McMillan

Amnesty International. "Appendix: Statement of Joseph 'Shabaka' Green Brown." from "Fatal Flaws: Innocence and the Death Penalty."

Halperin, Rick. "Death Penalty News and Updates." http://people. smu.edu/rhalperi/.

Halperin, Rick. "Death Penalty News: October 1997." *Abolish Archives*. http://venus.soci.niu.edu/~archives/ABOLISH.

Halperin, Rick. "Death Penalty News: October 2000." *Abolish Archives*. http://venus.soci.niu.edu/~archives/ABOLISH.

Humes, Edward. *Mean Justice*. New York: Simon & Schuster, 1999. Excerpted on Steven Shurka and Associates Web Site. www.crimlaw.org/defbrief63.html.

Illinois Coalition Against the Death Penalty Web Site. http://www. icadp.org/.

Protest Net Web Site. http://www.protest.net.

Sealey, Geraldine. "Society's Debt: Who Pays When Innocent Men Go to

Jail? Sometimes No One." ABCNEWS.com, 8 August 2002. http://abc-news.go.com/sections/us/DailyNews/compensation020808.html.

Warden, Rob. Northwestern University School of Law Center on Wrongful Convictions Web Site.

Weinstein, Henry. "Death Penalty Foes Focus Effort on the Innocent." *Los Angeles Times*, 16 November 1998. http://www.texas-justice.com/latimes/latimes981116.htm.

Curtis Kyles

Amnesty International USA Death Penalty Web Site.

Campbell, Ward A. " 'Innocence' Critique."

Fight the Death Penalty in the U.S.A. Web Site. http://www.fdp.dk/uk/released.html.

Illinois Coalition Against the Death Penalty Web Site. http://www.icadp.org/.

Illinois Death Penalty Education Project. "Summaries of 46 Cases in Which Mistaken or Perjured Eyewitness Testimony Put Innocent Persons on Death Row."

Lovinger, Caitlin. "Death Row's Living Alumni." *New York Times*. 22 August 1999. www.protest.net/view/cgi?view=1501.

Robinson, Mary. "Re: Feingold Sponsoring Bill to Abolish Death Penalty." *Abolish Archives*. http://venus.soci.niu.e4du/~archives/ABOLISH/dec99/0097.html.

"Testimony of Brian A. Stevenson." *Post-Conviction DNA Testing and Preventing Wrongful Convictions of the Innocent*. United States Senate Judiciary Committee. 13 June 2000.
http://judiciary.senate.gov/oldsite/6132000_bas.htm.

Federico Macias

Cody, W.J. Michael. "The Death Penalty in America: Its Fairness and Morality." M.L. Seidman Lecture Series. Rhodes College, 24 April 2001. The Constitution Project Web Site. http://www.constitutionproject.org/dpi/codyspeech.htm.

Hall, Michael. "Death Isn't Fair." *Texas Monthly*. December 2002. http://www.texasmonthly.com/mag/issues/2002-12-01/feature2.php.

Halperin, Rick. "Death Penalty News—USA/General." *Abolish Archives*.

http://venus.soci.niu.edu/~archives/ABOLISH/rick-halperin/
oct99/0155.

Illinois Death Penalty Education Project. "Summaries of 46 Cases in
Which Mistaken or Perjured Eyewitness Testimony Put Innocent Persons on Death Row."

Lovinger, Caitlin. "Life After Death Row."

Texas Prison Abuse Campaign. "Prison Brutality and Injustice Page."
http://www.geocities.com/Heartland/Ridge/8616/texasprisonabuse.html.

Warden, Rob. Northwestern University School of Law Center on
Wrongful Convictions Web Site.

Charles Smith

Illinois Death Penalty Education Project. "Summaries of 46 Cases in
Which Mistaken or Perjured Eyewitness Testimony Put Innocent Persons on Death Row."

Lovinger, Caitlin. "Life After Death Row."

Jesse Keith Brown

Campaign for Criminal Justice Reform Web Site. The Justice Project.
"Death Penalty." The MacArthur Justice Center Web Site.
http://macarthur.uchicago.edu/deathpenalty/.

"Exonerated from Death Row." Australian Coalition Against the Death Penalty.

Part V: False Confessions

Introduction to Part V

Dwyer, Tim. "Crimes Admitted, But Not Committed: Confessing Can Seem
Easy After Hours in a Hard Light." *New York Times*, 20 October 2002.

Wilbert Lee & Freddie Pitts

"Case Histories: A Review of 23 Individuals Released from Death Row."
Florida Commission on Capital Cases. Locke Burt, Chairman. 20 June
2002. http://www.oranous.com/innocence/floridareport.htm.

Gary Gauger

Aucoin, Laurie. "Righting Wrongful Convictions." *Northwestern* Magazine. Spring 1999. http://www.northwestern.edu/magazine/north
western/spring99/convictions.htm.

Lovinger, Caitlin. "Death Row's Living Alumni."

Rummel, Carolyn. "Exonerated: Powerful Anti-Death Penalty Theater." *People's Weekly World*, 19 October 2002. http://host10.cpusa.org/article/articleview/2181/.

Warden, Rob. Northwestern University School of Law Center on Wrongful Convictions Web Site.

"The Wrongly Convicted." The Patrick Crusade Web Site. http://www.patrickcrusade.org/wrongful.htm.

Robert Lee Miller Jr.

"The 17 Innocent People Who Lived." American Civil Liberties Union Web Site. http://archive.aclu.org/issues/death/17exonerated.html.

Higgins, Dr. Edmund. "Wrongfully Convicted."

"Innocence and the Death Penalty." Death Penalty Institute of Oklahoma Web Site. March 18, 2001. http://www.dpio.org/issues/innocence.html

"News Archives: June 2000." Death Penalty Institute of Oklahoma Web Site. March 18, 2001. http://www.dpio.org/archives/News/News_2000_06.html.

Scheck, Barry, Peter Neufeld, and Jim Dwyer. *Actual Innocence*. New York: Doubleday, 2000.

David Keaton

"Exonerated from Death Row." Australian Coalition Against the Death Penalty.

Floridians for Alternatives to the Death Penalty Web Site.

"The Wrongly Convicted." The Patrick Crusade Web Site.

Johnny Ross

Amnesty International. "Indecent and Internationally Illegal: The Death Penalty Against Child Offenders." 25 September 2002. Amnesty International Web Site.http://web.amnesty.org/library/Index/eng AMR511442002?OpendDocument&of=COUNTRIES?OpendDocument&of=COUNTRIES.

Berrigan, Patrick J., and Jennifer Brewer "Appellants Suggestions as to the Applicability of *Aitkens v. Virginia* to the Issues in Mr. Simmons' Case." *State of Missouri v. Christopher Simmons*. Case No. SC84454. 20 July 2002. http://www.abanet.org/crimjust/juvjus/simmonsatkins.pdf.

Campbell, Ward A. " 'Innocence' Critique."
"The Wrongly Convicted." The Patrick Crusade Web Site.
Jerry Bigelow
Campaign for Criminal Justice Reform Web Site. The Justice Project.
Campbell, Ward A. " 'Innocence' Critique."
Warden, Rob. Northwestern University School of Law Center on Wrongful Convictions Web Site.
"The Wrongly Convicted." The Patrick Crusade Web Site.
John Henry Knapp
"The 17 Innocent People Who Lived." American Civil Liberties Union Web Site.
Against the Death Penalty Web Site. http://www.againstdp.org/natl-imp.html.
Campbell, Ward A. " 'Innocence' Critique."
Humes, Edward. *Mean Justice.* New York: Simon & Schuster, 1999. Excerpted on Steven Shurka and Associates Web Site. www.crim law.org/defbrief63.html.
Humes, Edward. "The Toll of Misconduct." Edward Humes Web Site. http://www.edwardhumes.com/articles/mean_toll.shtml
"The Wrongly Convicted." The Patrick Crusade Web Site.

Part VI: Junk Science
Introduction to Part VI
Cole, Simon. "The Way We Live Now: 5-13-01; The Myth of Finger-prints." *New York Times.* 13 May 2001.
"On the Evidence." *Richmond Times Dispatch.* 30 May 2002.
Robert Hayes
"The 17 Innocent People Who Lived." American Civil Liberties Union Web Site.
C. J. " 'The Exonerated': The Theater of Life and Death." *Revolutionary Worker* #1078. 13 November 2000. http://rwor.org/a/v22/1070 79/1078/exoner.htm.
Campbell, Ward A. " 'Innocence' Critique."

Fight the Death Penalty in the U.S.A. Web Site.

"Florida's Exonerated Death Row Prisoners." Floridians for Alternatives to the Death Penalty Web Site.

Freedberg, Sydney P. "Freed From Death Row."

Illinois Death Penalty Education Project. "Summaries of 46 Cases in Which Mistaken or Perjured Eyewitness Testimony Put Innocent Persons on Death Row."

Lovinger, Caitlin. "Death Row's Living Alumni."

Warden, Rob. Northwestern University School of Law Center on Wrongful Convictions Web Site.

"The Wrongly Convicted." The Patrick Crusade Web Site.

Randall Padgett

Australian Coalition Against the Death Penalty Web Site.

C. J. " 'The Exonerated': The Theater of Life and Death."

Death Penalty Information Center Web Site.

Fight the Death Penalty in the U.S.A. Web Site. "The Wrongly Convicted." The Patrick Crusade Web Site.

Levinson, Arlene. "Wrongly Convicted Offer Some Tips." Associated Press, 14 November 1998. Truth in Justice Web Site. http://www.truth injustice.org/conference.htm

Lovinger, Caitlin. "Death Row's Living Alumni."

Warden, Rob. Northwestern University School of Law Center on Wrongful Convictions Web Site.

Gregory Wilhoit

Australian Coalition Against the Death Penalty.

Lovinger, Caitlin. "Death Row's Living Alumni."

"Through Thick and Thin." ABCnews.com, 19 August 2000. http:// abcnews.go.com/onair/2020/2020_000818_deathrow_feature.html.

"The Wrongly Convicted." The Patrick Crusade Web Site.

Anthony Ray Peek

Campbell, Ward A. " 'Innocence' Critique "

Freedberg, Sydney P. "Freed From Death Row."

"The Wrongly Convicted." The Patrick Crusade Web Site.

Dale Johnston

Campbell, Ward A. " 'Innocence' Critique."

"Exonerated from Death Row." Australian Coalition Against the Death Penalty.

Illinois Death Penalty Education Project. "Summaries of 46 Cases in Which Mistaken or Perjured Eyewitness Testimony Put Innocent Persons on Death Row."

Lovinger, Caitlin. "Death Row's Living Alumni."

"The Wrongly Convicted." The Patrick Crusade Web Site.

Adolph Munson

Death Penalty Information Center Web Site.

"Exonerated from Death Row." Australian Coalition Against the Death Penalty.

Lovinger, Caitlin. "Death Row's Living Alumni." *New York Times.* August 22, 1999. www.protest.net/view/cgi?view=1501.

"The Wrongly Convicted." The Patrick Crusade Web Site.

Sabrina Butler

Amnesty International. "Fatal Flaws: Innocence and the Death Penalty." 1999. Amnesty International USA Web Site. http://www.amnesty usa.org/rightsforall/dp/innocence/innocent-6.html

Campbell, Ward A. " 'Innocence' Critique."

Death Penalty Information Center Web Site.

Lovinger, Caitlin. "Death Row's Living Alumni."

"The Wrongly Convicted." The Patrick Crusade Web Site.

Michael Linder

"Exonerated from Death Row." Australian Coalition Against the Death Penalty.

Radelet, Michael L., and Hugo Adam Bedau. "The Execution of the Innocent." Against the Death Penalty Web Site. http://www.against dp.org/exinno.html

"The Wrongly Convicted." The Patrick Crusade Web Site.

SOURCES

Part VII: Reasonable Doubt

Annibal Jaramillo

Campbell, Ward A. " 'Innocence' Critique."

Freedberg, Sydney P. "Freed From Death Row."

"The Wrongly Convicted." The Patrick Crusade Web Site.

Robert Cox

Campbell, Ward A. " 'Innocence' Critique."

Freedberg, Sydney P. "Freed From Death Row."

"The Wrongly Convicted." The Patrick Crusade Web Site.

Jimmy Lee Mathers

Campbell, Ward A. " 'Innocence' Critique."

"Exonerated from Death Row." Australian Coalition Against the Death Penalty.

"State v. Washington." http://www.geocities.com/CapitolHill/Lobby/7697/test3.html.

John C. Skelton

Campbell, Ward A. " 'Innocence' Critique."

"The Wrongly Convicted." The Patrick Crusade Web Site.

Andrew Golden

Amnesty International USA Death Penalty Web Site.

Freedberg, Sydney P. "Freed From Death Row."

"The Wrongly Convicted." The Patrick Crusade Web Site.

Gary Drinkard

"Gary Drinkard." Canadian Coalition Against the Death Penalty Web Site. http://www.ccadp.org/garydrinkard.

"Man on Death Row for Five Years Found Innocent." Associated Press, 26 May 2001. Truth in Justice Web Site. http://truthinjustice.org/drinkard.htm

Southern Center for Human Rights Web Site. http://www.schr.org/death penalty/index.html.

Samuel Poole

Campbell, Ward A. " 'Innocence' Critique."

"The Wrongly Convicted." The Patrick Crusade Web Site.

Jonathan Treadway
"Death Penalty." American Civil Liberties Union Web Site. http://www.aclu.org/DeathPenalty/DeathPenaltyMain.cfm.
"The Wrongly Convicted." The Patrick Crusade Web Site.
"Exonerated from Death Row." Australian Coalition Against the Death Penalty.
Vernon McManus
Campbell, Ward A. " 'Innocence' Critique."
"The Wrongly Convicted." The Patrick Crusade Web Site.
Robert Wallace
Campbell, Ward A. " 'Innocence' Critique."
"Exonerated from Death Row." Australian Coalition Against the Death Penalty.
"The Wrongly Convicted." The Patrick Crusade Web Site.
Warren Douglas Manning
Campbell, Ward A. " 'Innocence' Critique."
"Exonerated from Death Row." Australian Coalition Against the Death Penalty.
Jesse Keith Brown
Campaign for Criminal Justice Reform Web Site. The Justice Project.
Campbell, Ward A. " 'Innocence' Critique."
"The Wrongly Convicted." The Patrick Crusade Web Site.

Addendum: The Central Park Jogger
"Central Park Jogger Tells Her Own Story." Associated Press, 29 March 2003.
Dwyer, Jim. "Likely U-Turn by Prosecutors in Jogger Case." New York Times, 12 October 2002.
Dwyer, Jim, and Kevin Flynn. "New Light on Jogger's Rape Calls Evidence into Question." New York Times, 1 December 2002.
Dwyer, Jim, and Susan Saulny. "Youth's Denials in '89 Rape Case Cost Them Parole Chances." New York Times, 16 October 2002.
McFadden, Robert D. "Boys' Guilt Likely in Rape of Jogger, Police Panel Says." New York Times. 28 January 2003.
McFadden, Robert D. "History is Shadow on Present in Jogger Case." New York Times, 7 September 2002.

Sources

McFadden, Robert D., and Susan Saulny. "13 Years Later, Official Reversal in Jogger Attack." *New York Times*, 6 December 2002.

Saulny, Susan. "Convictions and Charges Voided in '89 Central Park Jogger Attack." *New York Times*, 20 December 2002.

Smith, Chris. "Central Park Revisited." *New York Magazine*, 21 October 2002.

Afterword:
United States v. Capital Punishment

Bonner, Raymond and Ford Fessenden. "States with No Death Penalty Share Lower Homicide Rates." *New York Times*, 22 September 2000.

"Facts About Deterrence and the Death Penalty." Death Penalty Information Center Web Site. http://www.deathpenaltyinfo.org/article.php?scid=12&did=167.

"History of the Death Penalty." Death Penalty Information Center Web Site. http://www.deathpenaltyinfo.org/article.php?did=199&scid=15.

Slater, Eric. "Illinois Governor Commutes All Death Row Cases." *Los Angeles Times*. 12 January 2003.

Weiser, Benjamin and William Glaberson. "Aschcroft Pushes Executions in More Cases in New York." *New York Times*, 6 February 2003.

Wilgoren, Jodi. "Citing Issues of Fairness, Governor Clears Out Death Row in Illinois." *New York Times*, 12 January 2003.

Wilgoren, Jodi. "Illinois Governor Issues 3 New Pardons as His Own Legal Problems Mount." *New York Times*, 20 December 2002.

Wilgoren, Jodi. "Illinois Moves to Center of Death Penalty Debate." *New York Times*, 13 October 2002.

Index

About the Author

Stanley Cohen is a veteran award-winning newspaper and magazine journalist. For more than forty years, he has worked as an editor, writer, and reporter for newspapers, magazines, and an international news service. He also has taught writing, journalism, and philosophy at Hunter College and at New York University. His work has appeared in numerous publications, including the *New York Times, Inside Sports,* and *Sports Inc.,* and he was a contributing writer for *The Diamond* magazine.

He is the author of *The Game They Played; The Man in the Crowd; A Magic Summer: The '69 Mets; Dodgers! The First 100 Years; Willie's Game* (with Willie Mosconi); and *Tough Talk* (with First Amendment attorney Martin Garbus). *The Game They Played* was a main selection of the *Sports Illustrated* Book Club, named by the *New York Times* as one of the notable books of 1977, and cited by *Sports Illustrated* in 2002 as one of the Top 100 Sports Books of All Time. Cohen also served as program consultant for the award-winning television documentary *City Dump,* which examined the 1951 college basketball scandal.

In the 1960s, Cohen took part in the campaign to abolish capital punishment in New York State and received a citation from Al Blumenthal, who sponsored the abolition bill in the State Assembly.

He currently lives in Tomkins Cove, New York, with his wife, Betty. They have two children and four grandchildren.